Multimedia-Based Instructional Design

Multimedia-Based Instructional Design

COMPUTER-BASED TRAINING

WEB-BASED TRAINING

DISTANCE BROADCAST TRAINING

William W. Lee
Diana L. Owens

Jossey-Bass
Pfeiffer

San Francisco

Copyright © 2000 by Jossey-Bass/Pfeiffer
Jossey-Bass/Pfeiffer is a registered trademark of Jossey-Bass Inc., A Wiley Company.
ISBN: 0-7879-5159-5

Library of Congress Cataloging-in-Publication Data

Lee, William W.
Multimedia-based instructional design: computer-based training,
Web-based training, distance broadcast training / William W. Lee, Diana
L. Owens.
   p. cm.
Includes bibliographical references and index.
   ISBN 0-7879-5159-5 (acid-free paper)
   1. Employees—Training of—Planning. 2. Computer-assisted
instruction. 3. Instructional systems—Design. I. Owens, Diana L.,
1951-II. Title.
   HR5549.5.T7 L4264 2000
   658.3'12404—dc21

                                        99-051003

Printed in the United States of America.

Published by

JOSSEY-BASS/PFEIFFER
A Wiley Company
350 Sansome St.
San Francisco, CA 94104-1342
415.433.1740; Fax 415.433.0499
800.274.4434; Fax 800.569.0443

www.pfeiffer.com

Acquiring Editor: Matthew Holt
Director of Development: Kathleen Dolan Davies
Developmental Editor: Susan Rachmeler
Copyeditor: Thomas Finnegan

Editorial Production Manager: Jeff Wyneken
Manufacturing Manager: Becky Carreño
Interior Design: Claudia Smelser
Cover Design: Blue Design

Printing   10 9 8 7 6 5 4

 This book is printed on acid-free, recycled stock that meets or exceeds the minimum GPO and EPA requirements for recycled paper.

To my mother, Goldie Lee; my sisters, Thelma Shepler, Leona Mohney, and Lucille Srock; and my friends Kathe Ginther, Mark Movinsky, Stuart Myers, and William McDonnell, for their encouragement and support throughout the years

—Bill Lee

To my husband, Terry, for his feedback and support, wonderful sense of humor, and the many things I have learned from him that have contributed to this text

To my parents, Luella and Bill DuBois; my son, Rob MacKey; and his wife, Jessica, for their constant demonstrations of love, encouragement, and support

—Diana Owens

CONTENTS

Preface   xi

Acknowledgments   xix

PART ONE Multimedia Needs Assessment and Analysis   1

  1 Introduction to Multimedia Needs Assessment
     and Front-End Analysis   3

  2 Needs Assessment   5

  3 Front-End Analysis   14

  4 Audience Analysis   17

  5 Technology Analysis   20

  6 Situational Analysis   26

  7 Task Analysis   29

  8 Critical Incident Analysis   34

  9 Objective Analysis   37

10 Media Analysis   48

11 Extant Data Analysis   65

12 Cost Analysis   68

13 Rapid Analysis Method   71

PART TWO Multimedia Instructional Design   81

  14 Introduction to Multimedia Instructional Design   83

  15 Project Schedule   88

  16 Project Team   93

  17 Media Specifications   100

  18 Content Structure   113

  19 Configuration Control   131

PART THREE Multimedia Development and Implementation   137

  20 Introduction to Multimedia Development   139

  21 Common Development Components   145

  22 Developing Computer-Based Learning Environments   156

  23 Developing Internet, Intranet, Web-Based,
     and Performance Support Learning Environments   164

  24 Developing Interactive Distance Broadcast Environments   178

PART FOUR Multimedia Evaluation   185

  25 Introduction to Multimedia Evaluation   187

  26 Purpose of Evaluation   190

  27 Measures of Validity   195

  28 Instrument Development and Measurement Plan   201

  29 Collecting and Analyzing Data   214

APPENDIX A Instructional Design Process Step/Action Checklist   219

APPENDIX B Assessment and Analysis   227

APPENDIX C Development and Implementation   245

APPENDIX D Evaluation   248

APPENDIX E Tools   268

    Assessment and Front-End Analysis Tools   269
    Design Tools   288
    Development and Implementation Tools   303
    Evaluation Tools   327

References   337

About the Authors   339

Index   341

How to Use the Accompanying CD-ROM   359

PREFACE

W hy the increasing emphasis on multimedia? What is the need for technology-based solutions for training delivery and solving business issues?

In a global corporate environment that is increasingly becoming a virtual world whose people are connected by technology, the need for rapid communication, continuous information flow, and speed to market is critical. Maintaining the business construct of everyone in the same room at the same time is increasingly difficult and often implausible. The need for virtual training to keep people connected is imperative. But still the paradigm of the physical classroom is a major delivery method.

Technology-based solutions must be viewed as helping to achieve corporate goals and objectives. John Noonan (1993) wrote that if the training function is ever to escape "corporate America's basement," it must transform into an organization that ties solutions to business needs.

Andersen Consulting conducted a study of training needs in the airline industry and produced a report in 1994 on the direction that industry must take. The findings expressed in the report apply just as well to many industries other than airlines. One of the report's major findings was the need to increase the use of technology to leverage training and support workforce performance.

WHO SHOULD BUY THIS BOOK?

Multimedia-Based Instructional Design is intended for course developers (instructional designers, authors, project managers) who are beginning their first multimedia project, as well as experienced designers of large projects in which a consistent methodology can be followed by all team members. It is well suited for use by project teams where there is a mixture of experienced and new developers. It imparts a consistent message to those project teams that find members matrixed in and out of projects and that use a combination of internal and outsourced resources.

Although the book discusses many issues encountered by internal training departments, multimedia consulting companies should also find the tools valuable and the tips for managing customer expectations enlightening.

WHY BUY THIS BOOK?

There are numerous books on the market today on how to design and develop computer-based training, others for web-based training, and still others for distance broadcast training. So why buy this book rather than one of the others?

Other books are well suited for their specific delivery media, but the approach to the instructional design process differs in each one. Most use the traditional instructional design (ID) model with its phases of analysis, design, development, implementation, and evaluation, but they vary in the tasks and activities to complete during each phase.

Consequently, if you want to design for more than one medium you have to buy a book on each and adjust or adapt your ID model depending on the medium. So, why buy this book? Because it eliminates this multiple need.

Instructional designers are intelligent, creative people who eventually figure out how to meld the best components of each design model given time and experience. We all gain experience by working on multiple projects. But time is usually what we lack. We're often too rushed to reflect on what we did during a project that made it go smoothly—what we did to get over the bumps and around the roadblocks. *Multimedia-Based Instructional Design* offers time-tested procedures and tools to encapsulate the experience of hundreds of course developers, thereby reducing the time required to reflect on past successes and problems. Use our book as the basis for projects, and change only those steps you find work differently and better for your group than the way we suggest.

FOCUS OF THE BOOK

Our philosophy is to focus on the human-performance arena. This focus presents challenges to multimedia development groups whose philosophy reflects a more traditional approach. We agree with Tom Gilbert (1996) that the purpose of all instruction is to affect human performance through learning or performance support. If multimedia development groups move into the human-performance area, they open new horizons of opportunities to work within an organization and become more valuable. We recommend Judith Hale's *The Performance Consultant's Fieldbook: Tools and Techniques for Improving Organizations and People* (1998) to help your group make the necessary shift.

We've all experienced working on projects for long hours, with budget overruns, missed deadlines, and unnecessary rework. We, too, have experienced the frustration associated with all of these situations. Our goal is to provide you with a handbook that helps you reduce cycle time for completing projects, makes your job easier, and conveys the lessons that will reduce your learning curve.

STRUCTURE OF THE BOOK

The book is organized in four parts:

1. Multimedia needs assessment and analysis
2. Multimedia instructional design
3. Multimedia development and implementation
4. Multimedia evaluation

Overall, it is structured as a step/action handbook that presents activities and the associated steps required for completing a successful project. We present tools to assist in organizing the information obtained from each activity. Appendix A is a step/action table, which lists the steps to follow in each phase of the instructional design process. Project teams can follow the steps as listed or adapt them for their specific needs.

The graphic that follows this paragraph appears (in varying form) at the beginning of each of the four parts of the book to identify the phase of the instructional design process to be discussed in that part. Note the circular configuration, to demonstrate the circular rather than linear nature of the process. Each phase of the ID process flows through to the next, and the first reflects back on the first. This is the concept of "congruence."

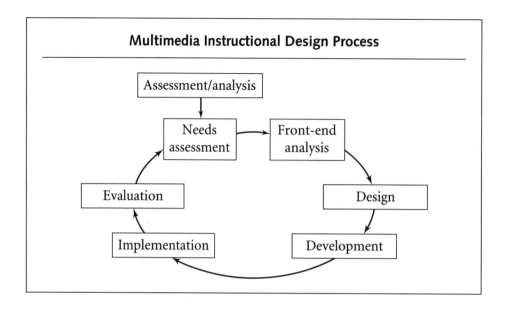

Multimedia Instructional Design Process

Assessment/analysis

Needs assessment → Front-end analysis

Evaluation

Design

Implementation

Development

We follow Dick and Carey's model (1990) of separating the analysis phase of instructional design into two parts: needs assessment and front-end analysis. Needs assessment focuses on determining the current state and the desired state, and the type of business issue the need arises from. Front-end analysis then determines how to close that gap with a results-driven solution. We address nine types of front-end analysis:

1. Audience: determining who the target population is for the solution, and their demographic as well as learning needs

2. Technology analysis: determining the type of technology available and technological considerations and constraints for delivery of the solution

3. Situation analysis: determining the environmental considerations in delivering the solution

4. Task analysis: determining the physical and mental requirements for getting the job done

5. Critical incident analysis: determining which tasks require that training or information be provided to the target audience

6. Objective analysis: determining the performance and instructional objectives for the solution and making the distinction between the types of objectives as well as when and where to use them; also their impact on the content as well as delivery media

7. Media analysis: selecting the most appropriate delivery medium (or media) for a solution

8. Extant data analysis: determining what materials are available and which need to be developed—basically, making a "build-or-buy" decision

9. Cost analysis: determining the up-front benefit the solution has in comparison to the cost of the solution

We also include a rapid analysis model (RAM) in Chapter Thirteen. We developed this model for experienced course developers who intuitively understand the step-by-step process involved in gathering data through needs assessment and the nine types of front-end analysis.

In Part Two, "Multimedia Instructional Design," we have provided the activities and steps required to produce a Course Design Specification (CDS) document. We include many tips on project management for course developers to fully understand the complexities involved in multimedia projects. Such information should guide them in selecting media. For example, if assessment and analysis result in a web-based solution, the project team should know what's involved so they can determine if the solution is realistic for their business and can assemble the required resources before the project starts. The complexities might, though, result in choosing another solution.

Part Three is on multimedia development and implementation. Here there is divergence of methodology depending on the media. Therefore, we begin with a chapter on common elements of development and implementation and then explain the particular aspects for computer-based, web-based, distance broadcast, and performance support solutions.

Course developers are expected to acquire increasingly broad skill sets and are becoming the authors of what they design. Even if the authoring and designing are performed by different groups, designers should know the complexities involved in the solution they propose in order to determine if the solution is feasible. Designers should also be able to carefully consider the issues related to implementing a solution.

Part Four is on multimedia evaluation. We discuss evaluation from two aspects: designing, developing, and delivering tests; and test validity and reliability. We present the steps for constructing various types of objective tests and explain the strengths and weaknesses of each type.

Throughout, we have included sections on applicable learning and instructional design theory as a basis of "why we do what we do." People outside of the human performance arena often don't see the need for particular aspects of development. They don't understand the basic human characteristics surrounding learning that require us to include certain components. We have laid out the theory to help you explain why to them.

We also provide sections in most chapters on our personal experiences, to help you avoid the pitfalls we have experienced and replicate the successes we've had.

In total, we present a replicable model, adaptable to any delivery medium, diverging only in the development phase of multimedia projects.

THE CD-ROM

The CD-ROM that accompanies this book contains tools we developed, which are meant to be modified to meet your particular project requirements. Here are the directories and documents included:

- Step/action list: this is a complete checklist of all activities and steps in the multimedia instructional design process as laid out in this book. The checklist is also found in Appendix A.

- Tools templates: the tools directory contains checklists and templates for each phase of the ID process. These tools and templates can be copied and used as-is or customized to meet your needs and used for multiple projects. The directory is divided into sections for assessment and analysis tools, design tools, development and implementation tools, and evaluation tools. A hard copy of each tool is also included in the appendixes (look for the CD-ROM icon: ●), so you can browse through and determine whether and how each one applies to your project.

- A demo of LearnLinc, which explains how the web-based delivery software works.

- A demo of WorldTutor, which explains the workings of the system of template shells and models.

HARDWARE AND SOFTWARE REQUIREMENTS

The tools found on the CD-ROM require you to have access to a PC running Microsoft Word.

The LearnLinc and WorldTutor demos require you to have a PC with the following configuration:

- Operating system: Microsoft Windows 95 or Windows NT 3.51 or later
- Microprocessor: 486 PC or higher (Pentium preferred)
- Memory: 8MB RAM minimum for Windows 95 and NT
- Hard disk space: 8MB minimum
- Disk drive: 2X CD-ROM or faster
- Audio adapter: Real Audio

ACKNOWLEDGMENTS

We would like to thank Robert Mamone and Ken Roadman for their contributions to this book. They were both original authors of *The Computer Based Training Handbook: Assessment, Design, Development, and Evaluation* (1995), which this book is based on.

We would also like to thank LearnLinc Corp., 385 Jordan Rd., Troy, NY 12180; Allen Interactions, Inc., 8000 W. 78th St., Suite 450, Minneapolis, MN 55439; e-Learnet, Inc., 310A Breezeport, San Antonio, TX 78216; and ONETOUCH Systems, Inc., 40 Airport Freeway, San Jose, CA 95110, for their cooperation in providing us with materials for this book.

Thanks also to Mlink Technologies, Inc., 550 Edmonds, Suite 204, Lewisville, TX 75067 for the examples of user-interface graphics shown in the book. Our appreciation goes to Claudia Dineen of Mlink, for the text addressing the rationale and business issue for each user-interface design and also for testing our tools and templates.

Thanks to Valorie Beer for editing the initial draft of the manuscript. Thanks to Frank Dwyer, Ph.D., professor of instructional technology, Penn State University, University Park; and Peter Vail, Oklahoma College of Continuing Education and the Center for Public Management and Educational Development, University of Oklahoma, for reviewing our book.

And to all of you whom we have worked with over the years who have mentored us, guided us, given us constructive criticism and feedback, and allowed us to experiment and be creative, you are too numerous to mention—but without all of you, we would never have gained the experience to share with others.

Thank you!

part one

Multimedia Needs Assessment and Analysis

Introduction to Multimedia Needs Assessment and Front-End Analysis

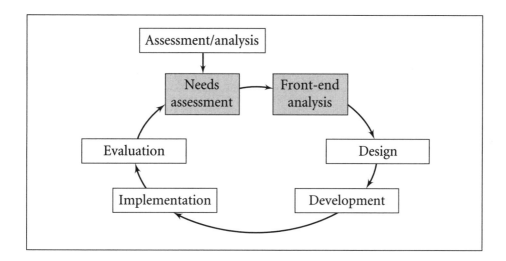

O ur approach breaks the analysis phase into two parts. The first is needs assessment, a systematic way of exploring and establishing the type of solution needed. The second is front-end analysis, a collection of techniques that can be used in various combinations to help you narrow the type and level of solution that will be required.

In completing the activities in this phase you will

- Find the customer's business issue
- Decide how to satisfy the business issue
- Decide the delivery mechanism for the solution
- Write objectives
- Complete cost analysis

During needs assessment it is critical to focus on gathering the information you need to be able to make informed decisions. The information from needs assessment provides input into front-end analysis in that, once the need for an intervention is established in needs assessment, front-end analysis explores deeper levels of information needed for the design of the solution. To perform needs assessment and front-end analysis you will need to:

1. Make a judgment about how much assessment and analysis is required to make an informed decision based on your time frame, project size, and project constraints
2. Determine the appropriate sources for collecting information
3. Establish a technique for collecting and assembling information

Needs Assessment

Needs assessment is the systematic process of determining goals, identifying discrepancies between actual and desired conditions, and establishing priorities for action (Lee and Roadman, 1991).

Briggs (1977) identified five types of need, illustrated in Table 2.1.

Table 2.1	
Five Types of Need	
Need	**Description**
1. Normative need	A need that is compared to a standard.
	Example one: industry standards establish that it should take 750 hours of development time for each hour of computer-based training delivery. Company X currently takes 1,500 hours to do this, so it needs to find ways to reduce the time to meet this standard in order to bid competitively.
	Example two: bank A is not as competitive as bank B in offering a variety of services to customers because it is not automated enough to efficiently process the paperwork required to deliver those services. Bank A needs automation to bring it to the same level as bank B.
2. Felt need	What people think they need.
	Example: the executives of a sales-and-marketing firm believe that their sales representatives need training in interpersonal

Table 2.1
Five Types of Need, Cont'd.

Need	Description
	relations because they don't share valuable information that can help others increase their sales. They feel a need for this training to solve their problem.
3. Expressed or demanded need	Supply and demand.
	Example: insurance company Y is looking for ways to improve the speed of processing claims because a private consulting company delivered the results of a survey it conducted, showing that motorists use this as the number-one criterion in selecting an insurance company.
4. Comparative need	Some people have a particular attribute; others don't.
	Example: retailer A finds that its customer service representatives resolve customer inquiries at an average of ten resolutions per measurement unit. The range among representatives, however, is from five to fifteen resolutions. The retailer needs to bring all customer service representatives to a maximum level of efficient processing while maintaining customer satisfaction.
5. Anticipated or future need	Projected demands.
	Example: a steering committee of bank A has decided that for it to be competitive it must automate the data-processing function to provide more services to customers. They state this goal in their five-year strategic plan.

PROCESS

There are six activities in the process of conducting a needs assessment:

1. *Determine the present condition.* Identify the root causes of the expressed need.

2. *Define the job.* What knowledge and skills are required to successfully complete the work?

3. *Rank the goals in order of importance.* Show how goals are interrelated.

4. *Identify discrepancies.* How do the expected performance and the actual performance encountered in meeting a goal differ? List all discrepancies, as well as missing tasks.

5. *Determine positive areas.* Identify areas related to the business issue in which the company is doing well, and document their existence.

6. *Set priorities for action.* Set them against the backdrop of the job goals, desired results, and other relevant factors.

Needs assessment is accomplished by developing assessment questionnaires, establishing procedures for collecting data (such as mailings, telephone, and personal interviews), and analyzing data to produce meaningful information.

Consider using the data-collection techniques presented in Table 2.2 (page 11). Appendix D provides instructions for these data-collection techniques:

- Self-completion questionnaires
- Direct interviews
- Focus groups
- Rank-and-order technique
- Observation

Confidentiality is important. To assure employees that none of their individual responses will be reported, use a confidentiality agreement similar to the one in the Assessment and Front-End Analysis Tools section of Appendix E. The organization's representative signs the agreement and a copy is shared with each participant in the needs assessment.

NEEDS ASSESSMENT PROCEDURE

Follow these activities:

Activity One: Determine the Present Condition

Step one: Identify the knowledge and skill needed to perform the task(s).

Step two: Identify the job-specific knowledge and skill areas used to select people for the task(s).

Step three: This depends on whether there is a match between the results of steps one and two. If there isn't, then identify the skills that are missing and review for possible training or performance support applications, and consider revision of employee-selection criteria.

Step four: If there is a match between steps one and two, then look for environmental causes of the problem. Visit the work environment and compare average performance with exemplary or ideal performance. Identify gaps in performance, and continue with step five.

Step five: Document task performance that is affected by such environmental factors as:

- Noise
- Equipment
- Tools
- Temperature
- Work space

Step six: Review all results and identify areas of need.
Step seven: Gather data from employees about:

- Management support
- Existing training
- Teamwork and empowerment
- Workflow and processes
- Safety

Step eight: Review all results and identify areas of need.

Activity Two: Define the Job

Define the ideal situation of the job, and compare the ideal to the tasks currently performed.

Activity Three: Rank the Goals in Order of Importance

List goals in order of importance, and show how they interrelate.

Multimedia-Based Instructional Design

Activity Four: Identify Discrepancies

Determine the differences between ideal and actual performance. List all discrepancies as well as missing tasks.

Activity Five: Determine Positive Areas

Use the appreciative-inquiry technique (Hammond, 1996) and document what is working. Appreciative inquiry identifies an organization's strengths, which is important for two reasons. First, the solution might be as simple as applying the same principles and procedures from those strengths to the current issue. Second, it focuses and allows organizations to reflect on and appreciate the positive aspects rather than focusing only on the negative.

Activity Six: Set Priorities for Action

Step one: List all possible solutions suggested by the needs assessment. Identify the impact on performance goals of not providing a solution.

Step two: Define the impact of each solution in terms of time, money, and customer satisfaction.

Step three: Make recommendations, keeping in mind job goals, desired results, and other relevant factors.

FROM OUR EXPERIENCE

Using the activities and steps outlined in this chapter, you will be surprised by how often the solution is not training. Spend the time you need to gather enough information to make enlightened suggestions for solving the stated business need.

Taking the time to systematically uncover the root of a perceived problem keeps you from wasting your time and your organization's resources on multimedia projects that do not solve a business need. Use the Needs Assessment Report form in the Assessment and Front-End Analysis Tools section of Appendix E as a starting point to document and report your needs-assessment results.

Those duties and tasks that the company performs well should be analyzed to determine how the successful skills are learned or taught at present. A possible recommendation might be that the successful learning techniques be replicated and included in training, or that where current performance is successful there is no need for training on those skills.

We often begin a needs assessment by analyzing the job descriptions that are usually already available for positions within a company. These descriptions generally detail the types of duties that members of the audience for the training are expected to perform. Job descriptions usually contain a catch-all phrase that reads something like ". . . and other duties as assigned." Be certain to identify if these other duties fall within or outside the scope of the stated business problem. Generic descriptions can be modified to accurately reflect the job using data collected during interviews or observations.

The status of the job description is a critical issue. If it is current, it probably accurately reflects the duties of the persons holding the position. If not current, you should determine its accuracy. The issue of accuracy might well be raised in any case, given the rapid pace of change and growth in business and industry today. More jobs now require people to assume multiple duties and perform tasks once performed by several employees.

At a minimum, the job descriptions you analyze should contain:

• Position title (the job name). This should be part of an overall organizational structure or hierarchy.
• Position description (generic). This can be a broad description or listing of the job actions and activities required for successful job performance.
• Knowledge, skills, and attitudes (KSA) required for the job.
• Proficiency measures. This is a list and explanation of the performance measures used for the job tasks.

If job descriptions do not exist for a position, they should be developed during the needs assessment.

From the job description, make a flowchart of the job, starting with the goal or final product and working backward. Use this flowchart to identify any prerequisite job skills as well as all critical steps in the job process and their related skills.

You can verify the job-description flowchart you have developed by asking the job performers and their supervisors to confirm the current duties and the correct entry-level skills for the job.

An electronic database is often helpful in assessment and front-end analysis efforts. A database format enables you to store, manipulate, and organize data to report your findings clearly and concisely.

We have found the techniques in Table 2.2 useful for data collection. Analyze them to determine what would work best in your unique situation.

Table 2.2
Data-Collection Techniques

Interviews

Technique	Advantages	Disadvantages
Phone	Fast and inexpensive	Less sensitive; no visual information
	Easy to supervise	Must be short—fifteen minutes or less (participants do not like to be kept on the phone longer)
		Requires trained interviewers
In person	High response rate, most accurate	Can be time consuming
		Sometimes yields extraneous information
	Highest volume of information	Requires trained interviewers

Questionnaires

Technique	Advantages	Disadvantages
E-mail	High rate of return	Requires explicit instructions
	Yields large amount of data	Allows collaboration among respondents (if individual responses are desired)
	Does not require trained interviewers	
Paper questionnaire	Yields large amount of data	Requires explicit instructions
	Does not require trained interviewers	Returns tend to be low

Observation

Technique	Advantages	Disadvantages
Video camera	Find out what people actually do rather than what they say they do	Time consuming
		Those who analyze the results must be trained

Table 2.2
Data-Collection Techniques, Cont'd.

Observation

Technique	Advantages	Disadvantages
Video camera (cont'd.)	Less bias of what is observed because more than one person can view the video	Workers may perform differently while being observed Does not allow you to question job performers in real time or experience some of the environmental factors that affect performance You can only see what the lens of the camera sees, not everything on the periphery
Observer	Find out what people actually do rather than what they say they do	Time consuming Requires skilled observer Workers may perform differently while they are being observed

Simulation

Technique	Advantages	Disadvantages
Inexpensive mock-up or talk-through	Permits collecting job performance information before equipment is developed	Results may not transfer directly to job performance because mock-up is not realistic Requires skilled determination of what should be simulated Will not account for motivational factors
Use actual equipment or software, but not in the work environment	Only opportunity to observe behavior under controlled conditions of stress, system failure, etc.	Can be very expensive Requires skilled determination of what should be simulated Does not account for motivational factors

After collecting all relevant data, verify that the information is adequate for recommending a solution and (if appropriate) designing the intervention. Document your conclusions with as much detail as time, resources, and project constraints allow.

If you are an experienced instructional designer and if you determine your project warrants a streamlined process for needs assessment and front-end analysis, use the rapid analysis method outlined in Chapter Thirteen.

SUMMARY

At this point, you have determined if there is a gap between the desired performance and the current state of a job. If a gap exists, move to front-end analysis and determine the type of intervention required to close the gap. If there is no gap, or if the gap is outside the range of interventions permissible for the multimedia development or training group (which might be the case for a performance or systemic issue, as outlined in Chapter Thirteen), then so inform the stakeholders.

Note that instructional developers and multimedia development or training groups should expand their repertoire of skills to assist with issues other than training. At the very least, they need to be aware of other sources of help. If some aspect of the solution is within the purview of the training group, remain involved in the project and stay informed of the changes that occur. In this way, your group can move quickly to implement your portion of any solution once the changes are completed.

Front-End Analysis

Once needs assessment determines that training or performance support intervention is required, the next step is to obtain more detailed information about exactly *what* is to be developed. Table 3.1 is a summary of the types of front-end analysis and what you will know at the conclusion of front-end analysis.

Table 3.1	
Types of Front-End Analysis	
Type	**Purpose**
Audience analysis	Identify the background, learning characteristics, and prerequisite skills of the audience.
Technology analysis	Identify existing technology capabilities.
Task analysis	Describe the job-related tasks performed as a result of the training or performance support.
Critical-incident analysis	Determine what skills or knowledge should be targeted in the multimedia intervention or training program.
Situational analysis	Identify environmental or organizational constraints that may have an impact on goals and multimedia design.
Objective analysis	Write the objectives for the job tasks to be addressed.
Media analysis	Select the appropriate media delivery strategy.
Extant-data analysis	Identify existing training materials, manuals, references, and syllabi.
Cost-benefit analysis	Identify cost and benefit, and return on investment.

At the end of front-end analysis, use the Analysis Report Tool in the Assessment and Front-End Analysis Tools section of Appendix E to organize your findings.

FROM OUR EXPERIENCE

Once the need has been established, use the tools of front-end analysis to collect and analyze all relevant data regarding a business need. To avoid expensive rework, we recommend you complete all front-end analysis, including content gathering, before beginning design.

We often find front-end analysis to be the "hidden phase" of the ID process. Many organizations decide to eliminate assessment and analysis altogether and begin immediately with design "to save time." But have you ever heard of tweaking the design? What usually happens is the team gets to a certain point in the project and realizes there's not enough information or there's been an error. So the team members decide to go back and revisit their initial ideas and then move forward. The team may have to gain permission to make the changes, which is usually obtained because of the investment of time and resources. So the project moves on—but suddenly, another stop! More tweaking. Then at some point the project is determined to be so far off target it is abandoned because the usefulness is no longer worth the effort or money, or it is finally completed—over budget and late.

The revisiting is really analysis. Time taken to complete a thorough analysis at the beginning is invariably more than made up in time savings later. It's sort of "Pay me now, or pay me later." Somewhere, the team is going to do the analysis. Our experience has been that if you spend adequate time completing a proper needs assessment and front-end analysis, the time required for the design and development phases can be greatly reduced. Those projects that go immediately to design simply spend more time there, and the result is a rushed development phase.

During development, it is usually the quality assurance (QA) reviews that are eliminated or rushed, resulting in an inferior product fraught with errors. We have found a more appropriate ratio is one-third analysis; one-third design and development; and one-third implementation, evaluation, and maintenance (Figure 3.1).

We have been asked how to respond to management or customers' position that they don't want to spend so much time on assessment and analysis. Our answer is that so long as you incorporate the time and activities into the project, you

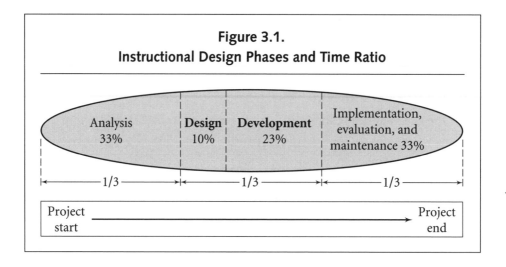

Figure 3.1.
Instructional Design Phases and Time Ratio

can call it whatever the decision makers are comfortable with. If you keep decision makers informed of the valuable information you are gaining from the assessment and analysis activities, they will be satisfied in seeing progress on the project.

The next nine chapters deal with the nine types of front-end analysis. We examine each type closely and explain the information derived from it. We also explain how all of the data collected during front-end analysis fits into the design of the project.

In Chapter Thirteen we present a method for reducing the time required to complete an analysis without sacrificing quality. Our rapid analysis method can be used only after you thoroughly understand the methodology and information derived from the nine types of analysis.

Audience Analysis

R emember sitting through training sessions that were way over your head, or that proceeded so slowly you had trouble staying focused? It's not a favorite experience, but one we all have had. Audience analysis identifies the background and some of the learning characteristics of the target population.

This information helps you design a solution appropriate to the intended audience. Examples of information about the target audience that has an impact on the final solution are

- Experience with the training medium, as with CBT (computer-based training) or self-instructional materials. You may have to add additional material to the solution to acclimate the audience to the medium.

- Learning preferences (such as team versus individual learning). If the job requires people to work together, the solution should use the team approach.

- Language ability or preference (say, considerations of English as a second language). Extra reference material, online dictionaries, or translations may be required.

- Previous training or job experience. If there are widely varying skill levels among those who perform the job, the solution has to accommodate the variations by guiding the audience to the appropriate level of materials.

- Special requirements (signing, Braille, and so on). If you have special conditions among the target audience that need to be met, the solution must be adapted to meet those requirements.

PROCESS

There are four activities in the procedure for conducting an audience analysis:

1. Analyze audience demographics and special requirements.
2. Determine attitudes toward content.
3. Analyze the language skills of the audience.
4. Document the results.

AUDIENCE ANALYSIS PROCEDURE

Follow these activities:

Activity One: Analyze Audience Demographics and Special Requirements

Step one: Begin with the job task information you collected during needs assessment and use it to verify the audience.

Step two: Confirm how many individuals will participate in the program and their general education and background.

Step three: Collect data on the native language, tone, use of humor, and graphics that are most appropriate for the audience. Pay particular attention to this aspect of the analysis if the audience is global, is predominantly male or female, or has a narrow age range. We recommend you become knowledgeable about cultural differences and make certain you address special requirements for cultural sensitivity for audiences from various cultures.

In step four, note any special physical, ergonomic, or environmental audience requirements.

Activity Two: Determine Attitudes Toward Content

Step one: Determine if the learners are likely to have misconceptions or misinformation about content that need to be addressed.

Step two: Determine if there are negative or positive attitudes toward the content.

Step three: Go on to determine if there is content-specific terminology or vocabulary that must be used or learned. Pay particular attention to this aspect if a large percentage of the audience use English as a second language.

Activity Three: Analyze the Language Skills of the Audience

Developing interventions at appropriate levels of readability is important to ensure that learning occurs. Analyzing language skills requires a two-step approach:

determining your audience's primary spoken and written language, and confirming the reading levels of the audience members in their primary language.

An effective method we employ to ensure that language is used consistently is the Fog Index (Gunning 1968), one of many readability scales available. Instructions for using the Fog Index are found in the Assessment and Front-End Analysis Tools section of Appendix E. Also, most sophisticated word-processing systems contain components that analyze readability.

Activity Four: Document the Results

Record the results of your analysis for use by the design team (graphic artists, instructional designers) during the design phase and for the development team (interface designers, authors, videographers) in the development phase.

FROM OUR EXPERIENCE

Audience analysis is an area where assumptions are often made without validation. If your assumptions about the audience are not correct, problems will show up during testing and evaluation, at which time it is often too late or too expensive to fix the product. Attention during analysis to determining the audience language, tone, and delivery format can make the difference between great multimedia for the wrong audience and great multimedia that hits the mark and solves a business need.

When developing training for a global audience, we recommend you consider (1) recruiting for the project team someone who is from the appropriate culture(s) and speaks the language(s) well to be certain the product meets the cultural and language requirements of the audiences, or (2) producing one version of the product and sending it to a vendor or development team from the target culture to enculturate and translate it.

SUMMARY

You now know the characteristics of the target audience with respect to their language, cultural, and educational background, as well as their attitude toward the content of the job and learning in general. All of these factors influence, and must be taken into account in, the media you use to deliver the solution.

Next, you analyze the technology considerations from the perspective of what is available or required for the solution, what the customer is willing to entertain as technology, and what the audience is familiar with and comfortable using.

Technology Analysis

There is a widening gap between training technologists and instructional designers. We assume the latter have the ability to produce "regular" training media such as instructor and participant guides, job aids, overhead transparencies, or flipcharts. But if you are typical of professionals in the instructional design field, your background is not "technical." Still, to meet the challenge of supporting business needs in today's business environment, you will discover it is critical to have a basic understanding of your unique technology environment.

Analyzing the level of technology expertise in your organization:

- Brings the flexibility needed to solve business problems in the context of your unique technology environment
- Allows for a measured and phased approach to multimedia technologies depending on who and how many in the organization have access to technology
- Provides the information you need for media selection

PROCESS

There are seven activities in conducting a technology analysis:

1. Analyze available communication technology.
2. Analyze the technology available for reference or performance support.

3. Analyze the technology available for testing and assessment.

4. Analyze the technology for distribution.

5. Analyze the technology for delivery.

6. Analyze the expertise.

7. Document the results.

TECHNOLOGY ANALYSIS PROCEDURE

Follow these activities:

Activity One: Analyze Available Communication Technology

To assess available technology for basic communication, determine which of these technologies are currently being used:

- Phone conferencing. Are employees able to phone in from their desks or a convenient location?

- E-mail. Are employees able to use their e-mail and attach documents to mail messages? Most employees have an e-mail address, and e-mail is accepted as just another communication tool, like the telephone. This media can very effectively constitute a communication channel between the instructor and student(s). E-mail was one of the earliest Internet applications to be widely used and is still one of the most powerful applications.

- Chat-room technology. Chat room technology allows users to carry on text-based, online conversation with one another from within their web browser, similar to a phone conference.

- Newsgroup technology. Newsgroups (discussion groups) are similar to chat rooms, but discussions are posted on a server for anyone to read and learn from. Most web browsers include features that let users interact with a newsgroup from the browser.

- List-server technology. List servers use e-mail to enable a group to carry on discussions around a common area of interest. List servers are another form of discussion group and are also one of the original Internet applications.

Activity Two: Analyze the Technology Available for Reference or Performance Support

Step one: Determine if online reference materials in Hypertext Markup Language (HTML) and linked documents are available: company websites with links to other references or websites; graphics, videos, and photos in databases; online phone lists; and online course catalogs, schedules, abstracts, course notes, and instructor's notes.

Step two: Determine if employees have access to performance support files or help systems. If so, what software is available for development? Robohelp, Doc-to-Help, or similar software applications are often used to develop this type of help file or online performance support system.

Activity Three: Analyze the Technology Available for Testing and Assessment

What technology is available for testing and assessment?

Step one: Determine if electronic self-assessment, testing, or certification is available. If applicable, determine database and record-keeping requirements. If the tests are developed internally, determine the languages used. HTML, Java, and Shockwave are applications used in test development, along with off-the-shelf testing and assessment generators.

Step two: Define the issues of security. They make web-based testing and assessment challenging. Security issues are often the purview of an information systems (IS) department responsible for the computing needs of the entire business. A multimedia development organization's need to be able to test participants remotely and with security may find that its requirement is not a high priority for an IS department struggling with system integration or similar problems. Two security issues related to testing and assessment via the Internet or an intranet are quite commonly encountered. The first is user authentication. Authenticating (confirming) users' identities and access privileges is one way to control access to the site. Users are asked to authenticate themselves by providing information unique to them along with a private password. Determine the requirements for authentication.

The second issue is information confidentiality. The type of security that receives the most attention is information privacy. Web encryption is the technology used to ensure that information remains private as it passes over the Internet. Encryption does this by scrambling information so only the sender and receiver can make sense of it. More and more, web browsers and web servers are being developed with encryption capabilities built in. Determine the requirements for information confidentiality.

Activity Four: Analyze the Technology for Distribution

What technology is available for distribution of training or performance support?

Step one: Determine if CD-ROMs, disks, or other materials are used for courses, reference material, or help files and, if so, how they are distributed.

Step two: Determine if file transfer protocol (FTP) is used to download courses or files. FTP is a program with standardized features and functions used to transfer files from one computer to another on an intranet or the Internet. FTP technology is widely available and used routinely for distributing courseware. The potential for security-related issues is particularly acute for courses that contain sensitive or company-proprietary information. FTP technology can be used internally, though, to transfer content among members of a production team.

Activity Five: Analyze the Technology for Delivery

What technology is available for delivery of training or performance support?

Step one: Determine if dedicated audio and video servers are used for delivering courses. If appropriate, note the requirements for file type and size.

Step two: Determine if employees have access to multimedia PCs. Be sure to note the delivery platform with the lowest common denominator, so that configuration can be used for a minimum development-and-testing standard. Remember that the performance of a course is only as good as the slowest computer on which it is delivered.

Don't assume that the corporate computer is the only one that most employees have available. Many home PCs are more multimedia-capable than their corporate counterparts. Determine alternate access to PCs.

Step three: Find out if a video teleconferencing or educational TV system is used for distribution of information. If applicable, pay particular attention to scheduling requirements.

Activity Six: Analyze the Expertise

Analyze the technology design and development and maintenance expertise. Determine if the equipment, hardware, software, and maintenance required for each technology is available. Include vendors or resources in other departments within your organization. Here is a sample checklist to use for determining availability of resources:

☐ Video production personnel, hardware, equipment, and software

☐ Audio production personnel, hardware, equipment, and software

☐ Graphics production personnel, hardware, equipment, and software

☐ Help or reference-system development personnel, hardware, equipment, and software

☐ CBT authoring and development personnel, hardware, equipment, and software

☐ Web and HTML development personnel, hardware, equipment, and software

☐ Testing, database, and statistical-programs personnel, hardware, equipment, and software

Activity Seven: Document the Results

Document all your results, and all contacts, with appropriate detail. Use the Technology Assessment Tool in the Assessment and Front-End Analysis Tools section of Appendix E to document findings, and note any additional technologies in use for

- Communication
- Reference material
- Testing and assessment
- Distribution
- Delivery
- Special design and development expertise

FROM OUR EXPERIENCE

It's impossible to meet business goals using multimedia without knowing technology details, such as the baseline configuration of user PCs or your company's ability to perform secure testing. Producing multimedia that doesn't transmit correctly, can't be maintained, or is inappropriate for the delivery platform wastes time, money, energy, and company resources. Understanding and documenting available technologies as well as current development expertise yields design specifications that ensure the effectiveness of your solution. A technology assessment can also uncover technology and resource gaps that are not readily apparent. This can have a big impact on cost analysis.

The assessment can be performed periodically and reused in multiple projects to lower overall analysis costs.

SUMMARY

You have now captured the technology capabilities of your group or target organization. These capabilities are important in determining which components you can include in a solution—indeed, in determining the very form of the final solution. For example, if the target audience has low-end computers with no sound or video capabilities, a high-level computer-based training solution is of no use.

Next, you look at the physical surroundings where actual work takes place and the availability of facilities in the event training is required.

Situational Analysis

When you analyzed the job and tasks being performed during needs assessment (Chapter Two), you noted the physical conditions in which the job is performed. If you uncovered physical or environmental factors that have an impact on job and task performance, then conducting additional situational analysis will help you gather information to:

- Take these factors into consideration in developing realistic goals and objectives
- Design an effective performance support strategy or multimedia delivery strategy
- Produce insight into the design phase to ensure successful job performance
- Help uncover barriers to transferring and performing job skills

PROCESS

Before you can begin to design your solution, you need to examine the work environment for factors that either detract from or else enhance how successfully an employee performs specific job-related tasks. Visiting the work environment is the best way to conduct a situational analysis.

There are three activities in performing a situational analysis:

1. Analyze the job environment.
2. Analyze delivery environment.
3. Document the results.

SITUATIONAL ANALYSIS PROCEDURE

Follow these activities:

Activity One: Analyze the Job Environment

Familiarize yourself with the environment where the job is typically performed. Analyze task performance that is affected by these environmental factors:

- Physical and environmental factors such as noise, ventilation, or temperature
- Management support of training and employee development
- Teamwork
- Empowerment
- Delegation and control
- Feedback
- Work processes and policies
- Safety issues
- Coaching and mentoring

Activity Two: Analyze Delivery Environment

What factors in the training delivery environment can influence transfer of learning to the work environment? For example, a telecommunications training lab might boast fine equipment that nevertheless does not replicate the real world of work in the company. Or a lack of proper training facilities might be obvious in a noisy retail environment.

In your review, you should consider a number of factors:

- Access to training facilities
- Availability of instructors, coaches, and mentors
- Physical and environmental factors such as noise, ventilation, and temperature

Activity Three: Document the Results

Document the results of your analysis for use in the design, development, and implementation phases. Be particularly sensitive to employee confidentiality and how results of the analysis are reported.

FROM OUR EXPERIENCE

The best multimedia in the world cannot overcome a network that constantly crashes, management that gives little support to the tasks being targeted, or lack of equipment and tools for performing the tasks on which you are targeting. Develop observation and survey instruments such as those explained in Appendix D to uncover the information you need about the environment.

If you suspect environmental or situational factors are inhibiting performance, conducting this analysis can keep you from wasting time and resources targeting training when in fact the effort should be directed at improving the workplace environment or organizational, management, or work-process issues.

SUMMARY

You now have information on the environment where the work is done and where any potential learning might take place. This information is pivotal in designing a solution. For example, you wouldn't want to design an instructor-led class in a facility where there are no classrooms. Neither would you want to present a hands-on workshop on the work floor of a noisy factory.

Now that you know about the audience, the technology, and the environment, you're ready to find out what the work consists of through task analysis.

Task Analysis

Task analysis involves breaking the job down into duties and tasks, as well as determining the knowledge, skills, and attitudes (KSA) that job performers must have.

The job is what is outlined in a job description. Duties are major categories outlined in the description; tasks are the steps required to complete a duty. As for KSA, knowledge is the intellectual information a job performer must have. Skills are the behaviors required. Attitude is the demeanor or spirit with which the job performer completes the job.

ADULT LEARNING THEORY

From behavioral and developmental theory comes our knowledge of adult learners. Although adults have gone through the developmental stages and their thinking has been affected by those experiences that gave them the pieces of information they integrated into their present intellectual scheme, nevertheless adults differ in numerous ways because of experience. When they are learning something completely new, they go through the same developmental stages as young children—though they pass through them much faster because of certain intellectual processes that are already in place from previous experiences. This means, for example, that adults need fewer examples of a concept than children do to completely grasp it.

The components of adult learning (Knowles, 1990) are outlined in Table 7.1.

Table 7.1
Adult Learning Theory

Component	Description
Relevance	Adult learners must see a direct relationship between the topic or information to be learned and the real world where the knowledge is used.
Involvement	Adult learners must be actively involved in the learning process, rather than sit passively and listen or watch the instructor.
Control over learning	Adult learners must have independence to learn where, what, and how they learn best.
Nontraditional learning situation	Adult learners need privacy for learning and individualized, self-paced instruction so that they can learn at their own rate.

Adult learning theory is applied to multimedia instructional development in two ways. First, material is less effective if written at a level above the stage where learners are functioning. Second, objectives must match appropriate levels if adults are to enjoy the best learning (see Lee, 1990).

PROCESS

A well-structured task analysis should give you the information needed to construct a list of all the tasks required for successful completion of a specific job. The activities to complete during task analysis are to

1. Define the position title.
2. Identify all job-related duties.
3. Identify all tasks.
4. Order the tasks.
5. Document the results.

Figure 7.1 may help you visualize the relationship between job, duty, task, and KSA.

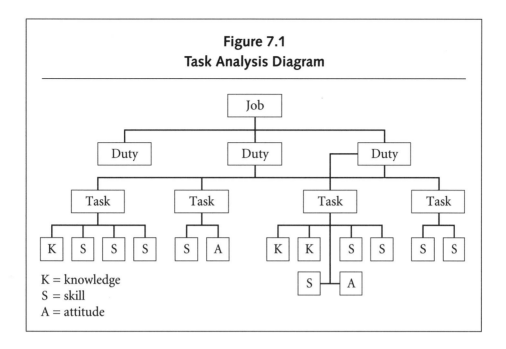

Figure 7.1
Task Analysis Diagram

K = knowledge
S = skill
A = attitude

TASK ANALYSIS PROCEDURE

Follow these activities:

Activity One: Define the Position Title

State the position title from the job description established during needs assessment. An example of a position title is "instructional designer."

Activity Two: Identify All Job-Related Duties

Break the job down into major areas of responsibility, and then write a duty statement for each area using a verb ending in *-ing* followed by an object of the action. (Example: specific duties of an instructional designer may be "writing course objectives" and "writing course storyboards.") Ensure that each duty is independent of other duties. If you can find no tasks to list under a duty statement, the duty is probably a subordinate task of another duty.

Activity Three: Identify All Tasks

Step one: Use questionnaires, interviews, and observations to confirm or identify primary tasks. Use subject-matter experts (SMEs), exemplary performers, or incumbent workers as your information sources. Be certain to

- Include references such as the names of tools or forms
- Avoid abbreviations and jargon
- Be brief

Step two: Ensure that each task statement stands alone. To write task statements, use an action verb and add clarification statements as necessary. For example, a task associated with the duty of an instructional designer who is writing objectives might be to "use all five parts of an objective (the situation; the learned capability; the object; the action verb; and the tools, constraints, and conditions)."

Step three: Determine the KSA the job performer must have. For example, the knowledge associated with writing a five-part objective is knowing the five parts of the objective and being able to include those items in writing objectives.

To review, using our example:

Job	Instructional designer
Duty	Writing course objectives
Task	Write a five-part objective
Knowledge	The five parts of the objective

Activity Four: Order the Tasks

Create a task hierarchy by listing all superordinate tasks with their subordinate tasks. Tasks should be ordered in the sequence in which they will be performed, if there is a preferred or required sequence. Order the tasks by using one of the methods listed in Table 7.2.

Activity Five: Document the Results

Document what you find in your analysis, using the Job or Task Breakdown Tool and the Task Inventory Tool, both found in the Assessment and Front-End Analysis Tools section of Appendix E.

SUMMARY

You now have the job broken down into its component parts. Now you can move on to critical incident analysis, to determine which of the components you want to include in the solution.

Table 7.2
Task Order

If tasks . . .	Then . . .
Are mostly related to procedures (such as steps performed to process an order),	Order the tasks in the same sequence by which the procedures are completed (job-task order).
Are concepts related to an overall skill or task (such as using active listening techniques to improve team communication),	Order the tasks from the simplest to the most complex (simple-to-complex order).
Require application of rules or principles (such as following guidelines of a policy for returned merchandise),	Order the tasks by grouping related content (psychological order).

Critical Incident Analysis

Y ou've assessed and analyzed your audience and the job from a
number of perspectives. Now that you have completed the task
analysis, you must decide which tasks to teach and which ones not to
teach.

It is important to focus on tasks that improve performance and are essential to
solving the business need. Otherwise, money and resources that could be used
to address other problems are wasted on extraneous design and development. Also,
your audience wastes energy wading through information that is simply not useful. As a consequence, the effectiveness of the solution is degraded.

In critical incident analysis, analyze the task list to determine the duties and
tasks that are presently performed well, and also those duties and tasks that are important but lacking.

Critical incidents are areas of performance that are completed either effectively
or ineffectively, and behavioral descriptions of instances of extreme cases (char-
acterized by success or failure) in performance. To perform a critical incident
analysis, use focus groups, observations, direct interviews, and questionnaires (or
any combination of these that you feel is necessary) to determine the critical aspects of the solution. Instructions for developing these observation instruments,
interview forms, and questionnaires are in Appendix D along with instructions for
conducting focus groups.

PROCESS

The basic process is to review the tasks that were generated during the task analysis and perform four activities:

1. Determine the critical tasks.

2. Determine important but nonessential tasks.

3. Determine the tasks you will deselect.

4. Document the results.

PROCEDURE

Follow these activities:

Activity One: Determine the Critical Tasks

Which tasks are critical to the job? Uncover those tasks the employee must be able to complete to successfully perform the job, under typical conditions and to the standard required. High-priority tasks that show up as weak areas of performance definitely should be included in the solution.

Because there are no universally accepted criteria for criticality, you have to construct one or more for your specific situation. You might consider these ideas in establishing your norms:

- How often the task is performed (the more often, generally the more critical)

- The severity of the consequences for failure to perform the task (the greater the consequence, the more critical the task)

- Restrictions within the organization on what jobs, tasks, and duties certain people can perform (for example, presence of union agreements usually indicates a higher level of criticality for those tasks)

Activity Two: Determine Important but Nonessential Tasks

Identify which tasks are nice to know but are to be included only if time and budget permit. Determine the criteria for marginal tasks, such as those that

- Are performed occasionally

- Constitute background

- Provide supporting knowledge not directly related to job tasks

Activity Three: Determine the Tasks You Will Deselect

Determine the tasks to deselect and not include in the solution.

Here are some typical reasons for task rejection:

- It is rarely performed.
- It is not critical to job performance.
- It is easily learned.
- It is a prerequisite skill that the learner has as a condition of employment.
- It involves skills beyond the range of capability or permissibility of the members of the target audience.
- It involves skills that are presently performed at a marginal, but high enough, level of proficiency.

Activity Four: Document the Results

The outcome of the critical incident analysis should be documented as a list of tasks used for developing objectives.

FROM OUR EXPERIENCE

Critical incident analysis is used most effectively to define performance in technical areas. The focus-group strategy is useful in situations where expert performers can describe their own performance. There are times, however, when what is considered expert performance is difficult to describe or capture. For example, what is it exactly that distinguishes the tasks of an effective salesperson or a top manager from an average or poor one?

Analyzing target-audience skill levels before going into design helps you produce a solution that is both appropriate and effective. Lists of prerequisite skills are important because, although expert performance sets the upper limits of knowledge and skill, prerequisite skills set the lower limits. Keep in mind that entry-level skills that the job holders are presumed to have usually do not require training and are in the nice-but-not-necessary category.

SUMMARY

Critical incident analysis keeps things focused as you develop objectives. With the information from this analysis, you concentrate on what is most important for improving performance and what you will include in your solution.

Objective Analysis

Writing clear, testable objectives is critical to developing effective solutions. Objectives determine what you include in the content, whether the solution produces knowledge or performance, how the effectiveness of your solution is measured, and the media you choose to deliver the solution. All of your analyses done thus far now culminate in formulating your objectives.

We have developed a system for writing objectives with two primary purposes: first, to get you to think about objectives before you write them, and second, to write objectives that are meaningful.

RELATED THEORY

Of all that is written on objectives, Mager provided the basics in his 1962 book *Preparing Instructional Objectives.* Gagné, Briggs, and Wager, in *Principles of Instructional Design* (1988), have, in our opinion, improved on these basics better than anyone.

There are five domains in which learning occurs: cognitive, affective, motor, psychomotor, and metacognitive. These domains, which are explained in Table 9.1, form the basis for an objectives analysis.

The Cognitive Domain

Gagné, Briggs, and Wager (1988) present an outline of the various levels of intellectual skills required for learning within the cognitive domain. Table 9.2 explains the seven levels.

Table 9.1
Domains of Learning

Domain	Dealing with . . .
1. Cognitive	The thought processes
2. Affective	Feelings and attitudes
3. Motor	Learning physical movements
4. Psychomotor	Cognitive thought processes involved in physical movements that have been brought to the automatic level (can be done without thinking)
5. Metacognitive	Cognitive thought processes involved in "learning how to learn" that have been brought to the automatic level (strategies for approaching learning tasks that one uses without thinking about them)

Table 9.2
Levels in the Cognitive Domain

Level	Intellectual Skill
1. Discriminations	Being able to see, hear, or feel the differences between incoming stimulus situations
2. Concrete concept	Being able to identify one or more instances of a class of items
3. Defined concept	Being able to classify objects or events according to certain attributes and functions
4. Rule	Being able to form classifications that distinguish relationships between and among concepts (concrete or defined)
5. Problem solving	Being able to apply rules to new situations
6. Cognitive strategies	Applying problem-solving strategies when approaching a learning situation
7. Verbal information	Information that can be verbally repeated with comprehension of what is verbalized

The Affective Domain

Krathwohl edited *A Taxonomy of Educational Objectives* (1964), which outlined levels within the affective domain. Although he listed five levels, we have combined the first two, receiving and responding, in Table 9.3 because receiving cannot be measured unless (1) the student responds and (2) we write only measurable objectives. Table 9.3 explains the four levels.

Table 9.3
Levels in the Affective Domain

Level	Description
1. Receiving and responding	Verbally stating the learner is sensitive to or has adopted a value or attitude
2. Valuing	Demonstrating by behaviors and actions that one is sensitive to or has adopted a value or attitude
3. Organization	Making comparisons, theorizing, organizing, balancing, defining, and formulating criteria to evaluate behaviors, codes of conduct, and standards for values determination
4. Characterization	Changing behavior as a result of reorganization, and establishing consistent, increasingly mature behavior patterns

The Motor and Psychomotor Domains

Harrow (1972) published a taxonomy of levels of functioning within the motor and psychomotor domains. Three are listed here as examples; we deal with only these levels because they seem to us the most relevant to writing objectives. (Refer to Harrow's book for a complete discussion of all the levels.) There is an important distinction for instructional designers, in that motor objectives are those that emphasize actually teaching the motor (movement) skill. Psychomotor has as its basis the intellectual knowledge and skills that underlie the motor activity. Psychomotor skills are motor skills that have been brought to the automatic level through learning that integrates them with cognitive processes. Table 9.4 explains these motor and psychomotor domain levels. Psychomotor has one level—perceptual—with five sublevels.

Table 9.4
Levels in the Motor and Psychomotor Domain

Level	Sublevel	Description
1. Reflex movements		Voluntary or involuntary physical movements or actions
2. Basic movements		Coordinated movements such as reaching, grasping, crawling, manipulating physical objects, walking
3. Perceptual		Distinguishing between the self and surroundings:
	(1)	Kinesthetic discrimination: the relation of one's body to surrounding objects and controlling one's body in relation to the surrounding space
	(2)	Auditory discrimination: the ability of the learner to differentiate among various sounds— their pitch, intensity, directionality—and to reproduce the sound if necessary
	(3)	Visual discrimination: distinguish between form and details of objects; visually track an object; remember the attributes of an object; select the dominant figure from the background; recognize the consistency of shapes and forms
	(4)	Tactile discrimination: the ability to differentiate between the textures or forms of objects through the sense of touch
	(5)	Coordinated abilities: the coordination of two or more of these perceptual capabilities

The Metacognitive Domain

Metacognition (Alley and Deschler, 1979) is integration of the cognitive, affective, motor, and psychomotor domains. It involves the internal strategies one employs when approaching a task or solving a problem—that is, learning how to learn. Metacognition is probably the least written about and least understood (but, in our opinion, the most important) learning domain because it integrates all of the others. The best learners develop these strategies on their own. However, mastering them should not be left to chance.

Superior multimedia instruction should go beyond simply presenting the knowledge and skills necessary for a task. Superior multimedia should teach processes and problem-solving strategies that individuals can generalize to other situations. Here is a basic eight-step metacognitive strategy to teach someone how to learn (Alley and Deschler, 1979):

1. Observe the student performing the task.
2. Explain the student's approach (verbalizing each step).
3. Explain the desired approach.
4. Demonstrate the new approach (verbalizing each step).
5. Encourage questions before, during, and after the demonstration.
6. Have the student verbally rehearse the steps until he or she can state them without error (provide corrective feedback to the student during rehearsal).
7. Have the student practice with simulated materials (again offering corrective feedback immediately).
8. Have the student practice with actual materials.

Writing Objectives Within the Domains of Learning

There are four types of objective for any solution, listed and explained in Table 9.5. Write objectives in the order outlined in the table.

PROCESS

Here is the process to follow when writing objectives:

1. Decide on domains.
2. Decide on level.
3. Write goal statement.
4. Write performance objectives.
5. Engage in a group discussion.
6. Separate terminal objectives from performance objectives.
7. Separate lesson objectives from performance objectives.

Table 9.5
Ordering Objectives

Objective	Description
Goals and course objective	Concisely states the goal for the entire course in one or two sentences, clearly indicating what the students should know (KSA) or be able to do (behaviors, performance) after completing the entire course. Statements describe the intended outcome of the learning from a learner's perspective.
Performance objectives	These objectives never actually go into the course; they are written for instructional designers to communicate with each other. These are the five-part objectives that eventually make up the terminal and lesson objectives, as explained in the process approach described in this topic.
Terminal objectives	This objective states the KSA that a student is to demonstrate when he or she returns to the job.
Lesson objectives	The specific KSA that the student demonstrates during a lesson.

OBJECTIVE ANALYSIS PROCEDURE

Complete the following activities and steps.

Activity One: Decide on Domains

Decide on the domain of each task, using the task listing to determine KSA. Match the domains to each task.

Activity Two: Decide on Level

Determine the level within the domain of each task.

Activity Three: Write Goal Statement

Write the overall course goal statement.

Activity Four: Write Performance Objectives

Write the performance objective for each task. Use the five elements in Table 9.6 to construct a performance objective for each task.

Table 9.6
Five Parts of an Objective

Element	Description
1. Situation	The stimulus situation, the given, or the circumstances under which the behavior will be observed
2. Learned capability	The type of learning outcome the demonstrated behavior represents, strictly defined by certain verbs for each level of intellectual skill
3. Object	The content of the learner's performance
4. Action verb	How the performance will be completed (*note:* a complete list of action verbs corresponding to each level of Gagné's hierarchy is provided in Appendix A)
5. Tools, constraints, and conditions	The special tools needed, the constraints to, or the actual conditions under which the performance will be observed

Table 9.7 lists the verbs that are used exclusively as capability verbs. Use the appropriate learned-capability verb for the level you intend. Gagné (1985) restricts these verbs to focus the objective writer on what the solution addresses, from discriminations to attitudes.

Use an appropriate action verb from the list at the beginning of Appendix B.

The following are examples of performance objectives that use adult learning situations in the technical-skills and soft-skills training environments, and model objectives in each domain and at each level.

Objectives for Technical Skills. Training in technical skills usually involves developing training for software, a piece of equipment, or machinery. The manufacturing examples we use here involve maintaining a piece of electronic equipment. The domain and the level are identified for each objective.

- *Cognitive domain, discrimination level.* Given a diagram of the electronic instrument (situation), the student will discriminate each functional part (learned capability) by circling (action verb) each major part (object) with complete accuracy (special condition).

Table 9.7
Gagné, Briggs, and Wager's
Learned Capabilities and Accompanying
Verbs for Developing Performance Objectives (1988)

Learned Capability	Capability Verb
Discrimination	Discriminates
Concrete concept	Identifies
Defined concept	Classifies
Rule	Demonstrates
Problem solving	Generates
Cognitive strategy	Adopts
Verbal information	States
Motor skill	Executes
Attitude	Chooses

- *Cognitive domain, rule level.* Given a defined problem in a major part of the electronic instrument (situation), the student will demonstrate (learned capability) knowledge of troubleshooting procedures (object) by describing (action verb) the troubleshooting procedure with complete accuracy (special condition).

- *Affective domain, valuing level.* Given an identified problem with the electronic instrument (situation), the student will choose (learned capability) to perform (action verb) the emergency-shutdown safety procedures (object) before beginning to repair the problem (constraint).

- *Psychomotor (perceptual) domain, visual discrimination level.* Given an identified problem in the electrical distribution system of the electronic instrument (situation), the student will execute (learned capability) the diagnostic procedures by correctly attaching (action verb) the voltmeter to the ground and appropriate resistor or lead point (object) with the correct ends on the correct terminals (constraint or tools).

- *Metacognitive domain.* Given an unidentified problem in an electronic instrument's electrical system, but without identifying a specific instrument (situation), the student will develop (learned capability) a strategy for approaching the situation (object) by verbally listing (action verb) the steps necessary to approach the problem without prior instruction (constraint).

Objectives for Soft Skills. Soft-skill training covers those intangibles such as delivering quality service, management techniques, leadership skills, or interpersonal skills. The examples here demonstrate how the objective-writing process is adapted to supervisory skills.

- *Cognitive domain, concrete concept level.* Given a selected work unit (situation), the learner will identify (learned capability) internal and external customers (object) by verbally listing (action verb) all (condition) customer characteristics.
- *Cognitive domain, problem-solving level.* To ensure that workgroup members have the information, training, responsibility, and resources to accomplish their assignments (situation), the learner will generate (learned capability) strategies for aligning (action verb) routine elements (object) of workgroup performance with customer requirements and quality standards (conditions).
- *Affective domain, organization level.* Given a workplace situation where quality standards could be ignored (situation), the student will choose (learned capability) to relate (action verb) the benefits of following quality standards (object) to another individual, using words that adhere to company philosophy (conditions).

Activity Five: Engage in a Group Discussion

Engage the project team, or a neutral party, in discussion of each performance objective to clarify and verify correct assumptions.

Step one: Review the objectives in a group setting to validate the relevance to job tasks.

Step two: Rewrite performance objectives as necessary after discussion.

Activity Six: Separate Terminal Objectives from Performance Objectives

The terminal objective and lesson objective exist within the performance objective. The terminal objective comprises the situation and learned-capability portions of the performance objective.

Separate the terminal objectives from the performance objectives. Let's use the example objective we have written for the manufacturing course:

- *Cognitive domain, discrimination level.* Given a diagram of the electronic instrument (situation), the student will discriminate each functional part (learned capability) by circling (action verb) each major part (object) with complete accuracy (special condition).

In this case, the terminal objective would read, "Given a diagram of the electronic instrument, the student will discriminate each functional part."

A terminal objective lists the observable performance that the learner will possess at the end of the course, when he or she returns to the job.

The terminal objective is written into the student materials to inform learners about what they will achieve. For this purpose, the objective should be rewritten to appear less formal; the terminal objective in the student materials might read, "After concluding this lesson, you will be able to discriminate each functional part of an electronic instrument."

The terminal objective focuses the instructional designer on the upper level of learning the concept—in this case discrimination (recognizing the parts).

Activity Seven: Separate Lesson Objectives from Performance Objectives

Separate lesson objectives from the performance objective by removing the learned capability from the latter.

Lesson objectives identify what activity occurs within a lesson that leads the learner to achieve the terminal objective. Continuing to use the performance objective from Activity Six, we suggest the lesson objective could read, "Given a diagram of the electronic instrument, the student will circle all major parts with complete accuracy."

The lesson objective focuses the instructional designer on the activities within the lesson that lead to accomplishing the terminal objective.

FROM OUR EXPERIENCE

Our system for writing objectives is designed as a way to think about objectives. All project team members have to understand the system for it to work. Where our system has been used, it eliminates confusion in two ways: designers and subject-matter experts have a clear understanding of the intended level of the training, and terminal and lesson objectives are developed concurrently.

This process emphasizes the team approach because objectives written by one person are (in our experience) not as effective as those written by a team.

After objectives are written, you may find that some do not align to the task order you created. Move and group objectives and their accompanying content as appropriate.

Objectives relate directly to any testing and measurement of the effectiveness of your solution. Testing and measurement concepts are discussed in Part Four.

SUMMARY

Once the objectives are written, you know precisely what the end user of your solution should know when he or she returns to the workplace to perform the job. You also know what must be included in your solution in the form of information and activities.

Now that you know the content of the solution and what to include in delivering it, you are ready to choose the medium or media for delivery.

Media Analysis

A systematic and careful media selection decision is essential to successful and cost-effective resolution of business problems. We have developed a media analysis tool that addresses many considerations regarding learner and cost factors relevant to delivery media.

There are many types of media to be considered in making the appropriate selection. Although *multimedia* is frequently used to refer to CBT, remember that the word *media* is plural; you should always consider using more than one medium.

The media discussed in this chapter are presented in Table 10.1.

PROCESS

To perform a media analysis, complete the following process.

1. Match outcomes to the appropriate media.
2. Match media advantages and limitations.
3. Compare results and decide on the media.
4. Document the results.

MEDIA ANALYSIS PROCEDURE

Complete the following activities and steps.

Activity One: Match Outcomes to the Appropriate Media

Match the desired learning outcomes to appropriate media using the objectives you have written.

Table 10.1
Types of Delivery Media

Media	Description
Instructor-led	Materials intended to be presented by a teacher or facilitator. They may be used in a traditional classroom setting or on the job. Presentations can include lecture, discussion, demonstration, workshop, as well as other types for other media.
Computer-based	Any form of delivery involving use of a computer. Options include computer-assisted instruction (CAI), which also supports printed materials or instructor, or totally computer-based instruction, where all content is presented by computer.
Distance broadcast	General term for the category of instruction delivered over television, telephone, or via satellite to remote locations. Specific media are video or audio tele-conferencing and interactive distance broadcasting.
Web-based	Use of the Internet or intranets to distribute training over wide-area networks (WAN) or local-area networks (LAN).
Audiotapes	Use of prerecorded audiotapes to deliver instruction with or without the supporting materials.
Videotapes	Use of prerecorded video to deliver instruction with or without supporting materials.
Performance support systems (PSS) Electronic performance support systems (EPSS)	Job aids, either electronic or paper-based, used to help and support people on the job. These do not require any formal training or instruction other than on the job-aid tool.

Step one: If the learning outcome requires employees to perform a complex task infrequently, then for the first step consider:

- Computer-based performance support (online help or reference system)
- Text-based job aid or reference manual
- Mentoring, phone support, or coaching

For example, it would be wise to choose a support system, rather than training, for a customer service representative at a call center who must complete a customer request form that is seldom used. The customer representative will probably forget the training by the time he or she is required to use the form.

Step two: If the learning outcome requires employees to learn a process or procedure, determine if motor or psychomotor skills are required. If either is the case, then consider a medium that allows for motor practice, such as

- Lab or simulation
- On-the-job training or mentoring
- Part-task trainers or virtual-reality systems

For example, if a factory worker is expected to perform safety procedures correctly, he or she should have experience actually performing the procedure under the supervision of a safety expert.

Step three: If motor or psychomotor practice is not required to perform the process or procedure, then consider a self-paced medium that offers a chance for this kind of practice:

- Computer-based or web-based training
- Interactive distance broadcasting
- Self-paced workbook
- Audio or videotapes with practice activities or study guides

An example is a merchandising representative needing to complete an online order form; practice using CBT should be sufficient.

Step four: If the learning outcome requires employees to learn concepts or facts that require detailed explanation, then consider

- Instructor-led classroom
- Web-based chat room

- Audio teleconferencing
- Video teleconferencing

If the content is apt to generate a high number of specific questions from the participants, then you need media that allow for a high degree of personal and immediate interaction.

Step five: Determine if the learning outcome requires employees to learn concepts or facts that do not require detailed explanations. If so, can visuals help in recalling information? If they are helpful, then consider

- Computer-based training
- Videotapes
- Web-based training
- Text with graphics

As an example, the cleaning staff of a hotel needs to know the correct way to prepare a guest room. The procedure leaves little discretion to the cleaning staff, so there should be few individual questions to ask. Thus visual media should be sufficient.

Step six: If visuals are not required to describe concepts or facts, then consider

- Text
- Audio teleconference
- Audiotapes

Employees at a chemical plant office need to know about a new OSHA requirement regarding hazardous materials, but not how to handle the materials; here, a communiqué is probably sufficient.

Step seven: If the learning outcome is intended to motivate employees or to change attitudes, then consider a method where role modeling can be demonstrated:

- Videotapes
- Video or audio teleconferencing
- Coaching or mentoring

One of these methods is appropriate if, say, you want to instill a positive attitude toward customer service in employees in the airline industry.

Step eight: Ask whether the learning outcome requires teaching either how to learn or critical-thinking skills. If so, consider a method that can provide real-time feedback:

- Video or audio teleconferencing
- Coaching or mentoring
- CBT simulation
- Workshop

As an example, any of these methods is appropriate for teaching an operator emergency procedures for shutting down power to dangerous equipment.

Activity Two: Match Media Advantages and Limitations

Match the strengths and weaknesses of the media to business requirements.

Step one: Analyze the advantages and limitations of each type of medium. Factors vary depending on your location, the size of the organization, internal and external resources, and your level of development experience. Table 10.2 is a starting point for analyzing each available media type and its advantages and limitations. Feel free to expand the table with additional media, details, clarification, or considerations that are important in your unique business environment.

Step two: Analyze the cost of delivery. Table 10.3 lists costs associated with various training media.

Step three: Consider delivery factors (see Table 10.4).

Step four: Consider maintenance factors (see Table 10.5).

Activity Three: Compare Results and Decide on the Media

Compare the results of the media selection, and decide on the appropriate media associated with the objectives.

Use the Media Selection Form in the Assessment and Front-End Analysis Tools section of Appendix E to prioritize various media. Remember, your solution may include more than one medium of delivery; the most effective and efficient solution determines the most appropriate medium or media for each task.

The rating scale can be used by your team or with a stakeholder; the correct approach relies on your judgment. However, if a stakeholder or team member has already fixed on a solution that you do not believe is correct, use the questions on the rating form to determine if all considerations of learner and cost have been taken into account in insisting on that solution.

Table 10.2
Advantages and Limitations of Media

Media	Advantages	Limitations
Instructor-led	Allows social interaction. Useful with variable-size audiences. Personalized feedback. Integrates a variety of media. Materials can be tailored to the group or adjusted by the instructor while in progress. Short development time. Traditional method of teaching that is comfortable for students and instructors. Because learners are removed from work environment, they can focus on the course free of distraction.	Scheduling may not meet the needs of all who require the information or instruction. Not enough time to give everyone feedback they may need. Moves at one pace, or at the pace of the majority of the class, and does not account for individual rates and styles of learning. Lack of transfer to the workplace. Relies heavily on instructor knowledge. Inconsistent delivery and certain areas stressed or deemphasized, causing gaps in learning and varied levels of learner involvement. Inconsistent evaluation. Travel time and expense, whether for participants to attend at a centralized location or for instructor travel. Only limited numbers can participate at one time.

Table 10.2
Advantages and Limitations of Media, Cont'd.

Media	Advantages	Limitations
Computer-based	Consistent delivery.	May be too text based.
	Accommodates individual time schedules.	Expensive due to the number of design-team members required, authoring platform hardware and software, and cost of added media.
	Extensive multisensory capabilities.	
	Learner-controlled pace.	
	High degree of interactivity and involvement by the learner.	Long design and development time, with range from 250–750 design and development hours per hour of delivered instruction, depending on the complexity of the content. For a first project, even more time has to be scheduled.
	Adapts to learner performance.	
	Consistent testing and record keeping.	
	Unlimited opportunity for review.	
	Overlearning through multiple presentations and examples of the same concept.	Specialized computer skills of programmers and authors are required.
		Feedback specific to content and context may be limited.
		Any poorly designed user interface makes navigation difficult (that is, extensive menu layers) or interferes with learning (that is, uses too many bells and whistles).

Table 10.2
Advantages and Limitations of Media, Cont'd.

Media	Advantages	Limitations
Distance broadcast	Transcends geographical boundaries. High level of interaction and immediate feedback to questions in spite of distance. One instructor for a large group of participants. Reduced travel for participants and instructors (reduced cost and more convenience). Trains large numbers in a short period of time. Incorporates a variety of media. Two-way video permits instructor to see participants and participants to see each other.	Large time-zone differences require some participants to view at inappropriate times. May rely on a "talking head" with little or no interaction, which becomes boring; participants lose interest. Special training of instructor to handle technology, or large staff to handle broadcast equipment, is often required. Much preparation by instructor is needed to coordinate technology. Satellite time is very expensive. One-way video does not allow students and instructor to see each other.
Video teleconferencing	Less expensive than satellite broadcasting with use of existing telephone lines. Transcends geographical boundaries. High level of interaction and immediate feedback to questions in spite of distance.	Delays due to compression and decompression rates of video may result in video and audio out of synchronization. Large time-zone differences require some to participate at inappropriate times.

Table 10.2
Advantages and Limitations of Media, Cont'd.

Media	Advantages	Limitations
Video teleconferencing (cont'd.)	One instructor for a large group of participants. Reduced travel for participants and instructors. Trains large numbers in a short period of time. Incorporates variety of media. Two-way video permits instructor to see participants and participants to see each other.	May rely on a "talking head" with little or no interaction, which becomes boring; participants lose interest. Special training of instructor to handle technology, or large staff to handle broadcast equipment. Much preparation by instructor to coordinate technology. One-way video does not allow students and instructor to see each other.
Web-based	Includes chat rooms, where participants and instructor can have dialogue or interactive, real-time, collaborative discussions. Includes electronic mailboxes, where participants can pose questions to instructor or participants. Includes reference and data-storage capabilities.	Much preparation by instructor to coordinate and plan course elements. Requires specialized design skills of programmers and authors. Security, testing, and feedback may be limited. A poorly designed user interface may be difficult to navigate (i.e., extensive menu layers) or interfere with learning (i.e., too many bells and whistles).

Table 10.2
Advantages and Limitations of Media, Cont'd.

Media	Advantages	Limitations
Web-based (cont'd.)	Includes sharing of files and data. Course material can incorporate audio, video, and graphics. Material is easily updated.	Slow video compression and decompression rates cause video and audio to be out of synchronization.
Audiotapes	Flexible in delivery; participants can get information anywhere there is a tape player. Inexpensive to develop and deliver.	Only one sensory modality used for learning.
Videotapes	Flexible in delivery; participants can get information anywhere there is video playback equipment. Inexpensive to duplicate and deliver after initial development costs. Good for role-modeling behavior and motivation.	Only two sensory modalities used for learning. Expensive to produce because of highly specialized skills of videographers, editors, producers, and script writers. Industry range is from $500–2,000 per finished minute of video.
Performance support systems (PSS) Electronic performance support systems (EPSS)	Provides information on an as-needed basis. Does not require formalized training that removes people from their jobs.	Not good for delivering concepts, principles, or demonstrations. Specialized programming and authoring skills on the part of members of

Table 10.2 Advantages and Limitations of Media, Cont'd.		
Media	**Advantages**	**Limitations**
Performance support systems (PSS) Electronic performance support systems (EPSS) (cont'd.)	Best for providing information on procedures and processes or reference material. Ready source for information that may be used infrequently or is complex.	design team are required for EPSS. May have a user interface or be constructed such that it is too complex to navigate. May not be organized in a way that allows users to quickly access the information they need.

The rating scale has built-in redundancy and asks you to consider numerous factors from the standpoint of both the learner and cost. It is designed to focus your decision, not make it for you. The considerations provided ask you to question what you really mean when you rank a factor on the scale.

Activity Four: Document the Results

Document the results by listing and grouping the media types.

FROM OUR EXPERIENCE

We advocate a rational approach to selecting media. By rational, we mean that a decision is arrived at through a process that considers all relevant aspects.

Here is an excerpt from a conversation in a project room in a training department:

A: Let's develop it [a training course] in CBT.

B: Yes, and let's include a game so people will enjoy it.

A: We can use all of the authoring system's capabilities . . . high-resolution graphics, animation, and video.

B: And CBT is so much more fun to design than those *other* courses. I'm so bored developing workbooks, I could scream! CBT experience looks better on a résumé, anyway.

Table 10.3
Cost Factors Associated with Media

Category	Factors	Consideration
Development-team resources	Project leader Instructional designer Subject-matter expert Deployment representative Media specialists (audio technician, video technician, graphic designer, system designer, etc.) Programmer (author, interactive designer, system engineer, etc.) Publisher (editor, etc.)	Hourly costs for team members involved in development activities
Administrative resources	Manager Clerical	Hourly costs for administration of development activities
Production	Reproduction of videos, diskettes, or CD-ROMs Postproduction Narration Studio rental Video equipment rental Videotaping Facilities costs	Production costs for developing media
Materials	Diskettes CD-ROMs Videotapes Audiotapes Software Hardware	Materials cost

Table 10.4
Delivery Factors Associated with Media

Category	Factors	Consideration
Logistics	Expected lifetime of course (years)	The longer the course will be useful, the more cost-effective it is to develop.
	Course length	More content is more expensive to develop.
	Number of users	The greater the number of students, the lower the cost per student.
	Times when course is held each year	Calculate deployment costs.
	Geographic location of audience	Calculate travel and other deployment costs.
	Materials	Consider reproduction, postage, and transmission costs.
Cost per training unit	Average annual salaries of Students Instructor Clerical staff Manager	Determine the cost for each person involved.
	Average per diem expenses of Students Instructors	
	Average travel expenses of Students Instructors	
	Facilities cost	
	Number of instructors per class	
	Cost per hour of development of each unit	

Table 10.5
Maintenance Factors Associated with Various Media

Category	Factors	Consideration
Ongoing reproduction	Cost of producing additional materials such as videotapes, audiotapes, diskettes, CD-ROMs, print materials	Who reproduces materials as needed?
Material	Additional cost of materials purchased: CD-ROMs Paper Diskettes Audiotapes Videotapes	Who purchases additional materials for ongoing reproduction? Who pays for additional materials?
Storage	Cost of storing materials	Where are originals and extra materials warehoused until distribution? Who maintains storage?
Distribution	Cost of distributing materials	Who is in charge of distribution materials? Do users know where to order materials?
Revision	Cost of revising materials	Who is responsible for required revisions to materials? Who is responsible for version control? Cost of disposal of outdated inventory?

Notice that there are a few elements missing from this conversation. As a matter of fact, in this situation the conversation continued but the important elements never came up. The discussion never turned to learning design, solving a business problem or performance need, or effectiveness in terms of time and cost. The major criterion seemed to be that the team should have fun developing the training.

True, there is something to be said for enjoying your work, but it is much more vital for effective and efficient use of technology to enhance performance and solve an organization's business need. Either it isn't important to A and B and their team of designers that the end users of the training need to learn something in a cost-effective and timely manner, or it is assumed that learning takes place magically. Both beliefs are erroneous.

We are here to tell you the medium is *not* the message, contrary to Marshall McLuhan's statement of some years back. This one aphorism—often misunderstood—started a rampage of multimedia development from which students and developers alike are still suffering.

We believe the message is the content that needs to be delivered through a certain medium or media. The content might be a process, procedure, principle, concept, fact, or system. Each type of content requires a particular instructional strategy. The medium is dictated by objectives. All of the capabilities and features of a particular medium are useless unless the product teaches something that the learner needs so as to enhance performance.

Here is an example. Company X has just adopted a new policy that must be communicated to all employees immediately so that the company can comply with a new government regulation. Question to you: What medium or media should the company use to deliver this information to employees?

In simply reading the description and the question, do you find yourself immediately deciding on the media? Does a choice at least occur to you in the back of your mind? Or do you begin to ask yourself such questions as the following:

- How many people are in the target audience?
- How geographically dispersed is the audience?
- Do employees only need to be informed of the policy, or do they need to be taught the skills to use it?
- What physical capabilities does the company have for holding large meetings?

If you began by raising these questions, then you're thinking in the right direction. In contrast, an impulse to begin immediately reaching a decision means a good chance of developing an inappropriate solution.

By jumping immediately to a solution, you make certain assumptions about the content, the context of the training, and the constraints you will face in designing and delivering the training. If you make the correct assumptions, great! The solution will be a success, and everyone will be happy. But what are the consequences if your assumptions prove to be incorrect? The solution is ineffective in solving the targeted issue.

For the sake of demonstration, here is some additional information about Company X's situation:

- There are three thousand employees who need the information.
- All employees must know about the regulation within a week.
- Employees only have to be aware of the regulation; they don't need the skills to carry it out.
- All of the employees are in one geographic location.
- There is an auditorium in the company's facilities that holds one thousand people.

If you were to immediately determine the media before being given this information (though we're sure you aren't in that impetuous group!), what impact would this information have on your decision? Suppose you had quickly decided to use interactive distance broadcasting, before you had this information. You might unnecessarily have spent thousands of dollars on satellite time and development costs.

With the information in this list, though, you make a better decision: to have a meeting in the company's thousand-person auditorium. Now you can either hold the meeting three times or hook up televisions in training rooms (if available) and encourage employees to call or fax in their questions.

We live in a society that expects to be entertained. The same entertainment principles follow when adults attend training classes. The courses or instructors who are the most entertaining usually get the best reviews from their students. We are suggesting that edutainment not be your primary instructional strategy. Edutainers lose sight of the fact that their overarching objective is for learners to obtain knowledge and skills to improve their performance. Multimedia with content that is presented logically, with appropriate practice and feedback, is far more effective than edutainment. Likewise, instructors who present training with confidence, expertise, and true enjoyment for what they are doing, and who can relate to students on a personal level, are more effective than those who spend much of their time practicing for a stand-up comedy routine.

We don't want to imply that you shouldn't use humor. If you can work in a relevant story or theme that is humorous, do it. However, making the graphics the focal point in a CBT or using your audio resources for irrelevant jokes detracts from the business goal of cost-effective and efficient performance support intervention.

SUMMARY

You have now determined the delivery media for your solution. There is one more analysis to perform before you begin to design your solution. Products may already exist that you could use in their entirety or in part. Analyzing extant data reveals information on what is already available. You should only design and develop new materials if you can't use material that has already been produced by others.

Extant Data Analysis

Remember: your primary purpose is not to design multimedia, but rather to solve a business need. Therefore you must determine if the solution, or parts of the solution, already exists (is extant), which avoids unneeded development costs. A search for what is available used to be a rather daunting task, but with advances in telecommunications and computer technology the search, or extant data analysis, has become relatively simple. Completing such an analysis can save you time and money, and it often yields an added level of confidence that you are not reinventing the wheel.

PROCESS

To conduct an extant data analysis, complete these activities:

1. Identify likely sources of information.
2. Collect information and existing course materials.
3. Compare information.
4. Make a buy-or-build decision.
5. Document your decision.

EXTANT DATA ANALYSIS PROCEDURE

Follow these activities:

Activity One: Identify Likely Sources of Information

Decide what you are looking for: is it an entire solution, or one or more pieces of the solution? Make this determination according to (1) the size and complexity of your solution (a large and complex solution means searching for one or more pieces of the total solution) and (2) the amount of proprietary company material to be included (the more proprietary the content, the less likely you are to locate existing, intact, useful content elsewhere).

Activity Two: Collect Information and Existing Course Materials

Web search engines are an excellent place to begin. Information searches can be conducted using a bulletin board service (BBS) and special-interest groups (SIGs) on the Internet, provided you have an online account or access to one. Search costs vary from free to a fixed fee per search—that is, a charge per unit of search time and amount of information generated.

The numerous guides and indexes to periodicals found in libraries are excellent sources of information. Most libraries offer online computer searches for information on nearly any topic.

Use the Extant Data Analysis Form in the Assessment and Front-End Analysis Tools section of Appendix E to document the results of your search.

Activity Three: Compare Information

Evaluate the collected information, being mindful of objectives, audience, and business needs.

Step one: Rate the appropriateness and usability of the materials you locate. Determine if the materials in fact contain the required information. Again, use the Extant Data Analysis Tool to compare audience, objectives, and media to the requirements of the solution. Also determine if the hardware, software, or scheduling required by the off-the-shelf material matches your organization's available technology.

Step two: Determine if the availability of the information matches the time constraints of the project. The shorter the time frame for development, the more appropriate an off-the-shelf solution might be if it is readily available.

Step three: Determine if the cost is appropriate to the project's budget. Ensure that a technology requirement does not include acquiring or implementing hardware that extends the delivery time line or costs beyond what is practical.

Activity Four: Make a Buy-or-Build Decision

You now decide whether, in essence, to buy (if the results of your analysis determine that the off-the-shelf material is usable as is or can be modified to meet the business need) or build (develop materials if the results of your analysis shows that an off-the-shelf product is not appropriate for the solution).

Activity Five: Document Your Decision

Document the results by listing the sources, rationale, and decisions reached during the analysis.

FROM OUR EXPERIENCE

There is no need to develop a solution that already exists in an off-the-shelf product or a course that can be purchased and adapted to meet your particular business need.

There are many sources of information available to complete an extant data analysis, from web resources to advertisements and vendors at professional conferences. The key to successful searches is organizing the search. Take time to focus it by listing key words or phrases and asking specific questions. It is vital to reduce the amount of material you have to review by collecting only the most relevant information, and as efficiently as possible.

In developing questions for a computer search, narrow your questions for the search. Computer searches can only give back information based on the key words searched. To take a whimsical example, consider how much time you will spend and how many hits you will get from searching for "mice" as opposed to searching for "mouse AND computer BUT NOT rodent."

Sometimes the time available for an extant data analysis is limited. Schedule and plan your analysis so that you do not spend too much time researching and gathering information at the expense of analysis of the search results. Remember, once a list is generated, someone still has to sort through the results, obtain and analyze the content or products listed, and make appropriate recommendations.

SUMMARY

You now know what is available, what to include in your solution, and what the project team has to develop. While analyzing, don't forget to note the costs of off-the-shelf materials, to include them in your cost analysis—which you are now ready to begin.

Cost Analysis

This chapter gives you a high-level overview of two commonly used formulas for determining the benefit of a solution:

1. *Cost-benefit analysis* (*CBA*) is used to determine if you will undertake a project.
2. *Return on investment* (*ROI*) is often measured after a project has been implemented, in order to determine its actual benefit.

Business is concerned with cost. If a solution does not add benefit to the organization, it should not be developed. As a professional instructional designer, you should be ready to justify the value added by your proposed solution. Document your cost-analysis results, and share them with your stakeholders in order to

- Request and obtain the support necessary to successfully complete the project
- Demonstrate that the proposed solution is cost-effective and adds value
- Maintain credibility and a business focus within your development organization
- Be seen as a solution provider and revenue generator rather than an overhead expense

PROCESS

To determine value added by a proposed solution, complete these cost-analysis activities:

1. Conduct a cost-benefit analysis (CBA).
2. Determine the return on investment (ROI).
3. Document the results.

COST ANALYSIS PROCEDURE

Follow these activities:

Activity One: Conduct a Cost-Benefit Analysis (CBA)

Determine the anticipated benefit of the project in relation to the cost of producing the activity. The formula is:

$$\frac{(\text{Estimated benefit of the intervention})}{(\text{Cost of assessment, design, development, implementation, and evaluation})}$$

For example, if you determine the anticipated value of your proposed solution to the organization to be $1 million and the actual cost to complete the solution is budgeted at $100,000, the CBA equals a ratio of $10 of anticipated value for each dollar spent. You must determine with your stakeholders if this is a high enough ratio. Some organizations set minimums on what they are willing to spend in relation to the return they anticipate receiving.

Activity Two: Determine the Return on Investment (ROI)

Measure ROI after a project has been implemented.

Prepare for ROI analysis by collecting data on the cost of the issue the intervention is intended to solve. The formula to calculate ROI is

$$\frac{(\text{Actual value of the intervention})}{(\text{Cost of assessment, design, development, implementation, and evaluation})}$$

For example, if the customer actually realized a profit of $1 million, as anticipated, and the actual cost was $100,000, as budgeted, the ROI is $10 for every dollar spent. If this is the ROI the customer said would be satisfactory, the solution is successful.

Activity Three: Document the Results

Document the results in the format appropriate to your audience. If the audience is a management team, use a presentation package whose style is familiar to the team members to communicate the cost-analysis results.

FROM OUR EXPERIENCE

If numbers are not your thing, get some help from your accounting group or set up some basic spreadsheets. Once set up, cost analysis can give you what you need to demonstrate your value, get the funding you need, and effectively focus your multimedia efforts. Detailed literature on the factors and calculations used with both formulas is available on the Web, on business publication bookshelves, and from such professional organizations as the American Society for Training and Development (ASTD).

Some people believe that not everything can be quantified. We believe everything can be measured. Certain soft skills, such as leadership, may be more difficult, but they can nonetheless be quantified. With a soft skill, the true value may be more than one level removed from what can be directly observed. Consider the following example:

Assume that having better leaders results in greater employee satisfaction (unobservable) and that satisfied employees are less likely to leave a company (observable). Therefore, statistics about employee attrition and employee satisfaction should show some correlation—that is, as satisfaction increases, attrition should decrease. Employee satisfaction can be measured by administering an Employee Satisfaction Survey, a component of which assesses employees' satisfaction with their leaders.

The average cost of replacing an employee times the attrition rate can be calculated. Keeping statistics on the employee attrition level before and after an intervention that trains leaders on leadership skills yields information on increased or decreased attrition along with associated cost savings. Thus, a goal to reduce employee attrition by a certain amount while increasing employees' satisfaction with their leaders by a certain amount is a measurable one.

SUMMARY

Using the CBA formula, you have now calculated whether (and, potentially, how much) the benefit of the solution you propose meets the customer's criteria. If it does, you are ready to begin designing and developing the solution. If your proposed solution does not meet the criteria, you must look for another solution—possibly a second one that you considered during media analysis.

Rapid Analysis Method

With the pace and number of changes occurring in business and industry today, it is incumbent on a training-and-development function to respond to the needs resulting from those changes. Therefore, we present a rapid analysis method, or RAM, which is designed to significantly reduce the amount of time required to conduct analysis while still obtaining valuable information.

There are benefits and advantages to the RAM:

- It facilitates collecting data from all levels of the organization (management and employees) and from all methods (interviews and observations) simultaneously.
- It identifies gaps between the actual and desired situations.
- It identifies differences in perception among various levels of the organization.
- It reduces cycle time for analysis by about two-thirds when used effectively.

Several essential factors must be present for this method to be successful. If any one is missing, the data retrieved may not hit the target. The first factor is that the training function must employ highly experienced analysts who intuitively understand what aspects of the assessment and analysis process are functioning in each question. The RAM is not for the novice or inexperienced analyst. Complex analysis processes are integrated in the RAM. Even though the method requires only five questions, each one represents a high-level view of all information gained from needs assessment and front-end analysis. The difference is that the analyst must be able to ask the required follow-up questions.

The second factor is that certain conditions must be true of the organization being analyzed:

- It must have a clearly articulated strategy that embodies core processes.
- Owners of core processes (for example, the core owner of the marketing process is the marketing VP) are charged with managing the operation of infrastructure and personnel.
- The training-and-development function must be involved and aware of strategies regarding operation of the core business.

If these essential factors are not present, the analyst can only be partially successful in suggesting interventions, because they may bring only a short-term solution to long-term problems.

For the RAM to work effectively, analysts must be aware of the organization's direction. At a minimum, analysts must thoroughly understand the business, the core processes, and the organization's objectives. This understanding is necessary for the background needed to rapidly analyze any situation requiring an intervention. If the analysis team is not integrated into the business, it takes too long to come up to speed on the requirements for solving the business need. Inadequate analysis often results because of time pressures, or the total elimination of analysis, both of which increase the chance of developing an incorrect solution or a band-aid applied to a much larger issue.

The third success factor is that analysts must complete an organizational assessment that goes beyond training needs and identifies performance and system issues that may be the actual cause of the problem. Training assessment can only identify the knowledge, skills, and attitudes that need to be developed to perform a job. Performance assessment identifies the tools, processes and procedures, and work environment and whether the emphasis is on the quality or quantity of work.

Systemic assessment examines those issues that touch the entire organization, such as incentives, corporate culture, and decision-making ability. Table 13.1 represents the three levels of organizational assessment.

Appendix B presents an example of how the organizational assessment might look, in a customer service setting. The example consists of three parts: the scenario, the analysis results, and the information structure of the assessment. The organizational assessment produces information that might be found through analysis. The information structure gives examples of each level in the model to be taken into consideration in developing the solution.

Table 13.1
Levels of Need Identified by Organizational Assessment

Levels	Factor	Examples of Need
Systemic	Retention	To keep highly talented and experienced employees, for corporate history and knowledge base
	Incentives	To offer rewards that encourage employees to be high performers
	Corporate culture	To value people
	Decision-making and approval levels	Who has the authority and responsibility to make decisions?
Performance	Work environment	Does the workplace support new skills learned?
	Tools	Do people have the equipment they need to perform the job?
	Processes and procedures	Do people know how to get their work done?
		Are ways of getting work done efficient and effective, or do people have to work around them to do their jobs?
	Emphasis on quality or quantity	What is more important: a job well done, or getting the job done and the product out the door?
Training	Knowledge	Understanding the concepts and information required to complete a job
	Skills	Having the physical capabilities to complete a job
	Attitudes	Understanding the value in completing a job; understanding and caring about the impact of one job on another

Source: Lee and Owens (1999).

Analyzing just the training needs might lead to developing a solution that addresses only a symptom of the problem, making the outcome of the intervention less effective.

Critical success factor number four is that the RAM assumes your customer has a clear idea of the direction in which to proceed. If not, the RAM can help articulate it, but the need to clarify direction lengthens the time required to develop and implement a solution. Some good organizational development work must often be performed before successful analysis of any type of intervention. For example, if a solution must tie into an organization's vision and mission, the vision and mission statements must be written, available, and articulated. Or if processes and procedures aren't producing the desired results for an organization, they must be changed.

Most RAM information must be gleaned from letting people talk. Analysts must have good listening skills and be able to probe for an appropriate level of detail. Questions must be succinct to capture all the needed information and to avoid repeatedly calling on those interviewed. The word *rapid* means just that: you get in, get the information you need, get out, and don't bug people again. Repeated calls to collect additional information indicates interviewers do not have the experience to successfully employ the RAM.

Table 13.2 outlines the RAM. It lists

- The activities and approximate amount of time spent on each one relative to the overall analysis

- The operations, or what should actually happen during each activity

- The anticipated outcomes of each operation

PROCESS

There are five activities that occur during the RAM:

1. Prepare for the analysis.

2. Ask primary questions.

3. Listen and record responses.

4. Observe actual performance.

5. Report results.

Table 13.2
Rapid Analysis Method

Activity	Percentage of Total Time	Operations	Outcomes
Ask	9%	Ask upper management, middle management, and employees these questions: "What is the source of the need?" "What do people have to do to respond to this need?" "What must people know to respond to this need?" "What is the value of a solution to the organization?" "How will you measure the success of the solution?"	Validate responses from all groups and reconcile the gaps.
Listen	50%	Categorize responses according to these categories: 1. Felt need 2. Normative need 3. Anticipated need 4. Comparative need 5. Expressed or demanded need	Complete information about the issue to use during observation phase to validate and reconcile difference between what is said and what is actually done.
Observe	40%	Observe exemplary performers and others selected randomly. Determine if the environment supports what each group says	Validate responses from various groups; identify gaps between the various needs and the actual situation in the environment.

Table 13.2
Rapid Analysis Method, Cont'd.

Activity	Percentage of Total Time	Operations	Outcomes
Observe (cont'd.)		people need to know and do.	
		Task analysis (is the task being performed effectively and efficiently by some segment of the employee population?)	
		Situation analysis (conditions under which the work is being performed)	
		Instructional analysis (learner characteristics: education, background, culture)	
		Critical incident analysis (what employees actually need to know)	
Report	1%	Compile results. Explain findings and make recommendations. Explain and recommend on three levels: 1. Training 2. Performance 3. Systemic	Groups' acceptance or rejection of recommendations (*note:* at this point the design of the intervention can begin at the appropriate level of training, performance, and organization; includes partial acceptance of recommendations with all groups understanding how much impact intervention(s) can have at the accepted level).

RAPID ANALYSIS METHOD PROCEDURE

Follow these activities:

Activity One: Prepare for the Analysis

Step one: Discuss the focus of the assessment with your customer and team to make sure they are aware that training, performance, and systemic levels will be assessed.

Step two: Prepare for the analysis by having a kickoff meeting attended by everyone involved in the project (except those who will be interviewed and observed).

Use the Roles and Responsibilities Matrix template included in the Assessment and Front-End Analysis Tools section of Appendix E to determine what tasks need to be done and by whom.

Once participants have accepted all roles and associated responsibilities, develop a project plan and project schedule to let each person know when his or her tasks begin and end.

Use the legend on the Roles and Responsibilities Matrix template to identify which participants are responsible for the task (R), consulted about the task (C), or simply informed (I) of the outcome of the task. More than one person can be consulted or informed, but only one is responsible for completing the task. Having everyone responsible for at least one task achieves buy-in from project members and gives everyone a stake in the success of the project. Note that the legend states the person who is responsible also has the authority for determining how the task gets done. Hammer and Champy (1994) state that assigning responsibility to someone without also giving the person authority is inconsistent. Getting things done requires that people be empowered to act and also be answerable for their actions.

Step three: Divide the work so that each analyst (if more than one) interviews and observes all three vertical groups (upper management, middle management, and employees) of a segment of the target audience. Using this vertical structure for analysis permits analysts to most readily identify inconsistencies between what is said and what is actually happening.

Activity Two: Ask Primary Questions

Step one: Ask the five primary questions listed in Table 13.2, in the first cell of the Operations column. Some probing questions may also need to be asked as follow-on to get complete information. In the overall process, this activity should only take about 9 percent of the total amount of analysis time. Ask the same questions of people at all levels of the organization: upper management, middle management, and employees. You are looking for congruence among what each group says.

Step two: Identify inconsistencies (gaps) among the answers of those interviewed at each level.

Activity Three: Listen and Record Responses

Step one: Begin this activity by listening to the responses. Listening involves fully half of the time for analysis. Too often, most of the time in analysis is spent questioning. We have found that if you just listen, people tell you what you need to know. Asking too many specific questions often biases what people say because of how the question is worded. In other words, you find out what you expect to find out, not what you need to find out.

Step two: Categorize responses into each of the five need categories in the Listen row of Table 13.2 to be certain that you have all the information needed.

Activity Four: Observe Actual Performance

Step one: Watch people complete tasks. You have probably heard the phrase "walk the talk." What people say often does not match what they do. People may tell you what they wish for ideally, or they may be out of touch with what is actually happening.

Step two: Identify gaps between verbal responses and actual performance. It is the analyst's job to reconcile any differences. Determining the mismatch between what people say and do is the reason for carrying out Activity Four.

Activity Five: Report Results

Review your notes and prepare to report your findings and recommendations. There may be a lot of data to analyze depending on the size of the project and the number of analysts, interviews, and observations. Even so, this step of the RAM should only take about 1 percent of the total time for analysis if your notes are complete and you have collected all the information you need in all areas. Use the Analysis Report tool in the Assessment and Front-End Analysis Tools section of Appendix E to summarize your findings.

FROM OUR EXPERIENCE

The T&D (training-and-development) function must have more D than T. If you conduct only a training analysis, it is an extremely narrow view of what your function is capable of contributing to your organization. We advise our customers that all three levels of organizational assessment outlined in Table 13.1 need to be addressed.

After we complete our assessment, we make it very clear to the customer how much of the total issue can be solved by addressing each level of the organizational assessment. Typically, the percentage of improvement increases as the performance and systemic levels are addressed.

There are times when training alone is the solution that solves the problem. This is the exception rather than the rule. Because organizations are so complex, changing one part nearly always affects another. For example, suppose you implement an electronic performance support system (EPSS) that greatly reduces the time required to produce automotive parts in a foundry. You must check to determine that the company has storage space for the parts. Otherwise, the amount of money you save in one area of the company may be lost in the expense of storing car parts until the assembly line can use them to build cars.

SUMMARY

In using the rapid analysis model, you are conducting the equivalent of all of the other analyses covered in Part One.

By asking just five questions, carefully listening, recording answers, and mentally categorizing them as you ask the questions (to be certain you get all the information you need), you have shortcut the needs assessment and analysis process.

Using the RAM gets you to the design phase much more quickly than completing each step of the nine analyses presented earlier in this part of the book. Whichever methods and strategies of assessment and analysis you use, you are now ready to begin designing the solution.

part two

Multimedia
Instructional
Design

Introduction to Multimedia Instructional Design

When you have documented all of the information from assessment and analysis and made the required decisions, you are ready to enter the design phase.

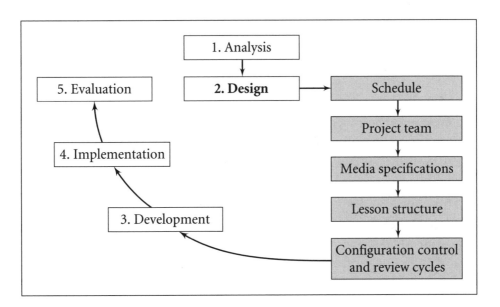

The design phase is the planning phase of your multimedia project. Planning is probably the most important factor in the success of your project. Projects often founder because of failure to adequately plan.

The outcome of this phase is a Course Design Specification (CDS) document that details how the intervention will look when it is complete. In completing the CDS you will:

- Schedule project activities
- Identify project team members
- Develop a project plan
- Write detailed instructional outlines (if your solution includes a course)
- Create an interface design (if appropriate)
- Review the design for the technical content accuracy with subject matter experts (SMEs)
- Review the design for instructional or performance support soundness
- Establish the standards for the development phase
- Establish the validity methodology of any tests

We recommend you complete the design phase with as much detail as project constraints (such as time or budget) will allow, thus avoiding expensive rework during development. Course design specifications are especially critical in projects where the planned multimedia development will be phased. A phased approach, in which the content is designed, developed, and implemented in sections, is appropriate when

- Development begins on a core set of content, skills, or knowledge with plans to add on additional content at a later date. For example, the development of a performance support tool with time-tracking procedures useful to all employees may contain plans and specifications for follow-on additional development of department level time-tracking guidelines.
- A solution is being developed in conjunction with the development of the content. This is often termed "concurrent development" and is often the case in projects that involve software or new product development. When using a multimedia solution for concurrent development, it is best to provide a framework via design specifications so that the content can be "plugged in" as it becomes finalized and available.
- The multimedia development is ongoing in response to rapid changes in the business environment. For example, a web-based tool that provides up to date

price or scheduling information that must be regularly updated. The design specification provides the "recipe" for updates.

- When rapid prototyping is used to "try it", "sell it" or to move forward quickly, a Course Design Specification provides a mechanism for capturing the decisions and documenting the design for follow-on development.

All specifications governing the production of materials should come from the work group that will be implementing them. Specifications should never be imposed on a work group by another group without their input. In addition, specifications should be developed in cooperation with internal or external stakeholders.

After specifications are completed, the design and development team and the stakeholder should approve the CDS document. Approval clarifies expectations among all parties and serves as a baseline as the project moves forward. Finally, the specifications should be delivered to the group that will perform quality control and product review.

The Course Design Specification consists of the elements shown in Table 14.1.

Depending on the type of multimedia project, you may need to add to the design specifications suggested in the table. For example, a distance learning project might require a more detailed scheduling component; the addition of video in a multimedia project might require detailed specifications for scripts, set design, lighting, and shot locations.

FROM OUR EXPERIENCE

There are several reasons your entire team should work together to develop a Course Design Specification:

- To capture innovative and creative design ideas before it is too late in development to make it practical to incorporate them. If project members begin creating individually, each might have good ideas that are not leveraged in the design of the entire project. Including the team in course specifications prevents good ideas from being overcome by events or being used inconsistently.
- To obtain consensus and shared understanding of the design specifications. Everyone on the team needs to understand the design specifications prior to beginning the development phase. Otherwise, you will set the project team up for needless rework and inconsistency in the final product. Design meetings that give

Table 14.1
CDS Elements

CDS Element	Content
Schedule	Describes the project and lists milestones, deliverables, and deliverable dates
Project team	Lists roles and responsibilities of project team members and contacts
Media specifications	Documents types, general presentation styles, text, grammar, graphics, fonts, themes, editing symbols, and so on
Lesson structure	Describes how the content is grouped, ordered, linked, or navigated: • The type(s) of information to be taught and methodology for delivering instruction • The lesson flow with respect to events of instruction; course flowcharts; unit, lesson, and detailed content outlines ready for storyboarding or scripting • Feedback, user control, user interactivity, and testing methods and types
Configuration control and review cycles	Describes version control and how media elements are designated and managed; also documents the types of review and process for conducting reviews

everyone a chance to ask questions and give their input increase the chances of the specifications being adhered to because all team members buy in.

• To create an appreciation for the necessity for a consistent approach. A consistent approach is important in order to create a comfortable learning or support environment and to ensure the transfer of learning. A consistent approach speeds development by documenting the degree of consistency necessary to meet project goals.

You may find that once you begin implementing the specifications during development, some things you thought would work well don't produce the desired results. Remember, however, as development progresses, the longer you wait to change design standards, the harder, more costly, and more time-consuming implementing the change will be.

A basic Course Design Specification template can be saved and modified to meet the requirements of subsequent projects. Modifying an existing Course Design Specification for follow-on projects can result in significant project time savings.

SUMMARY

The design phase uses the conclusions from the project assessment and analysis phase to build a road map for development. The design process is an opportunity to design your intervention, document a plan, build consensus, and clarify expectations before beginning development. The chapters in Part Two provide suggested steps and activities that will provide you with a road map for your project.

Project Schedule

You'll recall from the preceding chapter that the design specification phase begins with description of the project and a list of milestones, schedule, deliverables, and deliverable dates; definition of the scope and vision of the project; and details of the plan for how the vision is achieved. It often serves as a communication tool among stakeholders, internal and external customers, sponsors, vendors, and project team members.

Whatever the delivery medium or media, use the same basic principles for developing a project schedule. Each component of project planning must be integrated and coordinated, but in a different manner. For example, although CBT and web-based courseware are structured around learning components, distance broadcasting and teleconferencing are structured around timed events. Each must be carefully scheduled for effective development and implementation regardless of the resulting product.

Project scheduling at the activity level is often the result of design decisions and compromises made on the basis of the cost, availability, and capability of key personnel and tools. For example, the number and design of graphic elements, use of clip art, or the decision to use an off-the-shelf graphic interface may be determined by the availability and talents of key graphic development personnel. Interactivity and testing design decisions may be based on the development ratio required for one design versus another. The decision making during design affects deliverables and the supporting activity scheduling. Often the project activities are created and revised iteratively throughout the design phase. As design decisions are made, project activities are confirmed, developed in more detail, or revised to reflect design decisions.

Creating a project schedule is an important aspect of multimedia instructional design. The design must be not only effective but also achievable within the context of the business need, time frame, and personnel and resources needed to perform the work. When completed, schedules decrease the chance of "scope creep," which ultimately prevents you from meeting project deadlines. Schedules also communicate shared understanding of how the design affects goals, project tasks, and team members' roles and responsibilities.

PROCESS

There are three activities in the process of creating a project schedule:

1. Document general project information.
2. List project deliverables.
3. Schedule project activities.

PROJECT SCHEDULE PROCEDURE

To create a project schedule, perform the following activities and steps.

Activity One: Document General Project Information

Develop and include a brief statement about

- The purpose of the project and what business need is addressed
- The current performance gaps and obstacles
- The desired outcome and high-level performance requirements
- Any project constraints or issues
- The assumptions you are making that have an impact on time lines or project success

Activity Two: List Project Deliverables

List the deliverables or milestones, and associated dates, specific to your project. Deliverables and milestones might include developing, reviewing, and approving

- Audio scripts
- Storyboards
- Prototype screen interface
- Programming templates or models
- Video scripts
- Video broadcast schedule and script

Activity Three: Schedule Project Activities

Especially for large projects, it is important that activities be well organized and all team members (1) know their roles and responsibilities, (2) be aware of the project time line, and (3) deliver their project components at the appropriate time. If the Roles and Responsibilities Matrix has been developed during the analysis phase, revise and enhance it to produce the level of task detail needed to begin development. The matrix is outlined in the rapid analysis method (Chapter Thirteen) and is included in the Assessment and Front-End Analysis Tools section of Appendix E.

Be sure to establish review cycles with adequate time for revision as part of the schedule. Reviews are an important aspect of multimedia project success because they ensure the quality of the instruction design and the validity of content.

Include time in the schedule for reviewers to gain a clear understanding of what is to be reviewed, time allowed for conducting the review, time to record observations and suggestions, time to determine which suggestions are implemented, and time to perform the rework. The importance of adequate review and revision cycles cannot be stressed too strongly. If project deadlines narrow or are overrun, *never* encroach on the time necessary to ensure the quality of the design and final product. Remember, a good ratio for allocating time on multimedia projects is one-third analysis; one-third design and development; and one-third implementation, evaluation, and maintenance.

Plan for these reviews in your schedule:

- A technical or functional review
- An ID review

- A standards review
- An editorial review
- A management review

Templates with instructions for each of these reviews are included in the Design Tools section of Appendix E.

There are many useful software scheduling applications available, such as Microsoft Project or Microsoft Scheduler Plus. Automating scheduling is especially important when it becomes necessary to adjust the schedule; you can change one project date and all others that are affected by that change are adjusted immediately.

FROM OUR EXPERIENCE

Project management and project scheduling are complex disciplines that require a unique set of skills. Instructional designers or other multimedia team members often find themselves serving as project manager or team leader without the experience, aptitude, or tools necessary for success in this role. It is important to recognize that the project-manager or team-leader role is not a simple add-on for a team member having other duties in a multimedia development project. Because of the increased requirements for tracking, scheduling, communicating, and monitoring project activities, most multimedia projects require a skilled, full-time project manager.

It is best to construct the project time lines with those who will be performing the work. A team approach to constructing schedules takes advantage of the group's expertise and experience and affords the buy-in needed to get project development off to a good start. Chapter Sixteen presents a list of typical multimedia team members and roles and responsibilities. We refer you to Greer's book on project management (1996) for help in project management.

We recommend that the team develop a basic schedule and project task list and modify it for subsequent multimedia projects. Modifying existing schedules for later projects generally results in significant time saving and allows benchmarking and accurate project scheduling.

There is a lot to be gained from analyzing the schedule during and after completion of the project. Tracking and comparing actual time and costs with scheduled time and costs gives you the data you need to (1) accurately estimate the scope of future development efforts and (2) point out areas where you can increase productivity, maintain quality, or improve cost-effectiveness.

Lack of time-tracking data can be a real barrier to getting the scheduling information needed to do accurate planning. Scheduling isn't accurate if project time is not tracked, or if it's tracked inconsistently or haphazardly, or if it doesn't track scheduled tasks.

Considerations for time tracking include

- Determining how the time data are captured
- Determining what level of data should be collected and analyzed
- Deciding who gets access to the time-tracking information
- Determining how time tracking is implemented

We recommend doing a quick survey of how long team members think a project task normally takes or should take. Then, establish benchmarks and move forward by scheduling, tracking, and analyzing the team's performance against scheduled estimates. At the conclusion of the project, debrief the team and analyze how the benchmarks can be revised if needed. Review on a project-by-project basis provides the data needed to accurately schedule multimedia design and development tasks.

SUMMARY

The project schedule—especially the section outlining project-development tasks—reflects the decisions made during analysis and design. Schedules are an important tool in assessing whether multimedia ID decisions are achievable and appropriate to unique personnel, time frame, and business constraints. Regardless of your role on the multimedia design team, it is important to understand and have input into the activities that are planned and scheduled. The next chapter presents typical roles and responsibilities that are assigned to activities on a multimedia instructional design and development team.

Project Team

The second undertaking in design specification (recall Table 14.1) is to define typical roles and responsibilities for project team members and associate them with project tasks. If you are using scheduling software that facilitates assigning resources, then it's efficient to add the resources to the schedule.

In a perfect world, multimedia teams would design solutions without the constraints of using only what is available in tools and resources. In reality, multimedia ID teams must design solutions that consider not only the problem but also the resources at hand to solve the problem.

PROCESS

There are three activities in the process of defining roles and responsibilities for project team members:

1. List team roles.
2. Assign roles and responsibilities.
3. Match tasks to members.

PROJECT TEAM PROCEDURE

Follow these activities:

Activity One: List Team Roles

As a team, list the roles required. Review the typical roles and responsibilities of a design team in the (alphabetical) list that follows, and select those appropriate for your particular project.

Audio Producer or Technician

- Produces all audio
- Generates final audio scripts
- Casts talent
- Schedules audio recording sessions
- Mixes, edits, and digitizes audio
- Finds sources of music and sound effects
- Identifies existing media
- Controls and archives audio libraries
- Arranges licensing of existing audio materials
- Reviews the product from an audio perspective
- Has working knowledge of the authoring tool

Author (Publisher, Materials Developer)

- Produces written or electronically mediated instructional materials
- Integrates media elements and creates the product using an authoring tool
- Works with the graphic designer to incorporate graphics into the product
- Constructs interactions and makes revisions
- Has advanced skills with, and knowledge of, the authoring tool
- Works with the creative director to integrate audio and video elements into the product

Creative Director

- Works closely with the interactive designer and graphic designer on design and development of the human-computer interface
- Works with the interactive designer and audio and video producers on creating storyboards and scripts
- Collaborates with the graphic designer regarding media elements
- Ensures all media elements are produced and integrated into the product
- Carries responsibility for the overall quality of the media elements of the product

- Reviews the product from a quality perspective
- Has working knowledge of the authoring tool

Editor
- Edits written or authored material
- Creates or reviews writing specifications

Evaluation Specialist
- Develops or reviews the evaluation plan and tools
- Develops or reviews the testing plan

Graphic Artist
- Works with the graphic designer to create content graphics
- Creates screen or interface designs
- Creates illustrations and animations for the product
- Has some knowledge of the multimedia authoring tool

Graphic Designer
- Designs and produces graphics for instructional materials
- Designs the overall visual look of the product
- Works with the instructional designer and creative director to conceptualize the main interface and content graphics
- Designs the main interface as well as the typography and buttons for all screens
- Creates content art, illustrations, and animation
- Identifies opportunities to use existing artwork
- Maintains libraries of graphics
- Works with the instructional designer to determine all graphic standards
- Has working knowledge of the authoring tool

Implementation Representative
- Weighs implementation alternatives with organizational priorities, issues, and concerns to offer input on the best solution

- Identifies implementation activities according to the medium or media selected
- Defines the time schedule for implementation activities
- Works with support groups and organizations to ensure timely, smooth transition of the intervention from the development phase to the implementation phase
- Creates or carries out implementation, marketing, and communication plans and schedules
- Implements maintenance and evaluation plans

Interactive Designer, Instructional Designer

- Prepares objectives as part of the project team
- Defines content
- Selects and sequences activities for a specific intervention
- Writes (or works with subject-matter experts) to develop instructional material
- Develops multimedia instructional design
- Works with SMEs to develop content for the product
- Develops the interactive design of the product (for example, interactions within the product, how the interactions work, and how the user interacts with the product)
- Works with the systems designer to design flow diagrams to support the instructional and interactive design
- Creates storyboards with the graphic designer, creative director, and video and audio producers
- Works with the creative director to write audio and video scripts
- Bears responsibility for the overall quality of the instruction and interactivity of the product
- Has working knowledge of the authoring tool

Performance Analyst

- Identifies ideal and actual performance conditions
- Determines the cause of any discrepancy and recommends solution(s) and evaluation strategy

Project Manager, Project Leader

- Manages the project (including people, resources, schedule, and processes)
- Estimates the project costs
- Creates CDS with the support of the team
- Creates and maintains the project schedule with the support of the team
- Keeps the project on track by holding regular meetings of the team
- Ensures the team has sufficient resources and tools
- Keeps the customer and sponsors informed of all decisions
- Communicates regularly with management on the status of the project
- Maintains an atmosphere conducive to creativity, productivity, and quality
- Arranges for reviews of the product
- Sets the goals for the team and defines the roles and responsibilities of team members
- Maintains records and motivates team members
- Plans and coordinates resources for developing, acquiring, or deploying a developmental product or service
- Supports a group's work and links that work with the total organization
- Supports evaluation, measurement for success, and benchmarking
- Establishes ground rules for the team and reports on the project to senior management
- Resolves conflicts among team members and various departments, functions, managers, and so on
- Ensures recognition of project team members

Quality Reviewer or Evaluator

- Identifies what impact an intervention has on individual or organization effectiveness
- Reviews the product from an educational and quality perspective

Sponsor

- Owns resources and sets the direction of development activities for the project
- Interfaces with the project team on all decisions, status of project, and sign-offs

Subject-Matter Expert (SME)

- Reviews the content in various stages for accuracy and gives feedback to interactive designer
- Functions as a content expert throughout the development process

Systems Designer

- Designs how the product works from a technical standpoint
- Decides what development tools are used
- Decides how the program logic and flow is structured and how it is produced
- Manages authors
- Creates the base logic for the product and unit models for the authors
- Works with the instructional or interactive designer to design flow diagrams for the product
- Conducts technical reviews of the product
- Has extensive technical knowledge of the authoring tool

Systems Engineer, Application Developer

- Provides information-technology services, primarily application development and support

Video Editor or Technician

- Digitizes and edits all video
- Integrates video elements into the final product
- Has extensive knowledge of the online editing tool
- Has working knowledge of the authoring tool

Video Producer

- Produces and directs all video for the product
- Generates final video scripts
- Casts talent
- Schedules shoots
- Assembles a video crew
- Obtains costumes and makeup
- Reviews final product from a video perspective

- Has working knowledge of the online editing tool
- Has working knowledge of the authoring tool

Activity Two: Assign Roles and Responsibilities

Assign roles to project team members. Depending on the size of your project, the time line, and the skills and resources needed, you may find that team members fill multiple roles or that you require more than one person to fill a role. The project time lines reflect the number of responsibilities assumed by individual team members. If most responsibilities are assumed by a few key players, this generally lengthens the time line on a small project.

Activity Three: Match Tasks to Members

Match responsibilities and tasks to project team members. Develop a Roles and Responsibilities Matrix for each phase of the project, tailored to the needs of the project.

FROM OUR EXPERIENCE

Clearly defining roles and responsibilities can reduce conflict and confusion and focus team members on their unique role in successfully completing a project. Individual roles and responsibilities for design vary, depending on the size of the project, the number and type of media elements, and the number of available personnel (along with their talent).

Organizations that assume—as someone might breezily put it—that "a couple of people with the right skill sets" can design and produce multimedia are misinformed about the number and complexity of skill sets needed for even a minimal multimedia design and development project. It is rare, in fact almost impossible, to staff a design team with a couple of people who can competently act as subject-matter expert, instructional designer, media expert, authoring software expert, system engineer, and so on. The more likely scenario is a team-based approach with a much larger group of people who are not dedicated 100 percent to the project, lending expertise only when it is needed.

SUMMARY

Determining who performs project-development tasks affects the decisions made during design. Design decisions must be achievable and appropriate to the project's unique personnel, time frame, and business constraints.

chapter SEVENTEEN

Media Specifications

The first three elements of the course design specification describe the project, the schedule, and the roles and responsibilities of project team members.

The next undertaking, media specification, describes standards and design for multimedia elements such as

- Theme and interface design and functionality
- Writing style and grammar guidelines
- Feedback and interaction standards
- Video and audio treatments
- Text design and standards
- Graphic design and standards
- Animation and special effects

The design decisions on these multimedia elements are a set of compromises that weigh theories and best practices in learning and performance support; knowledge of the audience and content; project team member preferences, skills, and talents; and project realities such as the budget, time line, and stakeholder preferences.

An appropriate goal is to design a performance support environment or learning environment that

- Engages the learner's modalities
- Provides a comfortable and stress-free environment in which to learn or perform

- Presents the content at the right level and sequence, and with as much fidelity to the real environment as is possible
- Meets the constraints and requirements of the project goals

RELATED THEORY

The optimum design engages as many of the senses as possible. Barring any type of impairment or disability on the one hand and any extrasensory abilities on the other, we may assume that the learner has five senses. He or she uses all five senses to learn or perform.

Over the years, everyone develops a preference for using certain senses, because of types of instruction received, the parts of instruction attended to, and an inborn disposition to learn using some senses more than others. Whatever the reason, people learn in different ways. Learning through more than one sense is known as a multisensory approach.

The best learning occurs through using more than one of the senses. Even though one sense might be preferred, learning is reinforced through secondary sensory learning methods. Because the best learning occurs through more than one sense, the best instruction stimulates as many senses as possible.

In the typical learning situation, you have learners who represent preference for the full spectrum of modalities. The most efficient learners are those who can maximize integration of all of these modalities. It is the instructional designer's responsibility to help students maximize their learning by presenting content that stimulates as many learning senses as possible. Students can use their preferred sense to learn the majority of the material and their secondary senses for reinforcement.

FOUR APPROACHES TO LEARNING

Here are the five senses, grouped into four approaches to learning:

1. Visual: presenting instruction using anything learners can look at. Visuals include video, graphics, animation, written text (on a computer screen, whiteboard, flipchart, overhead transparencies, books, posters, and so on).
2. Auditory: presenting instruction using anything students can listen to (tapes, audio teleconferencing, CBT, lecture, sound effects, music, and so on).

3. Olfactory: presenting instruction using anything students can smell or taste—as when a student discerns that equipment is overheating, or something is burning, or something has been prepared with too much spice, and so on. (Olfactory is usually not a primary sense for learning, especially in regard to multimedia, but because some people are more sensitive to smells and odors learning is enhanced and stimulated by their olfactory sense.)

4. Tactile or kinesthetic: presenting instruction using anything students can touch or manipulate (models, actual parts or equipment, having students perform demonstrations, role plays, and so on).

PROCESS

Defining the media elements determines the look and feel of the final product. There are seven activities in the process of defining media specifications:

1. Define the look and feel of the theme.
2. Define the interface and functionality.
3. Define the interaction and feedback standards.
4. Define the video and audio treatments.
5. Indicate text design standards.
6. Prepare the graphic design standards.
7. Decide on animation and special effects.

MEDIA SPECIFICATIONS PROCEDURE

Follow these activities:

Activity One: Define the Look and Feel of the Theme

Step one: Brainstorm a list of themes. Delete any theme that could offend culturally sensitive audience members or be viewed as religious or sexist in nature.

Narrow the list to the top three or four themes. Use the information you have gained in analysis to define a theme (or metaphor) and general presentation style. The goal in defining a theme is to

- Add interest and relate to the audience and content
- Supply a thread that links the course elements
- Support learning with a unified look and feel
- Constitute a starting point for creating multimedia analogies, graphics, set and costume design, text styles, activities, and so on

Themes should be associated with the actual job the solution is designed for. Job-related themes enhance transfer of learning to the job. We do not recommend or support "fantasy themes"; teaching principles of leadership by way of space creatures coming from Mars to interact with humans does not make the connections that people need to learn—indeed, a far-out theme may be so intriguing as to interfere with learning. It is much more challenging to make the course engaging yet keep it related to the jobs that people do.

Step two: Mock up text styles, ideas for an interface design, set design, costumes, and analogies or graphic styles that support each theme on paper.

Step three: Join the team in deciding on the theme.

Activity Two: Define the Interface and Functionality

The interface design for multimedia should be representative of the theme, audience characteristics, and organizational environment. In addition, the interface design should

- Be as simple as possible, with adequate white space, uniform spacing, and adequate margins (top and bottom, left and right).
- Use consistent screen areas for repeated screen elements such as titles, feedback, links, menus, or prompts.
- Include a consistent navigation design so users become comfortable within the learning or support environment.
- Keep in mind that most people from western cultures view screens using a Z pattern, as shown in Figure 17.1. This is an important consideration in placing screen elements. Generally, the most important information (such as graphics or photos) are placed at the upper left and text or supporting information on the right, followed by prompts and navigation at the bottom. The most-often-used navigation button is placed at the lower right. This placement facilitates mouse-click navigation for right-handed mouse users.

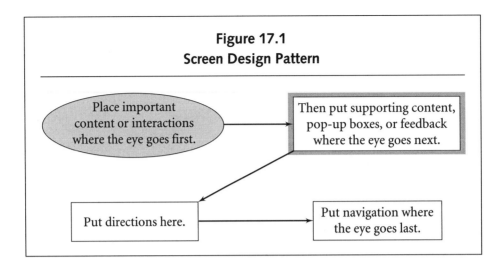

Figure 17.1
Screen Design Pattern

Place important content or interactions where the eye goes first.

Then put supporting content, pop-up boxes, or feedback where the eye goes next.

Put directions here.

Put navigation where the eye goes last.

Many of the interface design and navigation options in this chapter are available in authoring software. Consider these options when designing an interface:

- A frame identifier such as ("3 of 25"), so users can judge how close they are to completing a section or segment. (Remember, multimedia is not like text, where a user can judge how much remains by leafing forward in the text.)

- Exit, Next, Menu, and Back buttons, to facilitate navigation.

- Bookmarking, so that students can return to a course and navigate to the last topic or frame they completed.

- A Glossary button, if the terminology used is likely to be unfamiliar to the audience.

- A Help button with navigation tips, supplemental information, links to other websites, or graphics that remind students of their location in the flow of the course.

- An Audio Repeat button, so students can listen to the audio again on any particular frame. Repeat capabilities are a particularly good strategy if the audience uses English as a second language, if screens include complex audio instructions, or if screens contain long audio sequences.

- A Flash Card button, allowing users to mark frames for printing or review. This is appropriate if the application is deployed in a location such as a learning lab, where screens are not readily available for review or refreshment.

- A More Info button, for access to additional, detailed explanations. This strategy is successful with audiences having varying levels of expertise.

- A Print button, which allows printing job aids, course-completion certificates, or reference materials.

- Lesson and Topic buttons, to aid students in navigation through complex curricula.

- Audio Record, Stop, and Play (playback) buttons, useful when students are practicing audio responses and then listening to their responses and self-evaluating them against a prerecorded example.

One of the best sources of design insight is to review existing Web and CBT programs. Note how content, theme, and interface satisfy the audience and meet the business need that they address. Here are a few sample interface designs, with information about the audience and the business need in each case.

- The purpose of the CBT program illustrated in Figure 17.2 is to market the company's products. CD-ROMs were sent to prospective sales partners.

Completely open navigation is critical to the effectiveness of this program; therefore the interface is designed for easy access to all areas of content. Displaying the menu structure down the left side of the screen enables users to retrieve the specific information they need from any point in the program. Though this program was designed and produced prior to the growth in popularity of the World Wide Web, the general navigation layout it illustrates has become standard for most website design.

- The purpose of the CBT program illustrated in Figure 17.3 is to train operators in performing startup procedures for a steam turbine.

The user interface for this course (displayed across the bottom of the CBT screen) is designed to resemble the steam seal system control panel that operators use on the job. This brings a level of comfort to operators who are unaccustomed to using CBT for continuing-education purposes.

- The purpose of the CBT program illustrated in Figure 17.4 is to offer training and marketing information regarding AST Computer's Ovation Program.

Because of the competitive nature of its industry, AST chose a "Business Olympics" metaphor to compare its products and services to those of the competition. This includes a sportscaster-on-television theme, which in turn inspires the remote-control navigation interface. Users click through different "events" in the "competition" as if switching channels.

• The purpose of the CBT program illustrated in Figure 17.5 is to train new hires at an ophthalmology supplier and extend continued-education support for sales representatives. Areas of education include products, basic concepts and tools related to the field of ophthalmology, and the anatomy of the eye.

The course structure is presented as a tour of an optometrist's office. Users visit various rooms and explore the topics by selecting objects. Navigation is simplified

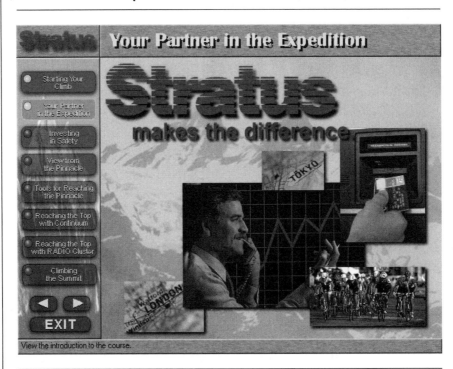

Figure 17.2
Sample Interface Number One (Stratus)

Source: Courtesy of Mlink Technologies

for ease of use, and so as not to conflict with or distract from the sometimes-complex content presented on screen. This interface also includes a briefcase (icon in the lower left corner of the screen) that contains reference materials and product and medical glossaries the student can access at any time.

Activity Three: Define the Interaction and Feedback Standards

Begin by defining the standards for interaction and feedback.

One of the strengths of multimedia is the capacity for interaction. A lot of exciting work is being done in the area of intelligent interfaces; virtual reality; and

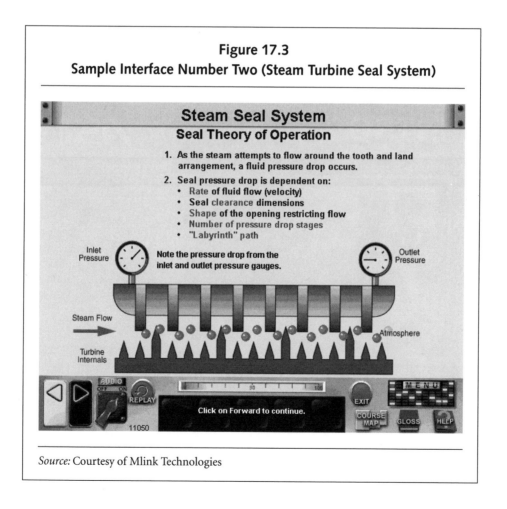

Figure 17.3
Sample Interface Number Two (Steam Turbine Seal System)

Source: Courtesy of Mlink Technologies

various means of interaction such as natural-language interface, voice and speech technology, gesture recognition, and even biological interface. For the time being, though, multimedia interaction is typically limited to what can be entered though a microphone, keyboard, or mouse. But even this limited interaction captures a user's attention, motivates the user, and helps him or her to form associations. In multimedia courses, interactions should be frequent and produce student involvement. We recommend student-controlled pacing and branching.

When using questioning techniques, make sure that there are clear instructions, and that the question contains only one correct response. Indicate the for-

Figure 17.4
Sample Interface Number Three (AST Computer)

Source: Courtesy of Mlink Technologies

mat for the sentence containing the question and possible answers in your standards so that they have a distinct and consistent screen format. Most questions are a variation of text entry, clicking on an object, multiple choice, or matching; they permit one or two tries before the user is given the correct answer and allowed to move on. All questions should be titled, worded clearly, and easy to understand.

Feedback should neither be distracting nor reward incorrect responses. It should be immediate, informative, and positive and motivational. There should be no excessive delay from the time the user performs an action to when the feedback occurs.

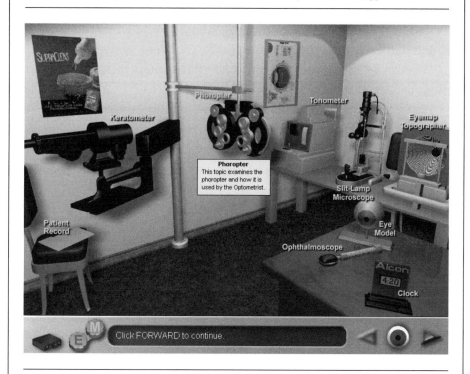

Figure 17.5
Sample Interface Number Four (Ophthalmology)

Source: Courtesy of Mlink Technologies

Because most multimedia systems have record-keeping capabilities, interaction or test-item results can be saved for later reporting. Indicate the items that are to be recorded, and in what format the information is exported. Reporting ensures desired, consistent outcomes. The ability to prove consistent learning is especially critical for organizations that must comply with changing regulations. Items that can be recorded include student identification, number of items missed, frequency at which items are missed, and seat time.

Activity Four: Define the Video and Audio Treatments

Define the audio, photography, and video standards. Here are standards to be established, depending on the media and the technology specifications you are using:

- *Audio:* narration style and tone—for example, male narrator, British English. Indicate sound file types and file-naming conventions. Determine how sound effects and music are used. Music is an especially good tool for signaling the beginning or end of an instructional sequence. As with a motion picture, it can also set the tone and support a graphic style and theme.
- *Photography:* file type, file-naming conventions, and size requirements.
- *Video:* file type, file-naming conventions, and size requirements. Any video should clearly support the goals of the project. Video should be shot with enough detail to demonstrate the objectives of the training. It should be used as an aid in and support for text, graphic, and audio presentation of the content. The length of the motion segments should not detract from the content; short segments that play a supporting role are best.

Activity Five: Indicate Text Design and Standards

Text design and standards stipulate such things as font style, size, and color. The text appearance and resolution on the screen should determine the size and font. Indicate the arrangement—both justification and letter spacing. Also indicate the display treatment (for example: "Bullets appear on the screen, from left to right, one at a time, with a two-second pause before each new bullet and after all bullets are in place.").

Activity Six: Prepare the Graphic Design Standards

The graphic design standards include file type, file size, file-naming convention, and color range. Graphics should have a clear benefit to the presentation of the content and hold simplicity of design as their overall characteristic. They should not detract from textual information. Graphics should be similar in size and placement, and any text that is included as call-outs must be readable.

Clarity and readability should not be dependent on color variations. There should not be more than four colors on a screen, and the entire course should use a palette of not more than seven colors. The color use on screens should be consistent. Manage color contrast appropriately: no red on black or blue on orange, and for most audiences minimal use of "hot" colors is best.

Activity Seven: Decide on Animation and Special Effects

Determine whether to use animation and special effects. They are good for capturing the user's attention and are effective if used to signal instructional events, such as the beginning or end of a sequence of instruction. They're also appropriate when you have to illustrate a moving object that is not easily photographed, as with the movement of oil through a diesel engine. Animation and special effects should be used to support the learning objectives. Development software options are a good place to start in determining standards. Most software used to develop Web applications or CBT—Authorware, for example—provide a number of options for special effects, such as how a screen is displayed or how the program moves to the next frame. Existing options act like a menu of choices. Review them, and choose two or three. Use effects sparingly and consistently, in support of project goals.

FROM OUR EXPERIENCE

It is easy to be enamored with the options and capabilities of today's multimedia development software. *Simple* really is better, faster, cheaper, and more effective. Without standards in place, projects can easily become sidetracked in a constant design and development mode ("Just one more bell or whistle. . . ." or "Before we wrap up, why don't we try presenting it with this approach?"). This can undermine project time lines and goals. Sticking to the agreed-on decisions is important because the cost of a redo seldom justifies the added benefit. Unless design decisions have an impact on the effectiveness of the product, it is best to record the suggestions, look over all the should-haves, would-haves, and could-haves, and, when appropriate, apply them to the design standards of the next project.

SUMMARY

The most effective multimedia has a simple interface design and is consistent in

- Writing style and grammar
- Interaction and feedback presentation
- Topography, graphics, colors, video, audio, and animation and special effects

Planning and decision making in the form of standards support consistent presentation of multimedia elements. Standards can serve as benchmarks, ensuring that effective and efficient development can occur. The next chapter presents information on how to structure and group content so that it is well organized, covers the objectives, and is written to the appropriate level of skill and knowledge.

Content Structure

Now that we have detailed the project, schedule, roles and responsibilities of project team members, and the media specifications, it's time to consider the nature of the multimedia itself. That is, if your solution includes courses, you group instruction into concepts or lessons and apply an instructional strategy.

Regardless of the unit of instruction, content should be logically grouped and structured consistently. In conjunction with the user interface, this gives students an effective learning environment where they can access information or learn comfortably.

RELATED THEORY

The structure should follow principles of learning that have been determined to be effective in presenting and learning information.

Certain principles of learning operate in any educational media. Here is a list of sixteen principles of learning that we have synthesized from the research literature on how people learn. We have editorialized to explain how each principle applies to the multimedia design.

Principle One: Use Review in Learning

Students learn more when lessons begin with a review of previous material.

Application to Multimedia. Begin multimedia lessons with a review of relevant information presented in previous lessons. The review should highlight main points that relate to what students are going to learn in the current lesson. If the chosen medium has a menu with navigation controlled by the user, or if the material is not presented in any particular order, then begin with a review of relevant prerequisites to the learning. Example: a lesson on troubleshooting a kiln might include

- An audio statement: "From operating the kiln, you may recall that the pilot light is normally blue."
- Supporting text: Remember: The Pilot Light Is Normally Blue.
- A photo of the pilot light.
- A legend indicating the topic title: Checking the Pilot Light.

Principle Two: Include Introductions and Specified Objectives

Students learn more when lessons and activities are introduced and learning objectives are specified.

Application to Multimedia. Design the beginning of your multimedia lessons to include a statement of lesson objectives put in terms appropriate to the learner, explaining what the student is expected to know or do. Example: a multimedia topic on sanitation might present the objectives on screen along with these elements:

- An audio statement: "This section introduces the procedure to mix and use sanitizing solution. When you've completed it, you will be able to use sanitizing solution to maintain the workroom to OSHA standards."
- Supporting text: Mixing and Using Sanitizing Solutions.
- Photo: a photo of the ingredients.
- Hypertext link: a graphic of a stack of paper titled "OSHA Standards" that links to a text-file copy of the standards.

Principle Three: Be Sure Verbal Content Is Effective

Students learn more when verbal content is precise and presented fluently.

Application to Multimedia. Lessons must present material in very clear, precise language and move (transition) logically from one segment to the next, avoiding unnecessary interruption or digression. Examples:

- An audio prompt to move forward to the next screen, which consistently comes up at the conclusion of a set of screen interactions
- Designing consistent presentation of audio sequences that are timed to the text they support

Principle Four: Use Examples and Demonstrations

Students learn more when relevant examples and demonstrations illustrate concepts and skills.

Application to Multimedia. Lessons must include visual examples of the concept that the student can view to see what he or she is to conceptualize. Examples and demonstrations should be sufficient in number and increasingly complex for the student to discriminate the finer points of the concept.

Example: A multimedia lesson on how to inventory the assets allocated to an office includes a graphic menu of the inventory process. The menu allows users to click on the step in the process to learn about the step and rationale for doing it. The graphical depiction of the process helps users conceptualize the entire inventory process.

Principle Five: Build In Student Success

Students learn more when they are able to handle tasks and questions with a high rate of success.

Application to Multimedia. Design multimedia lessons that ensure success for students who learn at different rates by incorporating supplemental materials, reviews, and summaries.

Example: A multimedia lesson on fiber-optic specifications contains a series of exercises on planning an installation. A button labeled "Look Up Specs" allows users who are not familiar with the specifications to check for information as they are completing the exercises.

Principle Six: Tailor Course to Audience

Students learn more when lessons and instructional activities are presented through concepts and language that are understandable and appropriate to the intended audience.

Application to Multimedia. Develop materials that are based on students' abilities, ascertaining this from audience analysis. Materials must be written at the appropriate audience level and language should not interfere with the concepts to be learned. Unfamiliar terms must be defined and students must be taught to incorporate them into their working vocabulary.

Example: a multimedia lesson on the controls used to account for supplies received in a restaurant is designed and written in quite different ways for two particular audiences:

1. Kitchen stewards with Spanish as their primary language. The stewards are mostly male and between eighteen and twenty-five, with no formal education, not computer literate, and having little exposure to accounting terminology. This audience requires a very simple interface, a glossary, and a theme appropriate to their gender and age group. In addition, audio and graphics, not text, are the primary means to depict the content.

2. Restaurant accountants with English as their primary language. The accountants are mostly females between thirty-six and fifty-four, with at least some college education, who use computers daily and are familiar with accounting terminology. This audience requires less audio and graphics, would not benefit from a glossary, and would benefit from a more complex navigation structure allowing more user control.

Principle Seven: Keep Pace Brisk, with Variations

Students learn more when lessons are presented at a brisk pace and when instruction slows to accommodate students' understanding but avoids unnecessary slowdowns.

Application to Multimedia. Effective lessons move at a pace geared to individual rates of learning, moving rapidly for students who grasp information quickly, offering greater depth for those who wish to delve further, and additional explanation for those who have difficulty grasping information. Most frames should be timed so that users do not spend more than three to five seconds before additional elements are added to the screen, or there is an option to move forward, or there is an interaction with the screen content in some form.

Example: A lesson on medical terminology for hospital administrative assistants uses an on-screen crossword puzzle, dictionary, and "Hints" button to teach the meanings of common medical terms at a pace appropriate to the learner.

Principle Eight: Include Smooth Transitions

Students learn more when transitions between lessons are made efficiently and smoothly.

Application to Multimedia. Students need to be reminded (cued) when a shift occurs from one topic to the next or from one activity to the next. This can be handled visually with a standard graphic or screen used to signal the transition; it may include a summary and information about upcoming content.

Example: A web-based lesson on a new plant maintenance software program uses a standard animation and a question to signify that a user is at the end of a topic and is ready to move on to the next topic.

Principle Nine: Use Clear Assignments and Directions

Students learn more when clear and concise assignments and directions are given.

Application to Multimedia. Direction for navigation and interaction must be clearly and carefully explained in unambiguous terms. Most multimedia screens have a prompt box located at the bottom of the screen that gives direction. Care must be taken to keep the user from getting into a loop, or stuck because the directions for proceeding are not clear. Here are some standard prompts:

- Click Forward to continue.
- Match the _____ with the_____.
- Type the _____ in the _____.
- Click on the_____ to _____.
- Sorry, that's not correct. Try again. (Then give the user the answer after the next try.)
- That's correct. Good job!
- Yes! That's the right answer.
- That's not correct. The answer is _____.

Example: A distance-learning videoconference always displays the call-in phone and fax numbers whenever a question is posed to the audience.

Principle Ten: Maintain Proper Standards

Students learn more when clear, firm, and reasonable standards are maintained.

Application to Multimedia. Students strive to reach reasonable expectations for knowledge or performance. Standards that are not clearly understood, not adhered to, or too high or too low cause the learners not to challenge themselves to reach the standards.

Example: A self-paced multimedia lesson on English composition implemented without testing or record-keeping functionality may not be successful in a high school environment where students are not generally self-motivated.

Principle Eleven: Monitor, Circulate, and Check Work

Students learn more efficiently when instructors circulate during classroom assignments to check student performance.

Application to Multimedia. Students tend to stay on task when learning is monitored. Automated response, capturing test scores and reporting results, tracking, and feedback cause students to be careful when answering questions.

Example: In a CBT chemistry lesson, the computer is able to check responses to procedures used to perform experiments and immediately correct any errors.

Principle Twelve: Ask One Question at a Time

Students learn more when questions are posed one at a time.

Application to Multimedia. Automated media can deliver questions in any sequence desired. Questions should be posed one at a time and be important and relevant. Students need time to formulate answers.

Example: Try to add these three sets of numbers concurrently rather than one at a time: (a) $2 + 7 + 9 + 14 + 11 = ?$ (b) $6 + 7 + 3 + 19 + 4 = ?$ (c) $1 + 7 + 8 + 6 = ?$

Principle Thirteen: Work in Feedback

Students learn more when instructional feedback on the correctness of their work is offered.

Application to Multimedia. Praise learners for correct answers, and give information about incorrect answers. A simple "Incorrect" is insufficient for students to learn from their mistakes. Instead, provide context-specific feedback such as, "No, that's incorrect because . . . Try again."

Example: CBT on the procedure for entering a check into a banking software program provides feedback after each step, allowing students to be sure that they are performing each step correctly before going to the next step.

Principle Fourteen: Follow Feedback with Appropriate Technique

Students learn more when sustaining feedback is offered after an incorrect response (or no response) by probing, repeating the question, giving a clue, or allowing more time.

Application to Multimedia. Students should have more than one chance to answer a question, be given clues about why an input is right or wrong, and receive hints to stimulate their thinking toward getting the correct answer. If students give partial answers, another question or some feedback can require them to further their initial response.

Example: In a learn-to-type CBT, if a student types a sentence incorrectly, the program indicates which keys were pressed incorrectly and repeats the sentence, illustrating the keystrokes with an animation.

Principle Fifteen: Material Should Motivate

Students learn more effectively when they are motivated by the material.

Application to Multimedia. Lessons must be designed to create and hold the student's interest. Topics and information must be relevant to the learner and demonstrate the reason he or she needs to know the material. Frequent interaction, correct pacing, and a theme and interface design that appeal to the audience are important components in creating and holding attention.

Example: A military, sports, or hunting theme may not be the most appropriate choice for a lesson aimed at an audience of young girls. A Barbie theme would be equally unappealing for those in the business world.

Principle Sixteen: Connect Material to the Real World

Students learn more effectively when the concepts taught are closely related to the real world.

Application to Multimedia. Lessons should practice something closely simulating the actual conditions under which the task has to be performed. Simulation *practice* must be included in materials, rather than just imparting information. Even showing and telling is not enough; students must *do*. This is what makes multimedia such a powerful tool for training on software applications. A multimedia environment can be a realistic simulation of the one where the work is to take place.

Example: A lesson on business processes might use the image of keeping a copy machine stocked rather than one of keeping a tackle box stocked. A business theme (for example, a delivery truck) rather than a fun arcade theme would add credibility to the content.

Motivation Is Everything

All of these principles fall into four categories:

1. Acquisition (acquiring knowledge)
2. Transfer (using knowledge)
3. Motivation (the need to possess knowledge)
4. Reinforcement (encouragement to possess knowledge)

The most central concept to learning is motivation.

LEARNING AND INSTRUCTIONAL DELIVERY STRATEGIES

The media analysis you perform may lead you to conclude that the most effective implementation is a mixture of media. Think of, say, a complex scientific concept being covered by a lecture, followed by lab with CBT practice, and including job aids to support transfer to the work environment.

There are two major learning strategies common to any medium, including multimedia: deductive and inductive. In the former, students draw specific conclusions from general information. The instruction presents the generality from which students draw their conclusions.

The inductive strategy requires students to draw general conclusions from specific information. The instruction allows them to achieve the desired conclusion by establishing the situation and furnishing the necessary information.

Both inductive and deductive processes require students to "prove" their conclusions are correct; the difference is that the processes begin from opposite ends of the spectrum.

The major instructional delivery strategies follow.

Lecture or Linear Presentation

The linear interaction is limited to simple statements or actions from the learner (yes, no, click Forward). This strategy is often used to introduce a course that embraces a number of delivery methods. For example, you may have to present some information before a classroom discussion or chat, follow it with a live demonstration or CBT, then conduct a group or individual open exploration, and end with a demonstration.

Lecture, Recitation, Interaction

Information is presented in a lesson, interspersed with questions or interaction. Questions require more than yes-or-no response; students must make a choice among alternatives. The general style is deductive. This is most often used in lecture, CBT, or interactive distance broadcasting.

Lecture and Discussion

This involves presenting information and then discussion questions that require response and interaction among students. Discussion can occur at numerous points during the lecture, or distance-learning session, or online chat, or after an initial presentation of information. The presentation may be as minimal as raising an issue and allowing the group to explore it thoroughly, eliciting divergent views on the issue. An instructor may or may not keep track of discussion points and summarize at the end of the session.

Lecture and Demonstration

Demonstration adds to lecture and recitation the dimension of actually showing concepts to students, using operational models.

Guided Learning, Open Exploration

In this strategy, learning situations are created and structured; students must then explore, raise, and answer their own questions. Information is provided as students discover it is missing and realize they need it. This strategy requires that instructors who are in the classroom, online, or in a distance broadcast session be highly knowledgeable about the subject matter, to answer unrehearsed and unanticipated questions with genuinely valuable information. In a scenario-based multimedia or CBT session, comprehensive reference material and help resources must be readily available. Inductively, this type of lesson poses another question to a first question that gives students a clue as to where to search for the answer but does not give them the answer. Deductively, it supplies the information that moves the student on to the next step or phase.

Brainstorming

Brainstorming is a technique that can be used within exploration. It is easily accommodated in a distance broadcast session or online chat session. It brings out all possible ideas on a topic, which can later be evaluated in some manner and validated as to their worth or pertinence. Brainstorming itself does not make these judgments. Because adult learners often want to impose judgment on their ideas immediately, they don't express their own ideas and may not be accepting of others'. Thus, brainstorming might not work well unless the rules are established before beginning a session. Here are some rules for brainstorming:

- The purpose is to generate as many ideas as possible.
- All ideas are acceptable.
- No criticism of an idea is permitted.
- You can add to, build on, or give the complete opposite of any idea presented.
- Everyone should participate.
- All ideas are listed, for everyone to see.
- Don't stop as soon as the initial ideas stop flowing; some ideas take longer to percolate in the mind.
- Point out any violation of these rules.

Games

Don't overlook the advantages of games. But then again, don't use gaming just for the sake of gaming. We are a generation that has grown up on television and is accustomed to being entertained, and this appetite has crossed over into education and training; students now expect to be entertained.

Carefully constructed and situated games are appropriate to all media and can have some very positive effects. They can drive home a point that would be rejected or have less effect if just stated. Also, if people enjoy learning, they tend to retain the information longer.

Role Playing

Acting out situations is a very effective method for practicing skills that are being learned. Role plays reinforce; they are an opportunity for the students to receive feedback on how the skill is performed. Role plays are appropriate to all media; a CBT with an audio recording and playback capability can be used to role-play answers to customer service questions.

Simulation

Simulations are high-end role plays, distinguished by being performed in, or as near to, the actual work situation as possible. Simulations are appropriate in all media, but multimedia simulations of software are a particularly effective design choice.

Performance Support

Performance support is distinguished by information that is readily available via one or two keystrokes, a phone call, or a glance at a job aid or reference manual. This strategy is particularly appropriate for information that is constantly updated, overly complex, or necessary to support or enhance performance.

PROCESS

There are two activities in the process of defining lessons:

1. Break the content into units.
2. Map the information.

CONTENT STRUCTURE PROCEDURE

Follow these activities:

Activity One: Break the Content into Units

Step one: Categorize the content in six major groups:

1. Concepts (ideas or definitions)
2. Processes (systems of related ideas)
3. Procedures (steps within a process)
4. Principles (guiding forces, mission, values)
5. Facts (single pieces of information)
6. Systems (physical entities with operational parts)

Step two: Arrange information based on a job task order, from simple to complex, or by logical content groups.

Activity Two: Map the Information

Step one: Create a lesson outline. Be certain it contains the eleven essential instructional or learning events outlined in Table 18.1. Each topic within a lesson should be considered a minilesson and follow the same pattern.

The steps presented in this activity are equally appropriate for all multimedia products. Regardless of whether your multimedia includes a web page, a reference manual, or an online help system, you must group and present the content within a defined structure and logic.

Include these elements in a lesson outline:

- Lesson title.
- Objectives for the lesson: the terminal objectives and the lesson objectives. List the terminal objectives for the lesson in the words and format in which they are going to be seen on screen. Remember, this format should be conversational so that the audience can understand the goals and objectives.
- Lesson length: determine how long it will take for the student who follows the long path (all of the branching, reviews, tests, and so on) to complete the lesson. Timing is important because each lesson contributes to the overall course, whose length is predetermined by analysis or project requirements.
- Lesson weight: proportion of the content of each lesson in the course. The weight of the lesson is determined by its importance with respect to the content

Table 18.1
Events of Instruction

Event	Description
Advance organizer	Explains what was previously learned, what will be learned in this lesson, and how both connect with one another and to subsequent learning. Includes the purpose of the lesson and its relevance to the course. Answers the question, "Why should I learn this?"
Objectives	Tells the students what they will be able to do or will know as a result of completing a lesson. *Note:* present the objectives informally and conversationally. Using second person *you* is appropriate in this case.
Content	The presentation strategies defined by the objectives.
Guided practice	Student practice is closely monitored to provide immediate and corrective feedback on how they are mastering the content; reinforces the presentation of the content.
Feedback	Positive and corrective feedback interspersed throughout each lesson. Positive feedback tells students that they are correct and what comes next. Positive feedback may also include a statement telling the students why they are correct. Corrective feedback explains why the answer was wrong, reveals what the correct answer is, suggests trying again, or points out other action to take.
Transition	Appears between topics throughout the lesson. Transitions are mini-introductions that explain how what was just learned applies to the next topic.

Table 18.1
Events of Instruction, Cont'd.

Event	Description
Summary	Closes a topic and reminds students what they learned.
Independent practice	Practice is done after completing the entire lesson but before formal testing. Independent practice engages students in performing tasks in a manner as close to the actual work environment as possible. Students find out if they have followed the correct steps at the end of the practice. At the end of the entire practice, they receive feedback on the points where there were errors. They may try again.
Test	Measuring the effectiveness of the solution.
Remediation	Clarifies why knowledge and skills have been incorrectly learned, and presents the information that could be learned in a different presentation. Remediation does not entail repeating the same material in the same way. It might mean an abbreviated form of the initial instruction to help students understand points they might have missed.
Retest	Follows remediation. It is used to determine if the students have now mastered the knowledge or skill. The same test as the first may be used. However, it is better to use a parallel test.

of the entire course and the length of the lesson compared to the overall length of the course. The weight of each lesson determines how many questions to apportion in a final test; it also affects the overall grading procedure. A process for weighting lessons is covered in Part Four, Multimedia Evaluation.

- The lesson introduction: write the introduction just as you want it in the lesson.
- Presentation strategy: detail what presentation strategy is to be used, and tell the developer how to write it along with the information you intend to present.
- The testing strategy: how to test and track student scores. This topic is covered in the fourth part of this book, on evaluation. Remember to include all questions for lessons, units, and the course when you write the lesson outline.
- The lesson summary: follow the same steps you did for the introduction.
- A list of the media to be used in the lesson.
- A list of the resources required to complete the lesson. These may be instructional tools that supplement the lesson (user's guide, student manual, course administrator guide). Include any resources that the student needs to complete the lesson.

Concept mapping is another method for organizing material for presentation. Mapping is much freer in structure than outlining, and it allows more creativity. It lets you consider all ideas before beginning to organize content. See Figure 18.1 for an example of how information is organized in a concept map.

Here's how concept mapping works:

1. Brainstorm a list all of the phrases that state the main ideas included in the concept, process, system, and so on you are addressing. You may not use all of these ideas in the materials, but let the ideas flow.
2. Choose the central idea, and write one or two sentences that encapsulate the idea.
3. Consider all of the main ideas listed in the first step of the concept mapping, and see which ones go together. At this point, you may determine that some of the phrases listed as main ideas are really supporting ideas.
4. Put the central idea in the middle of the map.
5. Order the main and supporting ideas.
6. Recheck the map to be sure it's logical to you.
7. Explain the map to someone else, and take suggestions on improvements.
8. Make final revisions to the map.
9. Begin developing the lesson.

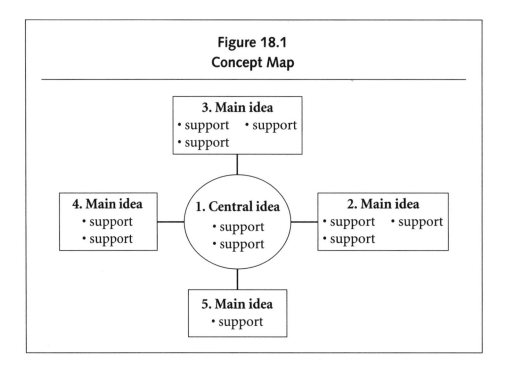

Figure 18.1
Concept Map

Step two: After completing the lesson outline or concept map, create a course flowchart or map.

A course flowchart can be developed on any flowcharting software application. Experiment with several such packages before deciding on one, because some are easier to use than others. Figure 18.2 is an example of a high-level course flowchart.

Detailed lesson flowcharts show the branching within individual lessons. Figure 18.3 is an example of a detailed lesson flowchart.

FROM OUR EXPERIENCE

Inexperienced multimedia instructional designers and design teams tend to arrange content and use design strategies according to their own preferences and experience. This limits the creativity and effectiveness applied to the design. We have two low-cost suggestions for countering this problem.

The first is that one of the most useful techniques for gaining insight and ideas is to check out similar products by way of the Web, by visiting vendors at trade

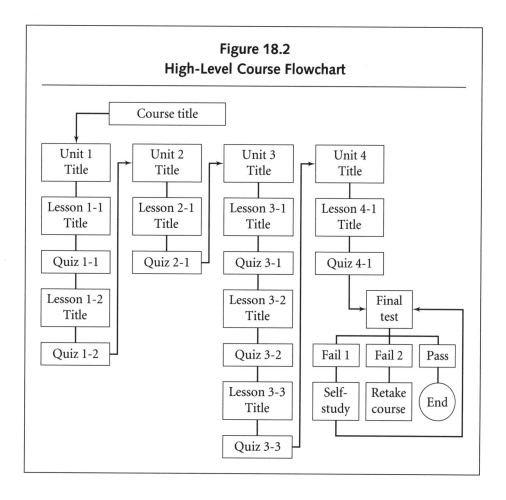

Figure 18.2
High-Level Course Flowchart

shows, or by experimenting with off-the-shelf offerings. Note what works well or not so well and how these insights can be applied to your own design project. Don't discount children's educational multimedia titles; they contain some of the best (and occasionally some of the worst) examples of simple interfaces and innovative ID strategies.

The second suggestion is to use brainstorming in searching for novel approaches to meeting your design goals. Include non–instructional designers and design team members who have a flair for creativity and can provide fresh ideas and approaches. Design sessions are often some of the most enjoyable and invigorating activities associated with multimedia projects.

SUMMARY

Applying the principles of instruction, along with a sound instructional strategy, allows you to order the content for instructional effectiveness. Involving as many team members as is practical boosts morale, builds consensus, and improves the quality of the design.

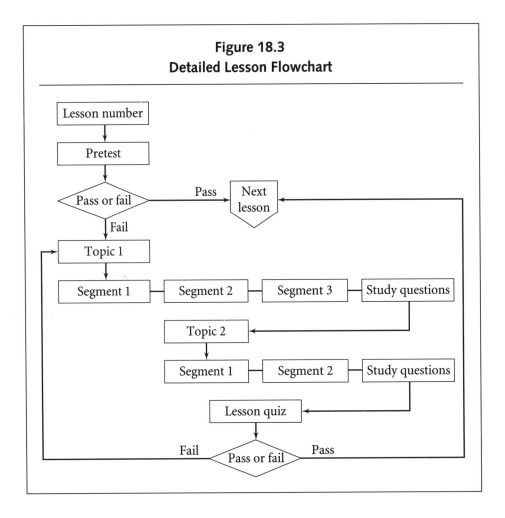

Figure 18.3
Detailed Lesson Flowchart

Configuration Control

The course design specification now describes the project, schedule, roles and responsibilities of project team members, and media specifications, and it breaks the information into logical chunks. As a final planning step, you need to establish the configuration control (CC) plan for developing course materials. Configuration control is the project's quality-control process.

PROCESS

There's just one activity in the process of configuration management: establishing a CC plan.

CONFIGURATION CONTROL PROCEDURE

Follow this activity:

Activity One: Establish a Configuration Control (CC) Plan

Develop a CC process that regulates the version of the materials under design, development, or review. If numerous people are working on the same material, then each team member must have access to the same configured version of the materials.

You can make CC as complicated or as simple as you wish. Complicated procedures slow down the project but afford more control. An important point is that a process is only as good as the people who use it. The team members must commit to following the procedures in the process to ensure uniformity. There is a sample CC plan at the end of this chapter.

A master hard copy and an electronic copy of each version of the materials under development or review always remains archived. In that way, if electronic disks are corrupted or hard drives fail while in use, the only changes lost are the most recent. Plus, you have the hard-copy comments from the last version. It might be annoying to have to rework the storyboards or program files, but at least the work is recoverable rather than lost forever.

Continue the CC steps until there is no need to return the lesson materials to the project team and the materials can be stored as the final version. The material is resurrected when entering the development stage of the project and turned over to the development team, who then make their contributions.

All project members must provide version copies of their electronic files to the configuration control designee for security. The designee is responsible for dispensing the correct version of the materials.

SAMPLE CONFIGURATION CONTROL PLAN

This configuration control plan outlines the steps and the roles used to maintain version control. In this plan, the course developer, script writer, or any design team member can be substituted for "author." The most important element of any CC plan is the configuration control gatekeeper (CCG), whose responsibility it is to manage the review cycle.

Step One ("Author's" Responsibility)

Deliver the material to be reviewed to the CCG.

    A. The electronic disk version should have a label indicating
- The name of the document
- The version of the document
- The original author
- The date of the version

    B. The hard copy version of the document should have the same information that is on the disk, with the version number and date printed in the footer.

Step Two (CCG's Responsibility)

Prepare the material for routing through the review cycle.

    A. Make a duplicate of the material (electronic or hard copy).

    B. Label the original of the material "Master Version 1" and the copy "Copy Version 1."

    C. File the Master 1 of the material and circulate the Copy 1 for review.

    D. Attach a routing sheet to each document that is put into review. The routing sheet should contain:

- The name of the document
- The version of the document
- A place for reviewers to sign their names and the date they complete the review
- A place for final sign-off if the document needs no changes

    E. Deliver the material to the first reviewer in the review cycle.

Step Three (Reviewers' Responsibility)

Complete one entire review cycle before the document goes back to the author for changes.

Step Four (Last Reviewer's Responsibility)

The last reviewer returns the material to the CCG.

Note that the first review (step three) should be the subject matter expert (SME) review, or technical review. If the content contains significant technical inaccuracies, this reviewer can return the material to the CCG to send it back to the author for changes before completing the review cycle. The technical reviewer is the only one who has this option. The reason for allowing the technical reviewer this choice is simple. If the material does contain significant inaccuracies, it has to go through an entire review cycle again after the author makes the revisions. Therefore, it makes sense to cut down review time and cycles by catching these technical problems immediately.

Step Five (CCG's Responsibility)

Return material to originator.

Step Six (Author's Responsibility)

When the author gets the document back from review, he or she
    A. Opens the electronic document
    B. Makes changes to the document
    C. Saves it as Version 2
    D. Returns the original and Version 2 to the CCG

Step Seven (CCG's Responsibility)

The CCG prepares the material for routing through the second review cycle.
    A. Make a duplicate of the revised material (electronic copy or hard copy).
    B. Label the original of the material as "Master Version 2" and the copy "Copy Version 2."
    C. File the Master 2 of the material and circulate the Copy 2 for review.
    D. Attach a routing sheet (same type as in step two, part D) to each document that is put into review. The routing sheet should contain
        • The name of the document
        • The version of the document
        • A place for reviewers to sign their names and the date they completed the review
        • A place for final sign-off if the document needs no changes
    E. Deliver the material to the first reviewer in the review cycle.

Step Eight (Reviewers' Responsibility)

Complete the second review cycle.
    A. It's important to note that the second and subsequent review cycles are only to determine if all changes were made to the reviewer's satisfaction and for final sign-off.
    B. If all changes were not made, initial that there are still changes to be carried out and pass the materials to the next reviewer.
    C. The last reviewer returns the material to the CCG.

Step Nine (CCG's Responsibility)

Return the material to the original author if there are still changes to be made. If all changes have been incorporated and the document is final, the CCG should mark the material "Final Version" and file it.

Step Ten (Author's Responsibility)

If the material must go back to the author again, he or she

A. Opens the electronic document

B. Makes changes to the document

C. Saves it as Version 3

D. Returns Versions 3 and 2 to the CCG

Cycles continue in this fashion until there are no further changes required.

FROM OUR EXPERIENCE

In general, the more planning done up-front in any project, including planning for configuration control, the more smoothly the project operates; the result is a quality product delivered within budget and on time.

Much work is lost, duplicated, or repeated if CC is not well planned, communicated, and followed. This is especially true in large projects. Multimedia projects have numerous components, and they are handled by many project team members. If there's no one in charge of managing this cycle, integration of these components is confusing, frustrating, and fraught with errors that require rework—often involving long hours.

SUMMARY

Including the project's configuration control process is an important part of the CDS. All project team members can reference it in their own copy of the document.

part three

Multimedia
Development and
Implementation

Introduction to Multimedia Development

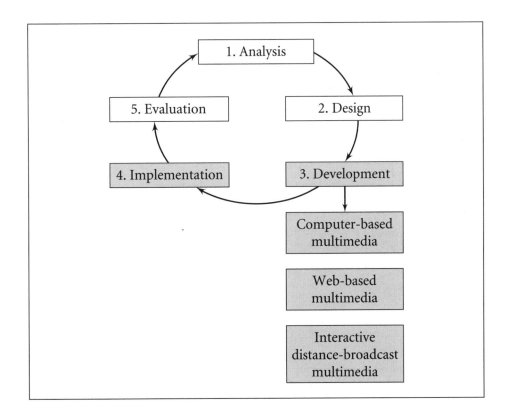

The course design specification (CDS) document is implemented during development. At this point in multimedia projects, more team members become involved. Storyboards are written; video is shot, edited, and logged; audio is recorded, edited, and logged; graphics are created, edited, and logged; and initial versions of web pages are developed, tested, and reviewed.

The larger the project, the more important it is that the development phase be well managed. Team meetings are extremely important during development and are necessary to coordinate the various activities. All project team members must know their roles and responsibilities, understand the project time line, and fulfill their assigned responsibilities.

Review cycles must be implemented, with each reviewer clearly understanding what to review and how to do it. Records of approvals, decisions, and changes must be maintained. Each media element must be integrated and coordinated, and the unique project production and implementation requirements must be managed.

Whatever the type of multimedia, the basic development principles remain the same:

1. First, establish a framework of templates, models, development specifications, and standards.
2. Next, develop the media elements that fit into the framework.
3. Then review and revise the product.
4. Finally, implement the finished product.

Successful multimedia development methodologies tend to include these elements:

- Design-time prototyping: creating an early application-system prototype so as to review, test, and approve the interface design, media elements, script, or map. This is an efficient method for rapid development.
- Evolutionary development: using each stage of prototyping and development as the basis from which to evolve the next prototype. For this to be successful, design decisions that do not involve the content must be locked in.
- Use of models and templates: modeling is a useful methodology for parallel development projects. It's particularly useful in projects where content is added in an iterative process, as it is made available. Templates are created and used as a framework for content as it is identified. For example, in a software development

project we're familiar with, the instructional design, look and feel, and functionality are developed first so the content can be inserted when available. Here is a list of the screens or frames developed at the same time the final changes to the software are being finalized:

- Title screen (with music)
- Main menu
- Help, and About This Course screen
- Credits screen
- Topic level one: "What is this topic about?" (includes seven screens)

    Title and objective for the topic; how long the topic should take (with animation and music)

    How will it affect my job?

    When will I do the task?

    What do I need to know to perform the task?

    What are the steps I need to take?

    Are there any special hints? Common errors or time-saving tricks

    Summary and transition (with music)

- Topic level two: "How is it done?"

    Title (with animation and music)

    Video sequence of the steps, audio, text

    Summary and transition (with music)

- Topic level three: "Let me try"

    Title (with animation and music)

    Functionality; screen for clicking on an object, with feedback

    Functionality; screen for text entry, with feedback

    Summary and transition (with music)

This topic-level model is a production prototype that serves as a template for the follow-on development. In development, the prototype is copied and revised. This rapid development ensures that the training can be deployed along with the new software. This development approach is necessary if a change in content or revision is likely. Such screen elements as titles, prompt boxes, buttons, graphics, photos, text display areas, and video windows must be consistently sized and placed for this approach to be fully successful.

Using prototyping methodologies reduces risk, increases consistency between lessons, ensures acceptance from those authorized to approve the project, and uncovers any production problems or issues when they are at a manageable level. Prototyping and rapid development cycles are increasingly important in industries such as telecommunications, where time-to-market is critical to product success and supporting multimedia must be ready when the product is ready.

In some sectors the rate of change means it's essential to be able to produce ongoing updates and revisions to the courseware. To accomplish this goal, use topic or lesson-level templates, combined with libraries of graphics and photos, all of which allow the designer to change the graphic once and see it updated throughout the multimedia. To design for this type of development approach, consistency is the key.

Regardless of the type of multimedia, reducing the time spent in development has some significant benefits:

- Decreased cost by increasing speed to market and return on investment
- Maximizing the shelf life and how long a product can be used by deploying training in conjunction with the product
- Freeing resources for additional development work

Implementing efficiencies during the development phase, coupled with using a rapid analysis method (RAM) can significantly decrease project cost.

Efficiencies can be gained by

• Using rapid prototyping to increase communication and buy-in and to reduce rework. For example, consider the benefit of creating paper-based simulations of a proposed screen interface, or acting out a proposed videoconference sequence.

• Using predeveloped models and templates. Commercially available CBT and web-based templates and models are available. The models contain lesson, interaction, and tracking templates along with the computer-managed instruction (CMI) program components in which the various text, graphic, and video elements of a program can be inserted.

- Leveraging available expertise by teaming with experienced mentors, vendors, or consultants. Previous development experience is invaluable, especially in a first-time multimedia project. Determine who has experience and is willing to act in the coaching role, and make sure he or she is part of the development team.

- Aggressively managing scope creep and time lines. It's always tempting to agree to include "just one more graphic, or one extra link" that does not actually increase the overall effectiveness of the solution. Keep in mind that you are solving a business need rather than producing a product. Sticking to the planned course design, content, and development time lines ensures that you maintain or even shorten project time lines, and therefore contain costs.

FROM OUR EXPERIENCE

In a development process, keep the emphasis on the fact that "only the project wins." When the subject of individual preferences arises, we like to use the analogy of an orchestra. If each member of the orchestra decides to individually interpret the music and play in the key of his or her own choice, the result is less than desirable. When everyone works together and plays on the same page, the end result is much better.

The same concept applies to multimedia projects. The CDS is the conductor, keeping project team members on the same page. If you are developing in a medium for the first time, recruit an expert to coach you. It can mean the difference between a successful project and a disaster.

The newest versions of many authoring packages contain templates for authoring. WorldTutor, produced by Allen Interactions in Minneapolis, is one such system for CBT development. The Interactive Learning International Corporation (LearnLinc) in Troy, New York, offers a shell for delivering live, interactive, virtual-classroom (synchronous) or individualized (asynchronous) web-based course delivery. Leading authoring packages—such as Authorware 5.0, Attain, and Asymetrix's Toolbook—now provide tools for web-based training design. In addition, Abernathy (1999) lists other currently available authoring software packages, their features, system requirements, current pricing, and distributors.

Efficiencies can be achieved in developing CBT storyboards by using tools such as Designer's Edge from Asymetrix. It coordinates information from analysis into objectives and content, and it ultimately produces storyboards for authoring. It's easy to use and readily adapts a development process to its built-in structure. At the same time, Designer's Edge is highly flexible and can be modified to support an established or unique ID process. We return to discussing the efficiencies gained by using these products in conjunction with rapid prototyping in later chapters of Part Three.

SUMMARY

Regardless of the type of multimedia, the basic development process is the same. First, establish a framework; then develop the media elements that fit it; next, review and revise the product; and finally, implement the finished product. Multimedia development is most successful if design-time prototyping, evolutionary development, and models and templates are used.

Common Development Components

Within the multimedia development process, during production there are components common to computer-based, web-based, and interactive distance broadcast solutions:

- Preproduction and production cycles
- Postproduction quality-review cycles

THE PRODUCTION CYCLE

Table 21.1 encapsulates the development methodology described in this chapter.

Preproduction

Lesson outlines and concept maps become programmed lessons in the development phase. This is an easy concept to express, but it's complex in execution. The responsibility for development is placed in the hands of many people who have to be counted on to do their jobs well and deliver each piece on time.

The *instructional designer* (ID) who outlines the lesson is responsible for organizing and conducting a preproduction meeting. He or she must duplicate the lesson outlines or concept maps that will be used during the meeting and distribute a copy of the set to each team member.

The *author* (programmer) assigned to the project reviews the outlines and maps and comes to the meeting prepared to ask for clarification and make suggestions about the programming. The author should be ready to offer suggestions for standardizing, reducing costly customization and time required for programming.

Table 21.1. Development Methodology

Stage		Media	
	CBT	Interactive Distance Learning	Web Site
Preproduction	Create storyboards with review cycles to establish adherence to technical and instructional standards.	Create a script with audi-tions to establish adherence to visual, audio, and instructional goals.	Map the links in a flowchart, check page design, and review to establish adher-ence to technical, web, and instructional standards.
Production	Create and assemble media elements according to the storyboards and course-development standards.	Shoot the video; edit and create additional media elements according to the script and course-development standards.	Create and assemble pages according to the map and course web-development standards.
Postproduction and quality review	Perform technical reviews, debug, and test the pro-grammed lessons for adher-ence to the storyboards and programming standards.	Rehearse and practice the session, adhering to the script and allotted time frames.	Perform technical reviews, debug, and test the web pages for adherence to the map.
Delivery or implementation	Deliver the course.	Conduct the session.	Implement the web page.

The *art director* comes to the meeting prepared to ask for clarification or to make suggestions regarding the graphics. Because graphics can be a time consuming and costly component of the development phase, the art director should be encouraged to offer ideas on reducing the time and costs associated with course development. For example, the screen in Figure 21.1 is a compromise between using expensive and time-consuming custom artwork and using "just photography." The bottom edge of a clip art photo has been stretched and added to, digitally, so that the clip art photo appears to be custom artwork.

The *audio specialist* manages and sometimes records the audio files. Some manipulation of the file format, such as conversion of tapes to digital format files, is often necessary. The audio specialist comes to the meeting prepared to ask for clarification or to make suggestions regarding the audio and sound effects. The audio specialist ensures that the audio script design

- Uses double spacing and large font so that the narrator can easily read the phrases. (Avoid using the storyboards for narration, because this is one place where there is no efficiency to be gained. It usually takes too long for the narrator to adjust to all the information on the storyboard and find the narration.)

- Begins each phrase with a corresponding storyboard number (including a pause) so the audio can be easily tracked and converted into sound files.

- Indicates acronyms with hyphens (for example, *I-S-D*).

- Spells out phonetically any special terminology or hard-to-pronounce words.

The audio specialist should be encouraged to suggest music or sound effects to enhance the presentation of the content. The audio specialist chooses experienced narrators (who must be available to redo the narration should revision or additional narration be required).

The *video director* coordinates the video production. He or she reviews the storyboards and video scripts and asks for clarification on the set, cast, shot angles, and special video effects required. This director works in conjunction with the instructional designer and a scriptwriter to prepare the script for production. This involves checking the number of locations, types of shots, lighting, and so on, to effectively manage the crew and ensure resources are available when they are needed. He or she often clarifies script instructions with the instructional designer and scriptwriter.

Figure 21.1
Custom Clip Art Photo

Source: Courtesy of Star Mountain Inc.; designed by Training Consulting Softec

Video scripts are a blueprint for video production in the same way that story-boards serve as the blueprint for assembling the CBT. Professional video scripts have their own industry-specific nomenclature for giving directions to each member of the video team. Long or complex video sequences or scripts prepared for outside vendors need to be written using this nomenclature. If the video requirements are not presented using the standard script format, it can dramatically increase the cost, the probability of delay and errors, and the time required to communicate the intended results. See the Script Standards section in Appendix C for more information.

The *subject-matter expert* (SME) comes to the meeting prepared to give technical advice and make certain that any changes to the outlines or concept maps do not create technical errors.

A *quality-control representative* attends the meeting to ensure that any changes made at that time conform to the CDS. In addition, if an issue reaches an impasse and discussion continues for too long without a solution in sight, the quality-control representative stops the discussion and makes a final decision.

His or her decision cannot be questioned, for two reasons. First, it puts teams on notice that they had best be able to come to agreement if they want to influence the decision. Second, it prevents an issue from stopping the preproduction meeting, an impasse that ultimately is sure to delay the production schedule.

Production

Here are descriptions of the team members' roles and responsibilities during production.

Authors integrate the elements of the CBT into the interactive models. They enter the text into the framework for each lesson and add the video, graphics, and audio according to the storyboard specifications. The author uses the storyboard with the audio and video files listed as a reference to program the computer to pick up the correct segments and shots and run them at the correct spot in the lesson.

Graphic artists create the graphics and animation sequences and store them according to the file-naming conventions established in the CDS.

Videographers (or a video team) create shot lists, shoot the video sequences, and log them according to the CDS. The video team usually consists of the producer, the director, actors, camera operators, lighting and sound experts, set designers and decorators, costume designers, and makeup artists. The video team is often the largest in terms of the number of people.

It is useful to have a shot list to record the link between each video sequence filmed and the video script. An example is in the Development and Implementation Tools section of Appendix E. It's also often helpful to shoot each sequence from the preferred angle and, if time and budget allow, from a couple of angles. This approach allows options in editing and helps to eliminate reshoots.

After the filming is completed, the video used for multimedia must be converted from videotape to a digital video file format. Be very careful in conducting reviews, editing, and ensuring all video has been shot, particularly if the video must be shipped out to be mastered or digitized. It's extremely important that all of the video and audio be logged accurately so that the author can identify the exact point at which the audio and video begins and ends.

Similarly, establish a relationship with a vendor who is sensitive to schedule requirements. Errors or delays in postproduction can impede completing the project. It can be expensive to delay implementing a project while the video is returned for remastering or digitizing.

The video and audio is often stored on a CD-ROM that is sometimes called a check disk. The check disk, or check files, must be reviewed for four reasons:

1. To be certain that all of the video is on the disk
2. To be certain that all of the audio is on the disk
3. To determine that the media is of high quality (free of glitches and so on)
4. To check the video and audio file numbers for the author

Preventing video reshoots is important because it's expensive to reassemble talent, crew, sets, and costumes. In some cases, the filming circumstances are impossible to reconstruct because people, special events, or equipment may no longer be at your disposal.

Reshoots may be required for three reasons:

1. None of the takes clearly indicates or shows what is required.
2. There is a change to the item (machine, process) that is being depicted.
3. There is an error in the shot or contradiction with the previous video and audio.

If there is no usable video shot for a sequence, use the Reshoot Request form in the Development and Implementation Tools section of Appendix E to request a video reshoot. Fill in each section completely so that the director clearly understands the problem with the old shot and the set up of the new shot. Of course, the instructional designer and SME should be on the set for all reshoots, just as they were for the originals.

Use the Audio Log in the Development and Implementation Tools section of Appendix E to keep track of each audio segment as the audio is recorded.

Requests for rerecording audio can be for two reasons. Perhaps the audio is incorrect (a word mispronounced, wrong inflection, and so on). Or the audio may need to be changed (as with modification to the machine you are describing).

If the audio requires a rerecord because of the first circumstance, use the Audio Revision and Error List in the Development and Implementation Tools section of Appendix E so the error does not happen again. If the requirement is a complete rerecord, use the Audio Rerecord Form found in the same section.

Overall, the *director's* job is to be certain everything runs smoothly on the set and in the control room. A very large production might include a *producer,* who is in charge of arranging the entire shoot, and an *assistant director,* who stands in for the director when there are shoots in two places at once.

In multimedia development, the director or a team member having specialized knowledge about video should assemble the video team. It is the director's responsibility to

- Contact local talent agencies to request photos, résumés, and whatever else is needed to choose the talent for auditions
- Audition and choose the actors to perform in the video and to be available for reshoots
- Rehearse the on-screen talent
- Supervise set designers, costumers, and decorators
- Supervise camera operators

Set designers determine what the set looks like and supervise the construction crew in building backdrops or scenery required for the video shoot.

Set decorators gather props and construct the physical look of the scene according to the director's instructions.

Costume designers must find or make the clothing worn by the on-screen talent.

Camera operators film the scene in accordance with the director's instruction.

The *actors* memorize scripts, rehearse, and perform.

Lighting designers and grips carefully set the lights to accent the scene.

Sound designers set the microphones to achieve the best audio production and run the recording equipment in the studio, in the control room, and on location. They also convert the taped audio to digital files ready for assembly in the CBT.

The *instructional designer* also serves as technical advisor on the set and helps establish the shots according to the storyboards. His or her responsibility is to ensure the concept is filmed as intended.

The *SMEs* often come to the video set or are on call for technical aspects of the course. This is necessary to give advice and make certain the execution of the scene is technically correct.

The *art director* supervises photographers and graphic artists and provides the look-and-feel direction for the project. This director is often responsible for locating off-the-shelf clip art or photography to reduce costs and meet project needs. Many multimedia backgrounds and buttons are available in off-the-shelf products.

Photographers take the required shots, either using a digital camera and saving the images directly to disk or shooting the photos and having them scanned or imaged onto a CD-ROM, from which proof sheets can be made.

Graphic artists and animators create the graphics and animation sequences and save them to a directory or disk. A sample Graphics Log is provided in the Development and Implementation Tools section of Appendix E.

There are instances when requests for graphics rework may be called for:

- The depiction is unclear—perhaps too small, or the colors of adjacent items interfere, or there are undefined borders between important areas.
- The depiction is proportionally incorrect.
- The animation sequence is incorrect.
- An incorrect standard (such as font size, style, or color) is applied.

Use the Graphics Rework Request in the Development and Implementation Tools section of Appendix E to request graphic changes.

A *system engineer* or *programmer* may appear in projects where the course requires special data links to be programmed. For example, links between applications or other special programming may be required to write training records from the CBT to a training records database, or to access an application or set of files from the CBT. System engineers and programmers troubleshoot development software and files; create models and templates; compile programs; and manage file configuration, back up, and test platforms.

Postproduction and Quality Reviews

During postproduction, all of the segments of the lesson are reviewed and the final formative evaluation of the courseware is conducted.

Only three reviews are required during postproduction:

1. Standards review, to ensure that the standards described in the course specification document are followed throughout the lesson.

2. Editorial review, to be sure there are no errors in grammar, spelling, spacing, or punctuation.

3. Functional review, to be certain there are no bugs in the programming logic and no glitches in the audio, video, or graphics. A Functional Review Checklist is included the Development and Implementation Tools section of Appendix E.

The instructional effectiveness of the course was determined by the review during preproduction, so an instructional review is redundant at this point.

Nor do you need a management review; the courseware should meet the requirements based on the review of the storyboards during preproduction.

A technical review is also unnecessary. The SME has reviewed the technical accuracy of the storyboards, participated in the preproduction meeting, been on the set for video shoots, and reviewed the final video and audio with the instructional designer.

Follow these steps to conduct the required reviews of online lessons:

1. The first reviewer should number the Online Review Form pages. (This form is available in the Development and Implementation Tools section of Appendix E.) If more than one page is required for a particular screen of the lesson, subsequent pages should be numbered with an alpha character (for example 1, 1A, 1B, and so on).

2. Blank copies of all the review forms (editorial, standards, and functional) should be included in the packet of lesson review forms. The reviewer assigned to each review should complete the appropriate form.

3. In a large project, it's the author's responsibility to list the lessons on the Review Scheduling Form as each becomes available (see the sample form in Appendix E).

4. The reviewers are responsible for checking the list regularly to confirm that lessons are ready for review.

5. Should the author remove the lesson from review at any time, this fact should be indicated on the schedule with the author's name beside the appropriate time and day.

6. Each reviewer should use a uniquely colored pen to record errors. That way, if questions arise about a comment, the author knows whom to ask.

7. Each reviewer records errors on the same page. This method of recording

   - Helps the author correct all errors on one screen at one time.
   - Speeds up the process because the author only has to review one page of comments. Reviews must contain enough detail so that the author knows exactly what needs to be changed.

8. All reviewers should complete their reviews by running the multimedia on machines with the same configuration (speed, monitor, hard disk space, RAM, and so on).

9. All review forms should remain with the configured machine, until the last review is completed.

10. The last reviewer to complete a review and sign the scheduling form should return the online lesson review forms to the author.

11. The author makes changes and reintegrates the files.

After the author corrects the identified changes, there is no need to have each reviewer go through the lesson again. One person should be assigned to validate that the changes have been made, placing a check mark beside each change to confirm that it has been reviewed and corrected.

It is the responsibility of the system engineer or programmer to

1. Coordinate installation of hardware for pilot studies and implementation sites

2. Coordinate installing the program on LANs or servers

3. Maintain hardware and the program during testing

4. Be present at the implementation sites during the first pilot test and initial testing of the program

5. Troubleshoot problems that arise after initial installation

SUMMARY

Regardless of your role on the multimedia development team, you participate in or are affected by preproduction and production cycles, postproduction quality-review cycles, and instructional delivery strategies.

Being aware of team member roles, participating fully, and lending your expertise at the team level improves the quality, effectiveness, and viability of your multimedia project.

Developing Computer-Based Learning Environments

When someone says "multimedia," for many in the corporate training world the term signifies a computer-based learning environment. Indeed, the flexibility of computer-based learning environments brings some significant advantages to solving today's business needs. Because a computer-based learning environment can include video, audio, and graphic elements, the forms, processes, and roles and responsibilities presented in Part Three of this book can be adapted to a variety of multimedia projects.

You can speed up development by using software with prebuilt functionality that eliminates the need to program. Menu systems use libraries of functions to create four types of template:

1. Screen and lesson shells: to build course content
2. Skill assessments: at the end of a unit or for pretesting
3. Proficiency exams: to build and score tests
4. Course management system: for tracking students

The screen and lesson shells allow the multimedia author to begin adding content immediately. Standards and style guides are prebuilt into the template and can automatically enter a font type, font size, and overall placement of the content, or they can be fully customized.

Navigation components usually include a menu, forward and backward navigation, a glossary of terms, and a help function.

Skill assessment models usually have prebuilt logic for developing questions of various types (true-false, matching, multiple-choice, short-answer) and giving students feedback. The questions can be formatted creatively—as in matching items by dragging a graphic or text from one column to another—rather than just the typical text questions you would find on a paper-and-pencil test.

A course manager can register students, track their progress through the course (including scores on tests), and produce reports for administrators.

The WorldTutor templates (sold by Allen Interactions) are templates based on Authorware 5.0 that contain most or all of the functionality mentioned here. (A demo of this software is included on the CD-ROM.)

In addition to software packages, there are integrated hardware and software development platforms such as InformaWorks marketed by e-Learnet, Inc. Figure 22.1 shows the hardware components.

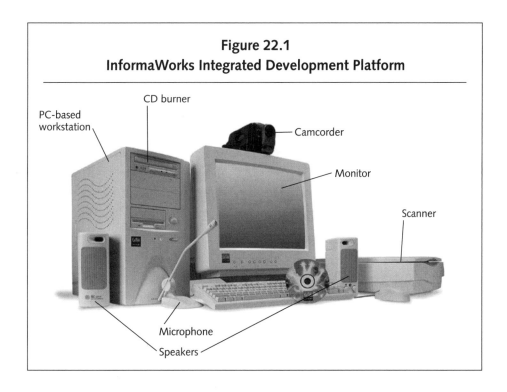

**Figure 22.1
InformaWorks Integrated Development Platform**

The system:

- Is fully Windows 95, 98, and NT compatible
- Uses Microsoft Access database files to store all files on the system hard drive so information can be easily changed
- Has system-animated characters
- Has text-to-speech capabilities accompanying the animated characters (you type in the text, and the system converts it to speech)
- Uses dynamic effects such as wipes, diagonals, pushes, splits, and transitions
- Uses 3D colored borders and bevels for dynamic frames
- Supports .WAV sound files (or you can record your own and immediately integrate them)
- Supports pictures files in BMP, DIB, ePIC, JPG, JIF, KQP, PCS, PNG, RLE, TGA, TIF, WMF, and WPG formats
- Supports AVI video files and can use clips from existing videotapes
- Has a built-in CD burner

The system permits development of a wide range of levels of complexity, from simple, linear designs to more complex and media-rich solutions. It is easy to use because it's very intuitive. The output is WYSIWYG (what you see is what you get), so you can quickly review what you create and instantly make desired changes until you get the desired effect.

Outputs play back on today's standard multimedia user systems. Outputs can be distributed using CD-ROM, LANs, or the Internet, in all cases using a few mouse clicks.

The chief benefit of an integrated development platform is that it ensures better compatibility than piecing together separate components. The system is also reasonably priced.

PROCESS

There are four activities in the procedure to develop a computer-based course:

1. Create storyboards.
2. Create and assemble media elements.
3. Perform online reviews.
4. Deliver and implement the course.

COMPUTER-BASED TRAINING DEVELOPMENT PROCEDURE

Follow these activities:

Activity One: Create Storyboards

Storyboards establish adherence to the CDS.

Step one: Review the rationale for the treatment of each type of learning outcome as presented in the outline, map, and specifications.

Step two: Translate the rationale to a screen-by-screen outline. It's important to standardize the CBT design so the programming elements can be modeled not only at the screen level but also at a topic or lesson level. Use the CDS elements of lesson construction you developed during design.

The resulting content may be linked and navigated as a series of screens or grouped into functional circles accessed through a menu, as illustrated in Figure 22.2.

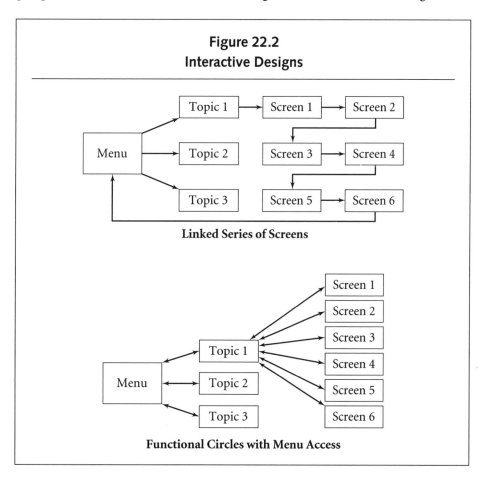

Figure 22.2
Interactive Designs

Linked Series of Screens

Functional Circles with Menu Access

Step three: Add title frames (also called "splash screens"), main menus, course introductory segments, overall reviews and summaries, pretests and posttests, and credit screens to the content storyboard as indicated in the CDS.

Each storyboard should include detailed information and directions:

- Date, version, and designer's name and phone number

- Lesson, topic, and frame number

- Graphic description, reference, or rough drawing

- Audio and sound effects, or video sequence and script

- Interaction instructions: which interface buttons are active, type of interaction (text entry, click on, match, move), and so on

- Screen text

- Animation and special effects

- Navigation links and instructions for pagination

We offer an example of a storyboard template in the Development and Implementation Tools section of Appendix E.

Step four: Review and validate the storyboards to be sure they contain correct information and meet specifications.

Step five: QA reviews are conducted on storyboards. Several reviews should be included:

- Editorial

- Standards

- Technical

- Instructional

- Management

Online Review Forms for each of these reviews are in the same section of Appendix E.

Activity Two: Create and Assemble Media Elements

Media elements are created and assembled according to the storyboards and course development specifications.

Step one: Hold a preproduction meeting to review storyboards, audio scripts, and video scripts and make final determinations about producing the various elements of the project before each of the groups involved begins work. This meeting is the forum to resolve conflict, negotiate differences, and achieve consensus on all aspects of the lesson before beginning production. Although some restraints must be imposed (for reasons of logistics or because of the technical systems used for production), be careful not to stifle creativity and input to the development process.

If it is practical, we suggest that storyboards be distributed well in advance of the meeting—we recommend a minimum of two days—so each member of the preproduction team has the opportunity to thoroughly review the storyboards and bring questions, comments, and suggestions to the meeting. Distributing copies of storyboards a few hours in advance is generally unacceptable. When the storyboards are distributed, the time, place, and date of the preproduction meeting should be announced.

The instructional designer leads the meeting, asking for questions, considering suggestions, and clarifying ID issues. Chapter Twenty-One details which team members might be included in the preproduction meeting.

Step two: Produce the CBT. The finalized storyboards are known as production baseline storyboards. They establish what is required to produce course components and serve as a test plan for postdevelopment evaluation.

Authors use the storyboard to identify what graphics, video, text, or audio elements they will receive and where each contributed component fits. Each frame of the course is built using the storyboard as the guide that cements the elements together.

Activity Three: Perform Online Reviews

Test, debug, and review the programmed lessons for adherence to the storyboards and programming standards.

Step one: Produce the test CD-ROMs. In preparation for final review, the CD-ROMs must be produced or the final version of the lesson must be loaded to the delivery system (a LAN or one or more correctly configured computers). To be valid, reviews should occur on test computers that are configured exactly like the lowest-common-denominator end-user machine.

Step two: Use the storyboards as a basis for review. The instructional designer and quality-control representative review the CBT navigation, text, graphics, photography, video, and audio to be certain that they all perform and look as intended. They ensure, for instance, that there are pauses between displays of text and that the audio matches the video it supports.

Step three: Record errors, either online or using a numbered set of Online Review Forms (see Appendix E). The numbers on the forms should coincide with storyboard numbers (which now match screen numbers), and there should be a separate page for each storyboard.

Step four: Correct errors and, *step five,* review the corrections. Follow the steps outlined in Chapter Twenty-One to conduct online reviews.

Activity Four: Deliver and Implement the Course

Delivery should be well planned to accommodate the business constraints inherent in the time frame, environment, and audience requirements.

FROM OUR EXPERIENCE

When we talk about multimedia production, we would be remiss in not reminding you to back up your computer files and plan for space to work.

Back up files to the LAN, disk, Zip drive, or tape backup unit. Most computers have an automatic backup you can set through the program manager function menu. Set this function to back up frequently and "auto save" files. Hard disks do crash, and you can lose significant amounts of work. You don't have to learn this the hard way (as we have). Make backup copies of your work daily.

Plan for file size and space requirements. It is not unusual for the data in a single graphics file or audio segment to total one megabyte or much more. Don't underestimate the amount of space required for CBT working files, storing copies of media elements, moving and backing up files, and storing compiled versions of the program. A good rule of thumb is to reserve ten times the anticipated file size of the finished program.

Let us emphasize once more that video and photo reshoots translate into big money because of the difficulty, and sometimes impossibility, of assembling all of the people and elements to do a scene or segment over again.

Audio studios charge setup fees and hourly rates for studio personnel, so make sure any audio scripts that accompany the storyboards are approved and additional retakes are carefully planned and considered. Plan all retakes to be completed in one session. It's much less costly to plan carefully, involve a subject matter expert and the instructional designer at the audio session, and do multiple readings the first time.

The project team may require technical-support expertise to configure delivery systems during implementation. The technical-support team members must have a high degree of knowledge and skill in the hardware platform your CBT courseware is to be delivered on.

Success of the pilot test—indeed, the overall success of the project—may depend on the skills of your technical-support group. Even if, for your project, the customer has its own technical-support group, your own technical-support team probably should conduct the initial training of the customer's group.

If everyone does his or her job efficiently and effectively (which storyboarding encourages), much of the mystery is removed about how a seemingly chaotic effort becomes a thing of beauty that is also instructionally sound.

SUMMARY

CBT continues to have a use and market for the foreseeable future. However, it will probably dwindle as newer technologies advance. But then, so will the current technologies as the next breakthrough is developed. Even though classroom training is often less effective than CBT, companies still spend billions on facilitated instruction every year. The move from classroom training to electronic forms is more a matter of economics than education. It is not feasible to continue to train using the classroom model with companies continuing to operate over wide geographic areas and even globally.

Developing Internet, Intranet, Web-Based, and Performance Support Learning Environments

The interactive age is here. Those who gain the skills to design for it now are wise. Those who resist gaining skills to develop for the Internet will become obsolete in the near future. The next generation of interactive multimedia will reside on the World Wide Web.

Internet delivery seems to meet many of the requirements of training on demand:

- It's available at the desktop.
- It eliminates the need for travel.
- It's cost-effective compared to conventional delivery media.
- Text-based Web interventions can be developed quickly.

Designing training for the Web follows the same ID process as any other medium. You must first establish a framework of specifications and standards; then develop the media elements that fit the framework; and finally review, revise, and implement the end product.

When we mention implementation and delivery technology, we are often asked about Web technology. Web-based applications use existing technology. Most businesses are in the process of developing or refining an intranet, which constitutes a ready-made distribution channel.

THE INTERNET AND INTRANETS

For many instructional designers, the difference between an intranet and the Internet is a key concept. Simply put, an intranet is created by using Internet and Web technology as the basis of an organization's internal communication network. Because an organization has complete control over its intranet, it manages issues such as network performance and security, which cannot always be controlled in using the public Internet.

The intranets of many businesses and educational institutions are much more advanced than the Internet as a whole. The use of Internet technology to deliver course materials is occurring first on corporate and higher education intranets. How courseware is being delivered over intranets today serves as a model for how courses will be delivered over the Internet in the future.

Adoption of the Internet and intranets as delivery media by business and educational institutions has been phenomenal. There are three primary reasons for this:

1. Universal access. Anyone can access the Web with a web browser and modem connection. Anyone can deliver content anywhere in the world using a web server. The Web is based on a few simple technology standards, such as transmission control protocol/Internet protocol (TCP/IP), web server software, and web browser software. This simple technology has allowed the number of intranet and Internet connections to grow exponentially.

2. Ease of use. Internet and intranet software is very easy to use. This is opening up adoption to a much broader audience with limited computer experience.

3. Multimedia content. Web-based technology support for multimedia (text, graphics, audio, and video) content has enabled delivery of a wide range of interesting content, again opening up the web-based intranet and Internet to a broad audience. Web-based technology support for multimedia allows instructional designers to meet the needs of a technologically savvy audience with varied learning styles.

The costs, skills needed, and technology associated with developing multimedia and video distance-education technologies have been and will continue to be a barrier for many businesses. Two issues exist regarding delivery of content over the Web. First, most software tools, including CBT authoring tools, do not produce applications that are based on Internet standards. As a result, web browsers are unable to access these nonstandard applications. To get around the problem posed by applications not being based on Web standards, many tool vendors have developed add-on software that extends the browser's capabilities to run nonstandard applications. These web browsers and add-ons are commonly referred to as "plug-ins" for the Netscape Navigator browser and "Active X" controls for the Microsoft Internet Explorer browser.

Although there are advantages to being able to access existing applications without having to convert them to Internet standards, there are some significant disadvantages. One of the reasons the Web has caught on so quickly is its simplicity. A user only needs a web browser to access Web content. Introducing a plug-in requirement adds significant complexity because it is up to the users to make sure that they are running the specific plug-ins required to view the content they need to access. Plug-ins are dependent on the web browser and underlying operating system and, in many situations, must be updated each time the plug-ins change.

Internet technology is evolving rapidly. Using applications based on Internet standards rather than using plug-ins would make the Internet more efficient and put it in a better position to take advantage of new capabilities as they are developed. For example, if a new Internet standard were adopted for video, it would be much easier to integrate video into web-based training without using the extra memory required by plug-ins. As computers are built with ever-increasing amounts of RAM and ROM and as older computer memory is upgraded, more complex forms of multimedia can be accessed.

The second important issue in delivering content over the Web concerns network performance. Many of the Internet's current limitations are related to network capacity, or bandwidth (the rate at which information moves across the network). Generally speaking, internal intranets allow information to move much faster than most public telephone lines do.

Information accessed over a company intranet travels at an average rate of 1.25 megabytes per second; information accessed over a telephone line using a modem travels at a rate of .004 megabytes per second.

As a result, a web course delivered over a company intranet can use a combination of rich multimedia. But if a course is to be delivered to remote users who must access it using a telephone connection, the course should be limited to text and simple graphics.

Streaming is a term that refers to a technique developed to get around some of the network limitations for delivering multimedia. This is a technology that essentially breaks a course, application, or file into small pieces and starts delivering the beginning of the application, so that it can be accessed by the user, while the remainder of the application continues to be broken up and sent separately. From the user's perspective, the experience is the same as if the application were available and running locally on his or her computer.

However, streaming technology is relatively immature at this point, and there is no prevailing industry standard. As a result, individual vendors have developed their own proprietary software that requires plug-ins.

Efforts are under way to develop industry standards for streaming, and they are beginning to appear. Until usability catches up with capability, CD-ROM may be a better delivery strategy for multimedia courses if your only alternative is the Internet.

The intranet and Internet infrastructure, expertise, and technology must be analyzed to understand the delivery options and successfully deliver multimedia.

DESIGNING FOR THE WEB

Web-based design and development can contain all of the components of computer-based courseware. Successful web development is dependent on (1) the creativity and skill of the course developers, (2) bandwidth, and (3) hardware capabilities.

Hypertext markup language (which we mentioned in Chapter Five) is a programming language particularly suited for use on the Web. HTML allows sophisticated design and development of web-based courseware. It can incorporate video, audio, animation, graphics, and sophisticated branching. Development can be less expensive than CBT because HTML does not require any particular authoring system and is relatively easy to use. Most designers can master it without extensive training and are productive as soon as HTML commands are mastered. Authoring systems contain the basic structures for integrating HTML components. Authoring shells can be developed that make media input into a program efficient without extensive authoring skills. Instructional designers can easily perform much of the design and development online.

Those who resist using the Internet for training raise the criticism that it is not as interactive and engaging as high-level CBT; it's too linear, they say. However, that's a designer's perspective, not the end user's. Millions of businesses and homes worldwide are connected to the Internet, and people spend countless hours every day online. This indicates that there are plenty of creative ways to engage a user.

For now, online text-based courses are OK as long as we use what we've learned from developing CBT to move forward rapidly. In other words, it should not take another twenty years for Internet training to reach the same degree of sophistication that CBT enjoys today. Instruction does not have to suffer using the Internet. It is limited only by the imagination and creativity of those designing instruction (or by inadequate hardware systems delivering the instruction).

Interactivity need not suffer using the Internet. Indeed, it can be enhanced. A chat room incorporated into an asynchronous Internet lesson allows participants to log on at specified times and carry on a dialogue with the instructor and other students. The instructor usually begins by posing a question, issue, or topic. Participants then type in their comments, responses, and additional questions. The entire dialogue is saved in a file for future reference by the instructor and by students.

E-mail is also an important feature of an asynchronous course. While students study online, they can send an e-mail to the instructor at any point, asking for clarification or proposing comments. The instructor must be constantly aware of participants' questions and respond promptly.

Much efficiency can be gained by using existing Web design and development software. Software is currently available that organizes synchronous and asynchronous training into a total web distance-learning environment that integrates and simulates classroom, instructor-led, and CBT training. One example of this type of learning environment has been created by LearnLinc, Inc. A demo of this software is included on the CD-ROM. Figure 23.1 shows the student graphical user interface, or GUI, for version 3.01 of this product.*

The right side of the interface is the content area. The instructor uses this area to share a whiteboard, synchronize multimedia or web-based content, and share software applications with students. Application sharing allows students to run the software application from the instructor's machine.

While students are in an application, the instructor can view what they're doing and how they're progressing through a "glimpse" capability. If the instructor no-

---

*Version 4.0 is in current release and contains additional features.

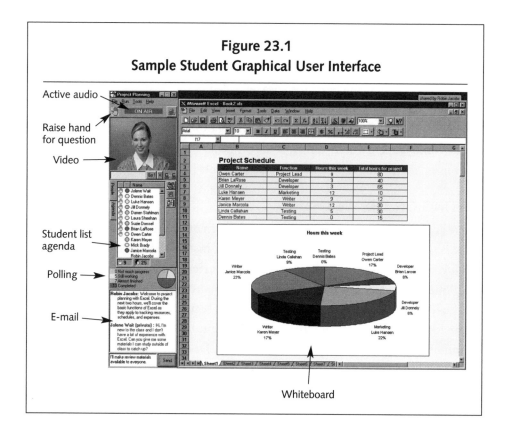

Figure 23.1
Sample Student Graphical User Interface

Active audio

Raise hand for question

Video

Student list agenda

Polling

E-mail

Whiteboard

tices that a student is having difficulty, he or she can individually work with the student. LearnLinc also allows the instructor to access a web browser to take the entire class to a website.

The left side of the interface contains the controls for the instructor and students. Students and instructors can view the course content outline. Instructors can click on the topics and launch them at the appropriate time. The instructor can also see the names of all students who are currently logged on to the lesson.

The bottom left of the interface has a space for students and instructors to pass messages back and forth through a chat-room capability. Public messages can be sent and seen by everyone in the class. Private messages may be sent from individual students to the instructor. Students cannot send messages privately to each other.

Students can ask questions by electronically raising their hands. The instructor can tell the order in which students raise their hands and can recognize students and even turn over control of the system to a particular student while everyone listens to the student's question. When a student is recognized, that person's picture appears in the video window in the top left corner of the screen. Everyone using audio conferencing hears the speaker called upon. Students can also be given control of the system to conduct demonstrations for the class. Instructors can launch questions for students to respond to. Questions are normally developed in advance and launched according to a lesson plan. The software knows how to poll responses, and results can be shared with students for discussion purposes.

TESTING ON THE WEB

There are issues of test security in using any form of web-based training. Because there is two-way video or audio in this product, instructors can monitor students remotely to determine if they are working on their own. Instructors can also use the glimpse function to see how students are progressing through the test.

Usually, testing is possible as long as certain security functions are embedded in the Internet infrastructure. If you do not want tests to be printed and widely distributed, you need to consider security issues. Designing tests taken online with the capability to generate random questions makes it more difficult for students to collaborate on answers. Timing tests can also discourage collaboration. A student who knows the material is less likely to want to devote time from his or her test to taking it for a student who doesn't know the material. Finally, remember that in web-based applications most students are at remote sites and are not together in the same room. Exchanging answers in such a situation is pretty difficult.

A Web course that we saw included a test distributed and taken using paper and pencil while a room camera monitored the students. One student collected all completed tests, placed them in an addressed envelope, sealed the envelope, and sent it to the regional training facility.

A test can be useful even if the course does not require certification or is not designed to meet some industry regulations. Students often learn something just from taking the test. Even if they do get an answer from someone else, there is a higher probability they will retain the information.

PERFORMANCE SUPPORT SYSTEMS

We include the performance support system (PSS) environment with the web-based one because we have found the storyboarding process and the user interface similar to the Web with respect to development and interactivity. There are two types of PSS. Performance support systems entail online and on-demand access to integrated information, guidance, advice, assistance, and training to enable high-level job performance with little support from people (for example, the Help function in Microsoft Word). The other type of PSS is the performance-centered application, which encompasses integrated business information processing with task or job-structuring support and related business knowledge, reference, data, and tools (as examples, a bank ATM, or an enterprisewide system that permits electronic submission of all business forms).

Our development process refers more to the first type of PSS than the second. Performance-centered applications are supported by software (such as SAP) that automates and integrates business processes throughout a corporation.

PROCESS

There are four activities in developing web-based products:

1. Determine the type of product and platform.
2. Assemble components.
3. Conduct reviews.
4. Implement the site.

WEB DEVELOPMENT PROCEDURE

Follow these activities:

Activity One: Determine the Type of Product and Platform

Step one: In deciding on the type of web application and the platform, determine which of two major types of content structure for the Internet will be used: asynchronous and synchronous.

1. Asynchronous content is analogous to computer-based courseware delivered to the desktop on demand. The entire content is resident on a LAN or WAN and available through dial-up access and password supplied to students registered for the course.

The interactivity is sometimes different from that of computer-based training. Rather than branching to various instructional paths through menu systems like those built into CBT, interactivity and branching are achieved through using hot links (areas of the screen that, when clicked, jump the user to another place in the program) to other web pages or sites. A system of menus achieves branching to various parts within the course. Whatever the level of interactivity, a button or selection on the main menu should always appear on the screen or be readily available on every page of the course, so that users can navigate back to the main menu to make other choices or exit the program.

2. Synchronous training means all students are online, taking the training at the same time. Students gain access to the class through a dial-up telephone number and password provided to them when they register for the class. Interaction is possible between students, with the instructor, and with course materials, through various means (including e-mail, chat rooms, telephone, faxes, scheduled conferences, video, online audio, and application sharing).

Lesson plans are constructed in the same manner as for any other instructor-led class. Plans are sequenced and time based, indicating what happens and when it happens, rather than event based as with CBT, where the sequence and time frame are user controlled. A lesson plan template for web-based training is in the Development and Implementation Tools section of Appendix E. Lesson plans for web-based training must be much more detailed and scripted than for live classroom training. Instructors must be much more mindful of extending verbal information on what is happening during the lesson (as examples, stating that control is being turned over to a student, or explaining that the instructor is now launching an application). Instructors must remember, or should assume, that the students are alone at a computer and cannot see everything that is about to happen.

Step two: Choose the development platform, language, editor, or software appropriate to your technical specifications.

Create web-based instruction by choosing one of the following means:

- A web development language, such as HTML. In this case, you need to integrate required audio, video, and animation.

- An HTML editor, consisting of a series of templates containing the necessary coding. Drag-and drop menus allow authors to immediately begin entering content and view what the page looks like.

- An authoring system that incorporates those plug-ins (such as Attain, Dreamweaver, Flash, or Macromedia's Authorware).

- A system that incorporates a graphical user interface, such as LearnLinc, for online training sessions with live instructors in a virtual classroom environment.

Activity Two: Assemble Components

Create storyboards, and assemble and link web pages according to the map and CDS. There is an example of a web storyboard in the Development and Implementation Tools section of Appendix E.

Activity Three: Conduct Reviews

Perform QA reviews, debug, and test the web pages for adherence to the map. (Use a machine with a web browser to test the site. Web reviews do not have the same test platform configuration issues that CBT projects normally face. The only requirement is to use the same web browser.) All of the QA reviews used in CBT should be completed. Good record keeping and file and configuration management are required.

Activity Four: Implement the Site

Put the site online using off-the-shelf web server software and a dedicated server, within the structure of your organization's intranet, or by using a commercial web service. Your implementation strategy depends on the level of technology expertise within your organization.

Overall, using the Internet is less costly than CBT for maintenance, updates, and changes to courses. Whereas changes to a CBT course often require burning new CD-ROMs and the expense and time that that entails, changes to an Internet course can be made with only minimal time required for the course to be offline. Changes to a CBT course also mean that all copies of the CD-ROM previously distributed are obsolete and may need to be replaced. Unused CDs must be scrapped.

Web-based courses are easily changed as content requires, so programs are offline far less. The turnaround time is only as long as it takes to make the changes to the parts of the content that are obsolete and put the program back online.

FROM OUR EXPERIENCE

Asynchronous Internet courses are useful even if they are more text based than CBT. What we presently accept as Internet training would likely not be tolerated in CBT. What we have learned about CBT over the last thirty years produces a shorter learning curve to bring Internet training to what we consider state-of-the-art CBT today. LANs with dedicated bandwidth for video, and upgrades to computer systems to handle video and audio, are probably the largest web-based investments a company makes.

Once this investment is made, there is a rapid return on investment if a company delivers a lot of training.

If web applications are delivered via a company intranet, they can pose some special problems for web developers. Intranets usually have a protective "firewall" that prevents access by the general public to information proprietary to the company or organization. Special software on remote computers as well as special passwords are required to access information from outside the company's direct LAN. These requirements may entail coordination with the company's IT group and special programming expertise that is not normally resident among development-team members.

Companies considering using the Internet for training should understand the benefits and obstacles to Internet development and delivery before making a final decision. For example, bandwidth is a common obstacle. Limited bandwidth encumbers transmittal of all components (video, audio, text, and graphics). A certain amount of space is required for the components to flow, and video takes up a lot of space. To pass it through the pipeline, it must be compressed at the sending end and decompressed at the receiving end. Compression and decompression rates differ depending on the modem speed and the available bandwidth. The higher the bandwidth and modem speed, the better the decompression rates. Low decompression rates result in an effect analogous to a badly dubbed foreign film: you hear the audio, but the video doesn't match, and it looks jerky and grainy.

One way to achieve better compression and decompression rates is to have a dedicated video server. These systems are often referred to as "video-on-demand systems." Rather than send all the video at one time, the video is streamed in small amounts over its own part of the pipeline.

To justify the cost of the dedicated systems and equipment, a company must do a substantial amount of training. Given the typical speed of processors and the memory and storage capability of most corporate computers, video is usually too memory intensive and takes much too long to download. Many computers do not have video cards. Video cards are available, though, and upgrades to computers can overcome this obstacle. However, upgrades must be cost-effective. Usually there is not enough usable video to make it worthwhile to upgrade a system.

At the desktop, video and audio hardware issues are rapidly becoming mute points as factories install both audio and video cards in new machines. Consumer demand has driven the computer industry in this area. When the Internet was mostly an e-mail system by which users communicated more rapidly than through regular (snail) mail, there was no need for video and audio. As consumers demanded more enhancements and sophistication in software programs, hardware began to come installed with more components at the point of sale.

Business has also to some extent been a driver of Internet enhancements in the 1990s. Virtual teams are rapidly replacing actual teams in a global corporate environment. With reduced profits and more competition, it is too expensive for companies to send large teams to remote sites for extended periods of time.

The Internet, coupled with videoconferencing, has allowed companies to reduce relocation expenses dramatically and still keep project teams in constant contact. Customer contact is maintained in much the same manner. There still may be times when the project team must be at the customer site, but these instances are increasingly shorter in duration and scheduled only at important milestones for the project. The Internet can thus drastically reduce project costs in a global environment.

Well-constructed templates are invaluable in reducing development time and therefore costs. Most web authoring systems include templates that are basic structures for integrating all HTML components. Macromedia, a San Francisco company, makes one such authoring system. Its version 5.0 of Authorware has produced the Attain Enterprise Learning System, a complete suite of software tools for planning, producing, administering, delivering, and reporting results from web-based training.

Attain Planner is a curriculum-building tool used to outline and organize programs. Planner supports a full range of online and traditional learning techniques, and each curriculum component can be tracked. Attain Client Administrator permits access to data by course administrators and others who need information about student progress.

Dreamweaver Attain is a visual design tool that generates HTML-based learning applications. It records student results, including scores and answers that can be stored and accessed through Administrator. It permits delivery of highly interactive and easily updated courses over low-bandwidth connections. Dreamweaver also contains "wizards," called "knowledge objects," preprogrammed templates that can be dragged onto the authoring flow line and opened, and content added immediately. The programming is done for the author.

HTML acts somewhat like word processing software, where the author can change the size, style, color, and position of font. Simple, nonproportional fonts are best because complicated fonts may be degraded if the computer on the user's end does not have complex fonts resident. Text can be graphical in form, but graphical text can demand a lot of memory and be slow to download. Usually you need to save the memory and downloading for graphics, video, and so on.

Graphics with nearly any filename extension (.BMP, .CGM, .PCX, and so on) can be converted to graphic interchange format (GIF) files for incorporation into web courseware. GIF reduces graphic file sizes but retains up to 256 colors. Microsoft PowerPoint graphics can also be formatted into GIF files.

Photographs and artwork requiring more than 256 colors can be incorporated into HTML using JPEG (joint photographic expert group) files. JPEG permits near-paper-quality visual output if the end user's computer monitor and display card have the capability to reproduce them. Animation can be created using Macromedia's Shockwave, which strings together individually created graphic files.

Video is shot and converted to a digital format and accessed by the computer from the file server or the CD-ROM as it is required. The user must have the correct player for the type of video file. Video plug-ins are often available from the web browser.

Audio is recorded as for any other delivery, converted to .WAV or other digital sound files, and stored on the LAN or CD-ROM. The user must have the correct player for the type of audio file. Sound plug-ins are often available from the web browser.

Instructions should include prompt boxes stating the type of plug-in required for the program and the location on the Web where the plug-in can be accessed and downloaded.

Branching can occur using hot links within the course, but additionally, hyperlinks can connect to other web pages and Internet sites. Although linking to other sites cuts down on the amount of development required, it presents a maintenance issue. If the developer does not have control over the sites linked to, there may be problems as sites are removed from the Internet, URLs (universal resource locators) change, or content may be changed that does not meet your requirements. If you control the websites you link to, this issue is less of a problem.

SUMMARY

Designing training for the Web follows the same ID process as with any other medium:

- A framework of templates, specifications, and standards is used.
- Media elements that fit into the framework are inserted.
- Review and revision cycles ensure quality.

In implementing the finished product, take into account web limitations and considerations during development. In the final analysis, we believe that companies that are not putting the infrastructure in place for Internet training development and delivery will be left in the dust.

Developing Interactive Distance Broadcast Environments

Distance learning is a generic term for any training that is delivered from one central location to multiple, remote sites simultaneously. Distance learning may take the form of satellite broadcast or video teleconferencing or a combination of phone and video strategies. We use the term *interactive distance broadcast* (IDB) training to be inclusive of all types of distance learning, whether by satellite or over telephone lines.

Interactive distance learning is somewhat of a misnomer since often it's neither "interactive" nor involving much "learning" in the instructional sense—unless you consider "informing" and "learning" to be the same. However, it does travel over a distance. For all of its promise, often all that is seen is a talking head with an occasional break for some sort of graphic. Maybe there are mechanisms for some interaction between the talking head and the listener at the remote site, say, through fax, telephone, or even keypads that permit people to buzz in with questions—and that's all. There is much unfulfilled potential for combining this medium with other communications media and innovative designs. Figure 24.1 shows one type of keypad produced by ONETOUCH Systems, Inc., which has good interaction capabilities.

There are many design, development, delivery, and maintenance issues to consider with interactive distance broadcast systems. Many of the considerations are

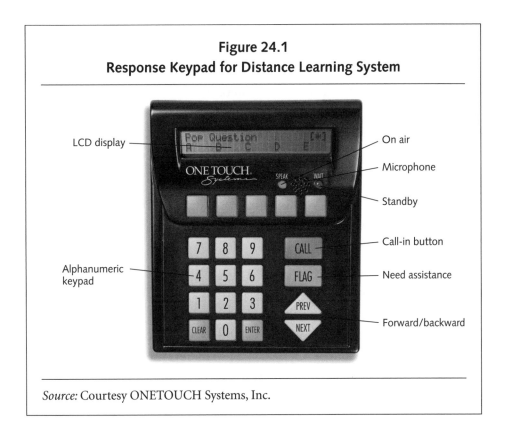

Figure 24.1
Response Keypad for Distance Learning System

LCD display

On air

Microphone

Standby

Call-in button

Alphanumeric keypad

Need assistance

Forward/backward

Source: Courtesy ONETOUCH Systems, Inc.

the same as for classroom learning environments. However, the number of sites does add other considerations, such as coordination and scheduling issues across time zones.

The concerns for video and audio production are much the same as those covered in Chapter Twenty-One.

PROCESS

There are four activities in the procedure of developing an IDB course:

1. Develop IBT script and materials.

2. Shoot video and edit.

3. Rehearse the presentation.

4. Conduct the session.

DISTANCE BROADCAST ENVIRONMENT PROCEDURE

Follow these activities:

Activity One: Develop IDB Script and Materials

To develop the script and materials, use the delivery and instructional strategies determined in the design phase (see Part Two).

Keep these points in mind while creating the materials for the IDB:

- Overheads should have no more than thirty characters per line, with a maximum of nine lines per image. You must match the aspect of the camera, which has a ratio of three high to four wide. Do not use extremely vertical images or portrait-view paper.

- Keep text in the "safe zone." Remember that a television monitor is wider and shorter than an 8½" × 11" sheet of paper, and leave margins of at least an inch to accommodate a border on all sides.

- Minimize the need to write on blank overheads or on flipcharts. For the best use of visuals, prepare them ahead of time and test them in advance to see how they look on camera. If you must write while on camera:

    Use manuscript print instead of cursive.

    Use medium-thick, dark markers.

- When you use flipcharts:

    Use inexpensive off-white or light blue paper.

    Cut the paper to fit the on-screen format. Paper lined in light blue keeps on-screen writing from running uphill.

    Anchor paper so it does not move around.

- When you create slides, use large-size print and simple fonts. Titles should be 30 points or greater, no less than 20 points for bullets. Bold face makes text legible.

- When you use handouts:

    Do not have a lot of text on a handout.

    Fax, make handouts available online, or send the materials to participants before the session.

- In storyboarding the session:

    Consider opening with an activity to break free of the idea that participants are watching television. Something as simple as asking a question and having participants respond using the keypad is enough to get the point across.

    Keep formal lecture periods short. Avoid the talking head.

Activity Two: Shoot and Edit Video

Shoot the video, edit it, and test additional media elements according to the script and course-development standards. It's a good idea to have a detailed outline indicating when supplemental media such as video, overheads, and so on are to be inserted in the course. It's also important to list when exercises occur and what specific questions to ask.

Activity Three: Rehearse the Presentation

Rehearse and practice the session, adhering to the script and allotted time frames.

Step one: Have the instructor practice using the technology. Practice is particularly important because you do not want to have any "dead air time" on the monitor. Even during activities that occur at the local site, there should be a message on the screen and some appropriate, nonintrusive music.

Step two: Review clothing considerations with instructors. Blue and off-white are best. Instructors should not wear white; it glares on the camera. Reds bleed. Certain patterns (such as houndstooth) make wavy motions on the screen as the person moves. Instructors should not wear jewelry; it may make sounds that are magnified by the microphone. Rings may reflect the studio lighting.

Step three: Instructors follow the outline to perform a dry run with a small group at the broadcast site.

Step four starts before the session; send the teaching assistants (TAs) at the student sites information regarding their roles and responsibilities. TAs and participants should also receive copies of the print materials:

- A welcome letter to participants explaining as much about the course content and structure as possible.

- Topical outlines delineating the amount of time to be devoted to each topic, or a workbook if appropriate.

- A biographical information form for participants to complete and return.

- Any local activity such as on-screen messages should be completed before airtime.

Activity Four: Conduct the Session

In conducting the session, note that maintenance is a bit more difficult for IDB than for classroom instruction. Some additional practice sessions might need to be scheduled to integrate new material.

FROM OUR EXPERIENCE

When used correctly, IDB can create the atmosphere of a small class while delivering instruction to a large number of people at one time.

If a satellite is used, cost is a significant factor. The costs to uplink to a satellite and downlink to remote locations can be significant (in the thousands of dollars for one hour of broadcast time). However, cost is becoming less of a factor for other forms of interactive distance learning. Barron (1999), in an issue of the journal *Technical Training* called "Interactive Distance Learning: Special Report," addresses technological advances and the increasing feasibility of distance education.

Video teleconferencing is less expensive because it uses telephone lines and television technology. However, this also requires a significant investment. There are many good commercial production houses capable of providing a turnkey solution that includes cameras, televisions, wiring, instructor stations, student stations, and instructor training.

There is justification for having two-way video as well as audio. A student with a question might display his or her work to the instructor, who can then give corrective feedback. Two-way video adds another dimension to student-instructor interaction and personalization of the training.

The return on investment for interactive distance broadcasting should be justified by analysis, as discussed in Part One. But media analysis is only the beginning. It then depends on the creativity and imagination of the instructional designers to have IDB reach its full potential.

The design and development options vary widely, depending on available hardware. IDB often consists of one-way video and two-way audio. The students can see and hear the instructor; the instructor can hear the students. Depending on the course design, this arrangement may still permit a great deal of interaction. If it's designed to be interactive, it will be. If designed as a lecture, it will be. The same considerations, including physical room arrangement, apply to IDB as for classroom environments.

Design and development time is lengthened from classroom training. Much more thought and detail must be included in instructor manuals regarding when to

- Display graphics
- Ask questions
- Switch cameras
- Move from camera to overhead or video

Time must also be included in the schedule for practice sessions so the instructor can become familiar and comfortable with the materials and the equipment. Pilot sessions for the training, desirable for most media, are almost mandatory for IDB.

If you are delivering over a great and varied distance, time zones are a big consideration. For example, if you're transmitting live in New York at 12:00 noon, it's 12:00 midnight in Singapore. It is inevitable that someone will have to be inconvenienced, but try to set start times that best fit the majority.

Instruction can also be arranged around breaks. For example, an instructor begins a session with a group at 9:00 A.M. central time. At 11:00 A.M. central, the instructor assigns an activity that lasts ninety minutes. The participants in the central time zone complete the assignment and then go to lunch from 12:30 till 1:30 P.M. A group in the pacific time zone thus begins this session at 7:00 A.M. pacific time (9:00 A.M. central time). The pacific group works on the activity at 9:00 A.M. pacific and goes to lunch from 10:30 A.M. to 11.30. The entire group comes back at what is 1:30 P.M. central or 11:30 pacific.

Larger time-zone differences require more complicated arrangements. There is also always a taping and playback option, but this takes away interactivity with the instructor. However, the presentation can be stopped to answer questions and complete activities if TAs are at the student sites.

SUMMARY

The essence of interactive distance broadcast training is well-orchestrated, instructor-led training. Design should focus on well-conceived interactions and integrated media. Implementation requires an instructor who is constantly aware of the audience, the technology, and the content.

Distance broadcast training may be the most underrated and overlooked medium available today. The technology is inexpensive and easy to use. (Satellite broadcasting is the only medium that requires expensive satellite time and usually, but not necessarily, a television studio.) If creatively designed, video and audio teleconferencing over television and telephone lines have great potential to obtain and maintain interactivity.

part four

Multimedia
Evaluation

Introduction to Multimedia Evaluation

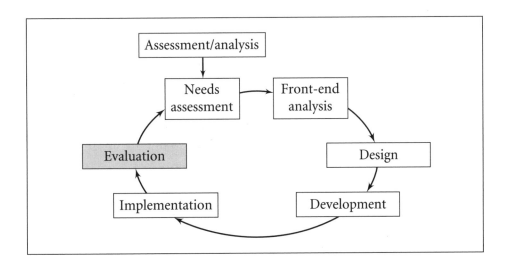

Congratulations! You've just made your delivery date, after many long hours and hard work. The solution is now installed and it's being used. "What a relief," you say—but it's only for a few seconds. Suddenly you're called in to your manager's office and given another assignment (as a reward for a job well done). Actually, what you need is a month off to recover from this one!

You really do derive a certain satisfaction from a job well done. But if you ever had the time to reflect on what's been done, you might want to know if what you developed is truly effective in teaching the skills needed to do the job the solution was developed for.

You have given feedback in the course to reinforce the learning of the students so they can improve. Well, just as feedback keeps students on track, feedback on your design and the effectiveness of the solution helps you improve the next project.

But if this requirement isn't in the contract and you're on to the next project, then you put feedback in the back of your mind. We want to bring those thoughts to the foreground and have them nag you a bit.

If you have completed all of the activities during assessment and analysis, design, and development, then *formative* evaluation—which is all about quality—is completed. Now you are ready for *summative* evaluation, to judge the effectiveness of the solution.

Evaluation is typically what we do worst. The causes of poor measurement stem from lack of knowledge or lack of attention, or both. Knowing what to measure and how to do it to target the data that yields relevant information is a process requiring careful thought by persons with highly specialized skills. Your evaluation design may be very sound, but something as simple as choosing the wrong measure of what you are trying to prove may cause you to find significant levels of learning where there is none, or no learning where there actually is some.

Part Four of this book explains summative evaluation from two perspectives: developing accurate measurement instruments such as tests and observation instruments, and applying appropriate statistical measures to the instruments for the purpose of analyzing results.

Donald Kirkpatrick (1994) identified four levels of evaluation. We have summarized the four levels in Table 25.1, labeling them slightly differently from how Kirkpatrick does. (His levels are reaction, learning, behavior, and results.)

The four levels of evaluation are highly interdependent. For example, it's important to determine the positive reaction to a course before starting to measure improved performance. The same goes for determining improved performance before measuring ROI.

There are certain skills outside the scope of this book. Therefore we don't cover statistics, statistical analysis, interpretation, or conducting research studies. There is, however, an Evaluation Glossary at the end of Appendix D to clarify some of the technical terms used in evaluation.

Table 25.1
Levels of Evaluation

Level 1	Reaction	Measures participant's response to the activity in the form of impressions about the relevance of the activity in enabling them to fulfill the duties of their jobs
Level 2	Knowledge	Measures increased level of achievement of the content and skills intended by the activity
Level 3	Performance	Measures change in behavior or attitude as a result of using the knowledge and skills of the activity transferred to the job over a period of time
Level 4	Impact	Measures the impact on the business in the form of return on investment (ROI) from the activity

FROM OUR EXPERIENCE

Customers for whom we develop solutions ask for validation that the solution is effective before they accept or pay for it. The days are rapidly coming to an end when developers can abdicate responsibility for the effectiveness of the solutions they create. Development groups that aren't willing to stand behind their products are subliminally telling customers they don't have confidence in what they are doing.

Purpose of Evaluation

Subjective criteria continue to be used to evaluate the worth of individuals. Students go through school making decisions about life choices based on grades derived from invalid measures.

The trend carries over into adult education and training. Many businesses use evaluations to determine salary increases, promotion, and employees' career paths according to criteria just as subjective as those used by teachers in schools.

Meanwhile, little or none of this evaluation is held up to the scrutiny of criterion-referenced and norm-referenced measurement principles to establish congruence between the amount of knowledge gained (indicated by test scores) and one's ability to perform the job better. In essence, evaluation is failing people rather than people failing evaluations.

Much has been written about applying Kirkpatrick's four levels of evaluation (1994). Borg and Gall (1996), Shrock and Coscarelli (1996), Campbell and Stanley (1963), and Martuza (1977) are leaders in the field of measurement, evaluation, and testing, whose perspectives form the backbone of Kirkpatrick's levels. The model presented here synthesizes the work of all of these experts.

The model is based on the principle that the level of evaluation must be connected primarily to the purpose and intended use of the results of the evaluation.

PROCESS

Assessing the appropriate amount of evaluation required involves one activity: determining the purpose of the solution. Table 26.1 shows the variables of the decision-making process; each is explained in the steps of this activity.

Table 26.1
Evaluation Matrix

Measurement Variable	Purpose	Low Validity		Test Item Validity		High Validity
		Face Validity	Content Validity	Distractor Analysis	Correlation	Predictive Validity
Organizational needs	Return on investment	■	■	■	■	■
	Improved workforce	■	■	■	■	■
	Regulatory requirements	■	■	■	■	■
	EEOC requirements	■	■	■	■	■
Individual needs	Promotion	■	■	■	■	■
	Professional development	■	■	■	■	■
	Improved performance	■	■	■		
	Increased knowledge	■	■			
	Self-improvement	■				

■ indicates level of validity required.

PURPOSE OF EVALUATION PROCEDURE

Follow this activity:

Activity One: Determine the Purpose of the Solution

Step one: Determine if the measurement variables are organizational or individual.

If the variables are organizational goals, determine if the organization is getting a *return on investment* that justifies the amount of money spent on developing and implementing the solution. To determine this

- Collect data on the cost of the solution the customer was delivering before implementation of the new solution, and compare that information to data collected over a period of time after the new solution is implemented.
- If there are no data available about the previous solution, collect as much information as you can on costs of the previous solution while you are developing the new solution. Using the information gathered before the new solution is implemented and comparing it to data gathered for a period of several months after, you can predict the effectiveness of the solution over yet other extended periods of time. Actual data plus your predictions determine how long it will take for the intervention to pay for itself.

Determine if the solution results in an *improved workforce* to accomplish the organizational goals. An improved workforce with higher levels of skill can get the job done better, faster, and more economically. Both speed and economy can be investigated separately, but increased speed at a sacrifice of improved performance is usually not a desirable outcome.

Determine also whether the solution produces employees who are aware of government *regulatory requirements,* such as those imposed by the banking industry regulatory body, the Securities Exchange Commission (SEC), the airline industry's Federal Aviation Administration (FAA), and the Occupational Safety and Health Administration (OSHA) in manufacturing.

Is the level of validity required by the regulations satisfied if the employees are simply aware of the regulations? Or must they be able to perform a skill or task as a result? The answer to this question determines the level of validity that the solution must achieve.

Finally, find out if the solution complies with EEOC guidelines (Equal Employment Opportunity Commission, 1978) on fair employment practices and nondiscrimination.

Step two: Identify the measurement variables that are individual rather than organizational.

With variables designed to measure individual traits, you must be able to prove that the traits accurately predict individual performance and that the solution used to impart knowledge and skills is valid. This is particularly important if the training is part of a career ladder required for an employee to advance in a company, or if the training is incorporated into a performance appraisal.

Does the solution provide the skills necessary for employees to successfully complete the job into which they will be *promoted*?

Can you predict that employees' *professional development* will increase as a result of successfully completing the development activities? The activities might include training but could also be much broader in scope.

Does the training predict *improved performance* from successful completion? If so, it can therefore be incorporated into a development plan for the purpose of granting merit pay increases.

Determine if increased performance has occurred after the training. These skills may be documented in the form of a performance appraisal. This information lets the employer know that the training is effective in having employees better prepared to do their jobs.

Note that performance appraisals should *not* be used as the basis for granting merit increases or incentive compensation. Merit and incentives should be attached to professional development plans that have goals with associated accomplishments and time lines attached.

Determine if the training results in *increased knowledge and skills* based on a standard measurement. Again, note that training designed to increase knowledge need only document that those who complete such training comprehend or understand the information offered by the training. There is no condition or implication of being able to perform better based on the content.

Finally, does the training result in *self-improvement* on the basis of the individual's own perceptions? Courses designed for self-improvement purposes require only that those who take the course believe that they have more knowledge or skills as a result of taking the training.

Step three: Determine if the solution will be used commercially. Commercial products to be used off-the-shelf have their own unique qualities and require specific mention. Because many products targeted for commercial use are developed by training-and-development companies that then resell them, the producer can't be certain how the product will be used. Therefore it's imperative that commercially developed products (1) be validated to the highest level (predictive validity), (2) specify the level of validity in the course documentation, or (3) translate the level of validity into terms that explain how and what the solution can be used for.

FROM OUR EXPERIENCE

Careful consideration of the purpose for which a solution is being developed is the first step toward accurate evaluation. We find both extremes; either the mention of the word *evaluation* sends people fleeing from the room or else they decide to kill a fly with a wrecking ball. Too little and too much evaluation are both wasteful.

Evaluation requires time and resources that translate into lengthened project schedules and increased cost. Be certain the expense is worth the cost and time.

SUMMARY

You now know the purpose of evaluation and whether your solution should be measured on an organizational or an individual level. Next you need to determine the level of instrument validity required to judge the effectiveness of your solution. After determining this, you can develop appropriate measurement instruments for the evaluation.

Measures of Validity

Now that you have determined why you want to evaluate, you can construct the instruments to assess that purpose. But before you construct the instruments, you must determine how to estimate whether they actually measure what they are designed to measure. Proper measurement is the test of validity. Test validity is established though statistical testing.

RELATED THEORY

Full validity establishes that a course teaches what it intends to teach. Face validity is relatively easy to establish but should be attempted before too much development is completed because experts may have suggestions to change and improve the product. We recommend face validity be established during the first stages of the development phase, when the content is organized.

Content validity of the course material is established through the technical content review cycles conducted during development (see Chapter 19), so test item content validity is what you need to establish during evaluation if it was not also done during the development phase, when you were incorporating the measurement instruments into the solution. Test questions are harder to change after they are programmed into a CBT course than on paper, so establish content validity during the development phase, immediately after questions are written.

Inter-rater agreement is established through practice, having evaluators view the same performance task (either live or on videotape) and rate the tasks using the validated checklist. You can use a norm-referenced statistical test here to determine inter-rater agreement—a t-test of statistical significance. If you establish an inter-rater correlation coefficient of +.90 or higher, you have a high degree of inter-rater agreement (+.95 is excellent; again, the criticality of what the raters are observing determines the degree of inter-rater agreement you need. Higher levels of agreement take more training and longer to achieve.) However, evaluators should be re-trained regularly if their evaluations occur over an extended period of time because their judgments can be affected by the number of students they observe over time.

PROCESS

Lee, Roadman, and Mamone (1990) recommend a process for establishing validity that has three activities:

1. Determine the level and type of validity required.
2. Determine when to validate measurement instruments.
3. Document your decisions.

MEASURES OF VALIDITY PROCEDURE

Follow these activities:

Activity One: Determine the Level and Type of Validity Required

The type of validity required for the intended use of the product can be found using Table 26.1. Types of validity are defined in Table 27.1.

Activity Two: Determine When to Validate Measurement Instruments

Examples of the various validity requirements and the corresponding phase of the instructional design process are found in Table 27.1.

Activity Three: Document Your Decisions

Document your decisions in the test plan section of the CDS that you created during the design phase.

Table 27.1
Types of Validity and When They Are Established

Type of Validity	Level of Validity	How to Accomplish It	Importance	Phase
Face validity	Low	Formative evaluation, where experts review the course materials and validate that the course content approximates what a course on this subject should teach	Minimum validity required to establish that a course teaches what it intends to teach or that a test measures what it claims to measure	Design or development
Content validity	Low	Formative evaluation, where experts review the course materials and validate that there is congruence between the objectives, content, and test items	Minimum validity required if the course is used for certification of competence in a subject	Design
Concurrent validity	Medium	Quantitative summative evaluation, measure of the similarities between two tests	Establishes test item validity	Evaluation

Table 27.1

Types of Validity and When They Are Established, Cont'd.

Type of Validity	Level of Validity	How to Accomplish It	Importance	Phase
Construct validity	Medium	Quantitative summative evaluation, measure of relationship between scores on a test and job performance	Establishes positive relationship between test questions and the actual job performed	Evaluation
Test item validity	Medium	Quantitative formative or summative evaluation, measure of the relationship between individual questions and the overall test	Gives a high degree of confidence that test items accurately measure skills	Design evaluation
Predictive validity	High	Quantitative summative evaluation, measure of the ability of a test to predict future success in a skill area	Establishes validity of a test and ensures that a test positively correlates with the job performance it claims to measure (short-term); establishes reliability of a test or course (long-term)	Evaluation
Inter-rater agreement	High	Quantitative formative or summative evaluation, measure of the ability of raters to agree on successful performance of a task	Establishes the confidence level that independent observations are consistent among raters	Assessment and analysis or evaluation

FROM OUR EXPERIENCE

You can measure the reaction (Kirkpatrick's level-one evaluation) to a course by using surveys (sometimes referred to as "smile sheets"). If you are going to use reaction surveys, tailor each to the product you're surveying. A specific question such as "Did the course teach you to interact more effectively with coworkers?" generates substantially better information than "Did the course meet your expectations?" In the second question, you don't know what information you are getting because you don't know what the respondent's expectations were!

Knowledge tests require differing levels of validity, depending on the intended use of the test. Performance tests require similar methods for validity as knowledge tests, and the level is also dependent on the intended use. However, there are usually no distractors to choose from. Rather, there is a checklist of the skills that must be performed and an evaluator must check that the skill was performed correctly.

The methodology of establishing test-item validity during development is to use a panel of judges. Qualification to be a judge is based on subject-matter expertise. There should be a minimum of four judges, each given a Test Specification Form (see Appendix D, where a completed form is also included).

Do a frequency count on the number of judges who respond that any given question meets the criterion. If you are using five judges, the criterion should be 80 percent (four of the five judges answer yes), 75 percent with four judges, and so on. If the level of knowledge required is extremely critical, you may choose 100 percent for the criterion regardless of how many judges you use. (For instance, the criterion level for knowledge of a brain surgeon would be much higher than for someone learning team-management skills.)

Each question that achieves the criterion level is considered to have content validity. Those questions that do not meet the criterion must be returned to the test writer for revision. Judges' comments are used to determine why an item was rejected. These rewritten questions must go through judging again. This process continues until all test questions reach the desired criterion level.

Although content validity is best determined using judges, various forms of statistical tests can also determine validity. Point-biserial correlation tells you if the skills are being performed consistently by those who are the masters of the training. Again, the difficulty index can be used for those performance items that produce low or no positive correlation.

This correlation involves very careful assessment and analysis of the tasks that the students who take the course are trained on. Assessment has to establish that enough people who are already masters have been observed, interviewed, and rated to establish the criteria for successful completion. You must use SMEs who are highly trained in inter-rater observation skills to perform the assessment and establish all levels of validation below predictive validity. Whether the tests are objective (based on knowledge acquired) or performance (based on ability to accomplish the skill), predictive validity must be established.

You don't need to use both judging and statistical methods to determine content validity.

Once analysis establishes the skills and the level of proficiency, you can use performance validation procedures to determine that all students are trained to the required proficiency level. You must then follow the students into the actual workplace and evaluate them at preestablished points over time, using the same evaluation instrument, to establish that adequate levels of proficiency are maintained. Predictive validity studies typically take place over an extended period of time. If your customer is really dedicated to improving individual performance and output, he or she will continue to collect data on employee proficiency on the job.

SUMMARY

Now that you have decided the type and level of validity required to test the effectiveness of your solution, you can develop the instruments that match the required level. You should also develop the strategy for distributing instruments and collecting the data from the instruments in the form of a measurement plan.

Instrument Development and Measurement Plan

A measurement plan details the specifications of any measurement instruments included in your product. Tests, questionnaires, and surveys must all be developed according to the purpose of evaluation (established in Chapter Twenty-Six) and the type and level of validity required (established in Chapter Twenty-Seven). All measurement instruments must attain the degree of validity required to return information offering any degree of certainty about the effectiveness of your solution.

Interview instruments, as with questionnaires and surveys, must attain a minimum of content validity to be useful. Beyond validity, certain other conditions are conducive to good interviewing, such as the interpersonal skills of interviewers.

Surveys present some difficulties with respect to being sure enough are returned to consider the resulting sample adequate. It is very optimistic to expect to get a 50 percent return rate on surveys. Here is a way to ensure that you get the total number of responses you need. When choosing subjects who are to receive surveys, keep the 50 percent return rate in mind and use the method for determining sample size and random selection discussed in the Direct-Interview Instructions section of Appendix D. Proceed as follows:

1. You have a list of five hundred names.

2. A sample size of 10 percent of the population means you need fifty responses.

3. Anticipating a 50 percent return rate, double the number of names (total one hundred).

4. Derive a random sample of one hundred names of people who receive the survey.

5. Resend the survey to those nonrespondents from the *same* group if you don't get the fifty you need on the first try.

6. If you still do not get the required number after the second time, repeat from step 3 with a *different* group.

7. Use all responses (the fifty required is a minimum; more than that is even better).

PROCESS

There are five activities necessary to complete a measurement plan:

1. Select the types of measurements.

2. Develop the measurement instruments.

3. Calculate the length of each instrument.

4. Calculate the weight of each item.

5. Decide when the instrument(s) should be administered.

INSTRUMENT DEVELOPMENT AND MEASUREMENT PLAN PROCEDURE

Follow these activities:

Activity One: Select the Types of Measurements

Step one: Determine what to measure using the terminal objectives created during objective analysis. Decide if the objectives measure skills, knowledge, or attitudes. If the objective involves students doing something, your instrument should measure skills; if students only need to demonstrate that they know something, a knowledge-based measure is appropriate. Decide how performance measures are to be constructed.

Step two: Determine if measures need to be norm-referenced (NR) or criterion-referenced (CR).

Norm-referenced measures estimate characteristics and capabilities of people compared to the general population. Criterion-referenced measures estimate characteristics and capabilities of people compared to a standard. For example, the reading level of adults in the general population would be a norm-referenced characteristic. The reading level of individuals in a target audience for a training course is a criterion-referenced measure that you would have to test or account for in some way in the results of your assessments.

Step three: Determine if the measures are qualitative or quantitative. Although they use data, qualitative measures of validity handle the data with a method that requires professional judgment; quantitative measures rely heavily on standardized methods of interpreting statistics (although some people argue that there is judgment involved in the interpretation, with which we agree).

The trick is knowing which statistical tests to use, and how to interpret the data you receive. Here are some common statistical measures of validity with an explanation of when to use them and how to use them.

Quantitative Measures. Quantitative measures consist of the following:

1. Correlations
2. Difficulty indices
3. Item analysis
4. Tests of significance

Correlations. Correlations establish the relationship between two variables. The result is a number between −1.0 and +1.0. Numbers closer to +1.0 indicate a high positive correlation, and those closer to −1.0 indicate a high negative correlation. The higher the positive correlation, the better the test item. But what about questions that receive 0.00? You must then use a difficulty index to determine whether to include or exclude the item.

Here is an example of how correlation works and its value. A company we worked for developed an interactive-video basic mathematics course. The course used a pretest and a posttest to measure the students' increase in knowledge and skills. During the pretest, students could test out of certain modules by answering selected questions correctly on the diagnostic test; they were channeled into other modules if they incorrectly answered these selected questions. If the students failed the diagnostic pretest, they had yet another chance once they entered a module of instruction, through another mastery test. If students scored 90 percent on the mastery test, they could at that point skip the module or choose to continue through it anyway.

But management wanted to know if the test measured the skills generally determined by experts to be required by students who have mastered basic mathematics skills. They needed an answer to the question, "Does this test have a high degree of predictive validity?" The testing team began by administering a test they had developed internally to groups of college freshmen (about one hundred) determined by college placement tests to be in need of remedial mathematics to succeed in their college courses. The testing team also found that the mathematics test from a national high school equivalency exam had been well documented as having a high degree of validity and reliability. The team also administered this test to the same group of students.

Comparing the scores on the course test and the standardized test, the testing team determined that there was a high degree of correlation between the two tests. As a result, management could declare that students who passed the posttest in the interactive video course had the mathematical knowledge and skills of students who have graduated from high school.

Difficulty index. But what about the questions that score with no correlation (0.00)? You must look at an index of the level of difficulty for that question. If all students get the question right or if all get it wrong, then the question is probably a poor question and needs to be rewritten. Compare questions with 0.00 correlation to your frequency tables.

How high should positive correlation be for a question to be considered valid? A sufficient level of positive correlation for each question should be +.80, again based on the criticality of the knowledge (say, brain surgeon versus management trainee). Low positive correlations require distractor analysis and frequency counts. No correlation below +.50 should be considered valid.

Item analysis. This determines if the individual test items and the overall test are valid. Item analysis establishes the validity of test questions by determining that those who performed best on the overall test also got a particular item correct.

To perform an item analysis, you must have two independent variables that can be compared in some way to make the determination about how good your test questions are. There are a number of statistical tests that establish this for NR measures and others for CR measures.

Tests of significance. Tests of significance are used when you want to determine if the results from running your data on your sample group are typical or not typical of the total population from which the random sample was drawn.

Qualitative Measures. More qualitative measures include the following:

1. Distrator analysis
2. Frequency counts

Distractor analysis. Analyzing the answers that students give to a test is known as distractor analysis. In this analysis, you must look for any questions that receive a low positive or negative correlation using quantitative methods and determine if there is one particular distractor (possible answer) that draws the better students away from the correct answer. Find out which distractor is causing the problem and then determine why it might be doing so. Rewrite the distractor (and any others for that question that need clarity), administer the test again, and perform the same correlation analyses. Frequency analysis also reveals this information.

If you are fortunate enough to have access to the students who answered the question incorrectly, ask them why they chose their particular answer. This is a very good source of feedback. If those students are not available, use only the data from distractor analysis.

Frequency counts. Though frequency counts are a quantitative measure, they require judgment to determine the cutoff for success or failure. Frequencies are easy to generate even if you don't use a statistical package; just count the number of responses based on some standard (say, correct-or-incorrect). However, a statistical package generates the data much faster, especially for a large number of cases.

Step four: Determine if you will administer measures before or after using your solution. If both before and after, will you use the same measure, or parallel forms of instruments? If you are developing parallel forms, use the following instructions and the Tool for Constructing a Bank of Parallel Test Items in the Evaluation Tools section of Appendix E.

Follow these steps to develop parallel tests and establish parallel test validity.

1. Provide a set of numbered objectives along with the Tool for Constructing a Bank of Parallel Test Items (see Appendix E) to a panel of SME judges, who will determine the parallelism. Have the number of each terminal objective marked in the "Terminal Objective Number" column before you give the form to the judges.

2. Provide a set of numbered test questions to the judges.

3. List the weight of each terminal objective on the Tool for Constructing a Bank of Parallel Test Items.

4. Provide directions for developing parallel test item banks to each judge.

5. Judges must match each terminal objective with two questions that they determine have an equal level of difficulty.

Activity Two: Develop the Measurement Instruments

Depending on the question types you decide to construct, use one or more of these forms from the Evaluation Tools section of Appendix E:

- Matching Question Checklist
- Multiple-Choice Question Checklist
- True-False Question Checklist
- Completion (Short-Answer) Question Checklist
- Simulation, Role Play, Performance Test Checklist
- Essay Question Checklist

Use the Test Completion Checklist in the Evaluation Tools section of Appendix E to evaluate the components of complete tests.

See Appendix D's instructions for developing questionnaires, surveys, and interview instruments to construct these types of measurement instrument.

Activity Three: Calculate the Length of Each Instrument

Step one: Calculate the number of questions. Suppose you have fifty terminal objectives and you decide you should ask two questions per objective as a standard. This means you have a test with one hundred questions. Remember, the students must have an adequate opportunity to demonstrate attainment of the knowledge of skill. Multiple questions or multiple attempts per objective on a criterion-referenced test increase the probability of demonstrating attainment.

Step two: Calculate the time respondents need to complete the instrument. How long it takes depends on the nature of the questions. Objective questions vary depending on the type (true-false, matching, multiple-choice), how long the question stem is, and how many distractors are included. Note that a good rule of thumb is to allow thirty seconds for each multiple-choice question that has four distractors. Don't forget that you have to leave time in the test for students to read the directions, or for them to be explained. For example, if you (1) have fifty objectives, (2) write two questions per objective, and (3) allow thirty seconds per question plus about ten minutes to read and understand instructions, this means you need to allow sixty minutes for test completion:

$$(50 \text{ objectives} \times 2 \text{ questions per objective} \times .5 \text{ minutes per question})$$
$$+ 10 \text{ minutes} = 60 \text{ minutes}$$

Activity Four: Calculate the Weight of Each Item

Determine the amount of content in each part of the solution. Not all parts of a solution carry equal weight; in a five-hour training course, if one section takes two hours to cover then it has more weight in the course than a section that takes half an hour. The number of questions for each terminal objective should be based on the relative weight of the content.

If the two-hour section of the course contains six of the terminal objectives, your job is simple. If two questions per terminal objective is your standard, you simply put twelve questions from that section on the total test.

But suppose you have one terminal objective for this two-hour section. As an alternative to the formula of so many questions per terminal objective, you can calculate the length of delivery time for the section in proportion to the entire course and construct enough questions to match proportionally.

If you administer a performance test where students have multiple chances to successfully complete the task, you can perform a frequency count to determine how many attempts were required for most (whatever standard you want to use, such as 80 percent) of the students to accomplish the task. If the number is low, that task is valid. If 80 percent of the students require four tries to accomplish certain tasks, you had better check those items; they are probably not valid.

Activity Five: Decide When the Instrument(s) Should Be Administered

Determine if measures should be interspersed in the course or if there should only be one comprehensive test at the end of the course. If measures are interspersed, determine how many will be needed. Use the information in Table 28.1 to determine the placement of measures.

FROM OUR EXPERIENCE

Instructional designers find that one of their greatest knowledge gaps is understanding what type of measure you need to develop. An NR measure only needs a sample of questions from among the objectives. However, a CR measure needs multiple questions for every objective. Whereas NR measures are designed to sample overall knowledge, CR measures are designed to ensure that a population possesses the skill being trained and that those tested have ample opportunity to demonstrate their knowledge or skill. Table 28.2 will help you determine if your statistical test can be applied to NR or CR measures.

Setting a pass-fail level differs for NR and CR measures. On an NR measure, a 50–67 percent score may be considered passing because most people who take the test score around the midpoint. On a CR measure, the pass-fail score is determined by the criticality of the skill the test taker will be performing; thus CR passing scores are usually set higher than the midpoint. The most important thing to remember is that a test score is not absolute; it is a point within a range. Any score within the range (standard deviation) is acceptable.

Generally, if you are developing a product so that a specific group learns a specific set of skills, you are probably developing a criterion-referenced test (CRT). Off-the-shelf products usually require CRTs unless the subject is general knowledge on some skill that any person using the product should have, such as basic mathematics, reading, and so on. However, the test must be established to the standard for the group using the product and taking the test.

Artificially imposed restrictions placed on the test are not a good idea before assessment is completed. Here are examples of artificially imposed restrictions:

- Predetermined test format (that is, objective, questionnaire, survey)
- Predetermined number of questions
- Predetermined time for test administration
- Predetermined ratio of class to test time

Table 28.1
Question Types

Type	Location	Level	Purpose	Frequency
Embedded (Study)	Within a lesson	Basic knowledge and understanding	Check basic knowledge of concept(s) taught in the lesson	Interspersed throughout a lesson
Quiz	At the end of each lesson or periodically after several lessons	Knowledge of information within a lesson Application	Test students' grasp of concepts *Note:* Questions should test only the major concepts from the objective(s) that the lesson covers.	End of a lesson or group of lessons *Note:* At least one question should be asked on each major topic.
Test	Interim and end of course	Application Evaluation	Test students' knowledge or performance by integrating information from throughout the course	As required *Note:* Test pool should contain at least one question from each lesson objective.

Table 28.2
Appropriate Statistical Measures

Test Name	Purpose	Application Type[a] A	B	C	D	Sample Requirements
Biserial	One continuous, one dichotomy	√	√	√		Representative sample size
Chi-square	One continuous, one dichotomy		√		√	Representative sample size
Kendall's tau	Two continuous variables	√		√		$n < 10$
Kuder Richardson (KR-20)	Measure of equal difficulty	√	√	√		Representative sample size
Mann Whitney	Compare unequal groups	√	√		√	Representative sample size
Pearson Product Moment (Pearson r)	Two continuous variables	√		√		Representative sample size
Phi coefficient (Φ)	Two true dichotomies			√		Representative sample size
Point-biserial	One continuous, one true dichotomy		√	√		Representative sample size
Rank difference	Two continuous variables	√		√		$n < 30$
Analysis of variance (ANOVA)	Significance between more than two means	√	√		√	Representative sample size
t-test	Significance between two means	√			√	Representative sample size

[a]A = Norm-Referenced; B = Criterion-Referenced; C = Correlation; D = Significance

You cannot determine the instrument format before completion of front-end analysis, and you cannot determine the number of measurement items until you have written your objectives. Time and ratios cannot be determined until you decide on instrument format and the number of questions.

Of course, there are certain limitations to the amount of time that can be spent on testing, but let situation and objective analysis shape this decision rather than arbitrary choice. Once you see the number of objectives and the conditions under which the product will be used or delivered, you may decide the format needs to be changed because there is a better method of evaluation.

In our opinion, transfer of skills to the workplace is the only justifiable reason for expending resources on a project. If employees simply have to know or be aware of something, give them a book, pamphlet, or other resource and have them read it. "But people don't take responsibility for gaining knowledge themselves," some say. "If I give them a book, it won't get read." To our minds, if that's the case then you had best expend your resources in other areas of employee development, such as creating self-motivated employees who are lifelong learners.

We are not saying that employers should not extend learning opportunities to employees. However, activities should not stop at the knowledge level. The value of knowledge can only be measured through resultant performance.

Students who complete the course must be observed regularly over time to determine if they are using the skills taught during the training. If you can determine that they are, then determine what cost savings can be directly attributed to using the skills.

For either knowledge or performance measures, you have to consider whether or not to preassess and postassess. For example, a new training course should always contain a preassessment if there is a postassessment for purposes of establishing validity of the instrument. Your goal is to determine if there are significantly higher results on the posttest. If the results are significant, this demonstrates that the course has taught what it was intended to teach.

After you administer the instrument often enough to establish validity and reliability of results, you can discontinue preassessing. If any portion of the course changes, you should revise the instruments, readminister it to pilot groups of students, and reestablish validity and reliability.

For either objective or performance instruments, if students can test out of a course or particular units of a course based on pretest scores, then this is a valid reason for using the pretest or posttest. If only posttests are administered, there is no evidence that the students learn as a result of taking the course. They might know the material beforehand, in which case they shouldn't have to sit though the course. Another explanation might be that the test is flawed by being so easy or so poorly constructed that students can guess the answers without knowing the content.

If the content is highly technical or presents a new concept, process, or procedure, and you are certain (from information gathered during analysis) that all students are beginning at the same level, preassessment may be unnecessary. If other forms of information were provided to certain students in the past, or if their work experience afforded some of them higher levels of knowledge than others, a pretest and posttest might be in order. If there is no evidence of wide diversity in prerequisite skills, don't waste your time. It might be nice to know, but it's not necessary.

Knowledge-based assessments are sometimes unnecessary if performance measures are administered after offering the information. The logic is that if a student can do something correctly, you can assume he or she has the knowledge.

However, you might spend a lot of time and resources developing and administering performance measures, only to achieve poor results among the students. It may be that they did not gain the knowledge. If so, you must then search for the reasons for low performance. Knowledge assessment at the end of the content portion of the course would be useful in detecting the source. Perhaps certain concepts, procedures, or processes weren't emphasized in the content or were taught incorrectly.

Backtracking is expensive and delays how soon the customer can begin fully implementing the program. You must develop instruments, validate them, preassess and postassess, score and analyze, and then reconstruct the performance project.

In our experience, another question that always arises when survey research is involved is, "How many people should be surveyed?"

Sampling some populations is difficult, and there is always a tendency to cut corners. Some professionals and customers point to some of the major rating providers (such as the Harris polling organization), who sample a very small segment of the population and still achieve highly reliable results.

Many don't realize or stop to think that professional rating corporations spend a great amount of money up front, using very sophisticated computer systems to continuously narrow and subdivide regions of the territory they plan to survey and the populations of those areas. They use and rely on systems that have been in place for many years and employ methodologies whose reliability has been constantly refined.

If your organization is in that lofty minority and has such sophisticated sampling equipment, then use it to choose a sample size. If your organization does not have the equipment and methodologies, then use the rule of 10 percent of the population and be satisfied with a 60–70 percent return rate from that 10 percent.

Yes, it takes time; yes, it takes money. But do you and your stakeholders want accurate information? If accuracy is not a concern, then just guess and save the money! Guessing is just as accurate as sampling five people from among a population of one thousand.

SUMMARY

You now know what measurement instruments are required, how to construct them, and how to develop a measurement plan. Now instruments will be distributed and completed and returned. You have to analyze and interpret the data and make some sense out of it.

Collecting and Analyzing Data

Plan your evaluation thoroughly before you run it. Some things are recoverable because they are in the data and you only need to analyze them differently; but some things might not be recoverable unless you run the entire evaluation project again—costing time, money, and a delay in final implementation.

Although this book is not intended to deal with statistics, we include some basic information on types of tests, their purpose, and the underlying meaning of the results obtained from each one. Knowing what data to gather, however, requires someone with a background in statistical methodologies. After interpretation of the statistical findings, anyone with good problem-solving skills can determine what the data mean.

PROCESS

There are five activities required in data collection and analysis:

1. Set up the database.
2. Develop an evaluation plan.
3. Collect and run the data.
4. Interpret the data.
5. Document your findings.

COLLECTING AND ANALYZING DATA PROCEDURE

Follow these activities:

Activity One: Set Up the Database

Use the statistical software package you have chosen to set up the database to capture information or transfer information from other sources. For example, if you have set up the database in a CBT course, it is sometimes possible to capture the data in another format (say, ASCII text) and import them into the statistical package. Data transfer requires planning well in advance—as far back as when you choose the statistical tool and the development and delivery software.

Activity Two: Develop an Evaluation Plan

Once a project is selected and decisions are made as a result of assessment and analysis, an evaluation plan should be developed. The plan specifies how the evaluation is designed and conducted (including identification of time frames, data collection, and analysis methods) and the reporting mechanisms for any and all evaluation activities associated with a project.

The same considerations are required to evaluate performance and impact as are called for in developing tests:

- Number of participants and the amount of data to be collected
- Types of sampling method
- Confidentiality
- Costs

There are additional considerations when measuring performance. The first is use of a control group, that is, a set of preselected participants or data as similar as possible to those in the experimental group. The experimental group is involved in the intervention; the control group is not. The two groups should be equivalent in job settings, skills, abilities, and demographic characteristics. For more information on using experimental and control groups, refer to Campbell and Stanley (1963).

The second consideration is influence outside the scope of the evaluation. External variables include, among other things, organizational changes such as seasonal variations that have a negative impact on business. Internal factors such as new leadership, transfer of participants, budget cuts, and changing organizational goals can affect results. Effective control of these influences increases your confidence in the accuracy of the results, reduces the need for elaborate performance assessment designs, and may reduce the number of required participants in the population or the sample.

Activity Three: Collect and Run the Data

Capture data from the measurement instruments. Capture as many responses as possible, at least through the pilot test.

Activity Four: Interpret the Data

Step one: Interpret the data against the goals for the evaluation and determine if the results match the goals.

Step two: Make decisions. If the goals match the results, you might decide to do a full-scale implementation of the solution and (1) continue to collect data for consistent results, (2) discontinue collecting data, or (3) wait for a certain period of time and then conduct another evaluation.

If the results do not match the goals, the possible decisions might be to

- Revise the course
- Revise the measurement instruments and tests
- Rerun the study with or without revisions
- Choose another representative sample and rerun the evaluation
- Discard the product

Activity Five: Document Your Findings

Record your findings in the Evaluation Report. A template for completing it can be found in Appendix D.

FROM OUR EXPERIENCE

You need a good statistical package to analyze the raw data. We've used SPSS (formerly known as Statistical Package for the Social Sciences, but now simply as SPSS), produced by SPSS in Chicago. The Windows version is particularly easy to use, and the documentation is excellent.

SUMMARY

At the completion of these activities, you have the information to determine if your solution is effective in terms of the customer's need (established during needs assessment). All of the activities and steps you complete during every phase of the project contribute to the results you achieve. If you pay careful attention to each activity and each step and if you plan carefully, you will no doubt achieve the desired result: your solution solves the customer's problem.

PHASE: ASSESSMENT AND ANALYSIS

Assessment

☐ Activity 1 Determine the present condition.

   ☐ Step 1 Identify required knowledge and skills.

   ☐ Step 2 Identify the job-related knowledge and skill areas used to select performers.

   ☐ Step 3 Check for discrepancies between steps 1 and 2 and identify missing skills; then review for possible applications or revise selection criteria.

   ☐ Step 4 If there is a match between steps 1 and 2, then check for environmental causes.

   ☐ Step 5 Document task performance affected by environmental factors.

   ☐ Step 6 Review all results and identify areas of need.

   ☐ Step 7 Gather data from employees.

   ☐ Step 8 Review results and identify areas of need.

☐ Activity 2 Define the job.

☐ Activity 3 Rank the goals in order of importance.

☐ Activity 4 Identify discrepancies.

☐ Activity 5 Determine positive areas.

☐ Activity 6 Set priorities for action.

   ☐ Step 1 List all possible solutions suggested and the impact of not providing the solution.

☐ Step 2 Define the impact of each solution in terms of time, money, and customer satisfaction.

☐ Step 3 Make recommendations, keeping in mind the job goals, desired results, and other relevant factors.

Front-End Analysis: Audience

☐ Activity 1 Analyze demographics and special requirements.
    ☐ Step 1 Using job task information, verify the audience.
    ☐ Step 2 Confirm the number of individuals who are targeted and their general education and background.
    ☐ Step 3 Analyze information about language, tone, and use of humor, especially for global audiences.
    ☐ Step 4 Note any physical, ergonomic, or environmental requirements.
☐ Activity 2 Determine attitudes toward content.
    ☐ Step 1 Determine any misconceptions or misinformation that might exist.
    ☐ Step 2 Determine negative and positive attitudes.
    ☐ Step 3 Determine special terminology or vocabulary.
☐ Activity 3 Analyze the language skills of the audience.
☐ Activity 4 Document the results.

Front-End Analysis: Technology

☐ Activity 1 Analyze available communication technology.
☐ Activity 2 Analyze the technology available for reference or performance support.
    ☐ Step 1 Determine online reference availability and capability.
    ☐ Step 2 Determine performance support availability and capability.
☐ Activity 3 Analyze the technology available for testing and assessment.
    ☐ Step 1 Determine electronic testing and assessment requirements.
    ☐ Step 2 Define security issues.
☐ Activity 4 Analyze the technology for distribution.
    ☐ Step 1 Determine how materials are ordered and distributed.
    ☐ Step 2 Determine FTP (file transfer protocol) availability and capability.
☐ Activity 5 Analyze the technology for delivery.
    ☐ Step 1 Determine availability and capability of dedicated audio and video servers.

- ☐ Step 2 Determine multimedia PC availability and capability.
- ☐ Step 3 Determine video teleconferencing or educational TV availability and capability.
- ☐ Activity 6 Analyze the expertise.
- ☐ Activity 7 Document the results.

Front-End Analysis: Situation

- ☐ Activity 1 Analyze the job environment.
- ☐ Activity 2 Analyze delivery environment.
- ☐ Activity 3 Document the results.

Front-End Analysis: Task

- ☐ Activity 1 Define the position title.
- ☐ Activity 2 Identify all job-related duties.
- ☐ Activity 3 Identify all tasks.
    - ☐ Step 1 Confirm or identify primary tasks.
    - ☐ Step 2 Confirm that each task stands alone.
    - ☐ Step 3 Confirm the knowledge, skills, and attitudes (KSA) required.
- ☐ Activity 4 Order the tasks.
- ☐ Activity 5 Document the results.

Front-End Analysis: Critical Incident

- ☐ Activity 1 Determine the critical tasks.
- ☐ Activity 2 Determine important but nonessential tasks.
- ☐ Activity 3 Determine the tasks you will deselect.
- ☐ Activity 4 Document the results.

Front-End Analysis: Objectives

- ☐ Activity 1 Decide on domains.
- ☐ Activity 2 Decide on level.
- ☐ Activity 3 Write goal statement.
- ☐ Activity 4 Write performance objectives.
- ☐ Activity 5 Engage in a group discussion.
    - ☐ Step 1 Review objectives to validate relevance to job tasks.
    - ☐ Step 2 Rewrite objectives as necessary.

☐ Activity 6 Separate terminal objectives from performance objectives.

☐ Activity 7 Separate lesson objectives from performance objectives.

Front-End Analysis: Media

☐ Activity 1 Match outcomes to the appropriate media.

    ☐ Step 1 Determine if learning a complex task is required.

    ☐ Step 2 Determine if learning a process or procedure is required.

    ☐ Step 3 Determine if learning motor or psychomotor skill is required.

    ☐ Step 4 Determine if learning a concept or fact with detailed information is required.

    ☐ Step 5 Determine if learning a concept or fact without detailed information is required.

    ☐ Step 6 Determine if visuals are required.

    ☐ Step 7 Determine if motivation or attitude change is required.

    ☐ Step 8 Determine if critical thinking skills are required.

☐ Activity 2 Match media advantages and limitations.

    ☐ Step 1 Analyze advantages and limitations of each type.

    ☐ Step 2 Analyze cost of delivery.

    ☐ Step 3 Consider delivery factors.

    ☐ Step 4 Consider maintenance factors.

☐ Activity 3 Compare results and decide on the media.

☐ Activity 4 Document the results.

Front-End Analysis: Extant Data

☐ Activity 1 Identify likely sources of information.

☐ Activity 2 Collect information and existing course materials.

☐ Activity 3 Compare information.

    ☐ Step 1 Rate the appropriateness and usability of materials.

    ☐ Step 2 Determine if materials availability matches the time constraints of the project.

    ☐ Step 3 Determine the cost of the materials; compare to project budget.

☐ Activity 4 Make a buy-or-build decision.

☐ Activity 5 Document your decision.

Front-End Analysis: Cost

- ☐ Activity 1 Conduct a cost-benefit analysis (CBA).
- ☐ Activity 2 Determine the return on investment (ROI).
- ☐ Activity 3 Document the results.

Front-End Analysis: Rapid Analysis Method

- ☐ Activity 1 Prepare for the analysis.
    - ☐ Step 1 Determine focus of the assessment.
    - ☐ Step 2 Conduct kickoff meeting.
    - ☐ Step 3 Assign tasks.
- ☐ Activity 2 Ask primary questions.
    - ☐ Step 1 Ask target groups the five primary questions; add follow-on questions as required.
    - ☐ Step 2 Identify inconsistencies.
- ☐ Activity 3 Listen and record responses.
    - ☐ Step 1 Listen to the responses.
    - ☐ Step 2 Categorize responses into the five response categories.
- ☐ Activity 4 Observe actual performance.
    - ☐ Step 1 Watch tasks being performed.
    - ☐ Step 2 Identify gaps between verbal responses and actual performance.
- ☐ Activity 5 Report results.

PHASE: DESIGN

Project Schedule

- ☐ Activity 1 Document general project information.
- ☐ Activity 2 List project deliverables.
- ☐ Activity 3 Schedule project activities.

Project Team

- ☐ Activity 1 List team roles.
- ☐ Activity 2 Assign roles and responsibilities.
- ☐ Activity 3 Match tasks to members.

Media Specifications

☐ Activity 1 Define the look and feel of the theme.
   ☐ Step 1 Brainstorm a list of themes.
   ☐ Step 2 Complete a mock-up.
   ☐ Step 3 Decide on theme.
☐ Activity 2 Define the interface and functionality.
☐ Activity 3 Define the interaction and feedback standards.
☐ Activity 4 Define the video and audio treatments.
☐ Activity 5 Indicate text design and standards.
☐ Activity 6 Prepare the graphic design standards.
☐ Activity 7 Decide on animation and special effects.

Content Structure

☐ Activity 1 Break the content into units.
   ☐ Step 1 Break it into six major categories.
   ☐ Step 2 Group information based on job and task order.
☐ Activity 2 Map the information.
   ☐ Step 1 Create a lesson outline or map.
   ☐ Step 2 Create a course flowchart.

Configuration Control and Review Cycles

☐ Activity 1 Establish a configuration control (CC) plan.

PHASE: DEVELOPMENT AND IMPLEMENTATION
Developing Computer-Based Learning Environments

☐ Activity 1 Create storyboards.
   ☐ Step 1 Review the instructional rationale for the treatment of each learning outcome.
   ☐ Step 2 Translate rationale into a screen-level outline.
   ☐ Step 3 Add up-front components.
   ☐ Step 4 Review and validate storyboards.
   ☐ Step 5 Conduct quality-assurance (QA) reviews.

☐ Activity 2 Create and assemble media elements.
    ☐ Step 1 Conduct preproduction meeting.
    ☐ Step 2 Produce the CBT.
☐ Activity 3 Perform online reviews.
    ☐ Step 1 Produce test CD-ROMs.
    ☐ Step 2 Use storyboards as the basis for review.
    ☐ Step 3 Record errors.
    ☐ Step 4 Correct errors.
    ☐ Step 5 Review corrections.
☐ Activity 4 Deliver and implement the course.

Developing Internet, Intranet, Web-Based, and Performance Support Learning Environments

☐ Activity 1 Determine the type of product and platform.
    ☐ Step 1 Determine whether learning is to be synchronous or asynchronous.
    ☐ Step 2 Choose the platform most appropriate for the technical specifications.
☐ Activity 2 Assemble components.
☐ Activity 3 Conduct reviews.
☐ Activity 4 Implement the site.

Developing Interactive Distance Broadcast Environments

☐ Activity 1 Develop IBT script and materials.
☐ Activity 2 Shoot and edit video.
☐ Activity 3 Rehearse the presentation.
    ☐ Step 1 Practice with technology.
    ☐ Step 2 Review clothing considerations.
    ☐ Step 3 Perform dry run of presentation.
    ☐ Step 4 Give assistants information on roles and responsibilities.
☐ Activity 4 Conduct the session.

PHASE: EVALUATION
Purpose of Evaluation

☐ Activity 1 Determine the purpose of the solution.

☐ Step 1 Determine if measurement variables are organizational.
☐ Step 2 Declare remaining measurement variables to be individual.
☐ Step 3 Determine if the solution will be used commercially.

Measures of Validity

☐ Activity 1 Determine level and type of validity required.
☐ Activity 2 Determine when to validate measurement instruments.
☐ Activity 3 Document your decisions.

Instrument Development and Measurement Plan

☐ Activity 1 Select the types of measurements.
    ☐ Step 1 Determine what to measure.
    ☐ Step 2 Differentiate norm-referenced and criterion-referenced measures.
    ☐ Step 3 Differentiate qualitative or quantitative measures.
    ☐ Step 4 Determine use of pretesting or posttesting.
☐ Activity 2 Develop the measurement instruments.
☐ Activity 3 Calculate the length of each instrument.
    ☐ Step 1 Calculate number of questions.
    ☐ Step 2 Calculate instrument completion time.
☐ Activity 4 Calculate the weight of each item.
☐ Activity 5 Decide when the instrument(s) should be administered.

Collecting and Analyzing Data

☐ Activity 1 Set up the database.
☐ Activity 2 Develop an evaluation plan.
☐ Activity 3 Collect and run the data.
☐ Activity 4 Interpret the data.
    ☐ Step 1 Analyze data according to evaluation goals.
    ☐ Step 2 Make decisions.
☐ Activity 5 Document your findings.

APPENDIX B: ASSESSMENT AND ANALYSIS

Action Verb List   228

Sample Organizational Assessment of Customer Service   239

ACTION VERB LIST

This list presents action verbs for use during objectives analysis. Once you decide on the type of learned capability for the objective, these verbs can be used to match the learned capability with the appropriate action for the objective.

Learned Capability	Verb	Definition
Discrimination	alter	to change
	arrange	to mentally order or classify in categories
	circle	to indicate understanding by encircling
	describe	to characterize qualities
	discover	to detect the true character
	divide	to separate into two or more parts or groups
	isolate	to set apart
	point	to make known or visible
	segregate	to separate or set apart from
	separate	to set apart
	set apart	to reserve to a particular use
	show	to point out a difference
	sort	to mentally group on the basis of common characteristics
	split	to mentally divide into parts or portions
	write (or) type	to put in print
Concrete concept	arrange	to place in an orderly manner; to classify into categories
	call	to make a request
	catalogue	to classify material
	combine	to synthesize in order to form a whole
	connect	to make a mental connection
	describe	to represent or give an account
	duplicate	to produce something equal to
	gather	to bring together or collect
	group	to form a complete unit from two or more parts; to classify; to mentally join or fasten together

Learned Capability	Verb	Definition
Concrete concept (cont'd.)	index	to list items in order to lead to a fact or conclusion
	inspect	to observe or take note of
	itemize	to detail or particularize
	join	to put together to form a unit
	label	to describe or designate
	link	to mentally connect
	mark	to distinguish a trait or quality
	match	to equate
	name	to label; to mention explicitly
	narrate	to relate in detail
	place	to distribute in an orderly manner
	point	to indicate; to assign
	repeat	to summarize principle points
	select	to choose by preference from a number or group
	sort	to arrange in groups according to predetermined specifications
	tell	to relate or give an account of
	unite	to coordinate or blend
Defined concept	alphabetize	to arrange alphabetically
	arrange	to put in order
	change	to modify or make fit
	evaluate	to appraise the worth of
	file	to arrange in order according to specified characteristics
	group	to combine according to certain specifications
	index	to classify according to certain characteristics
	list	to place in a specified category to inventory traits, preferences, attitudes, interests, or abilities that evaluate characteristics or skills

Learned Capability	Verb	Definition
Defined concept (cont'd.)	measure	to make determinations based on standard criteria
	order	to systematize
	organize	to form into a coherent unit
	pigeonhole	to assign to a category or classify
	rank	to make an orderly arrangement
	rate	to assign a value; to estimate
	record	to make a chronicle of
	score	to assign a value to
	sort	to distribute into groups according to specified characteristics
	survey	to examine a condition or appraise
	weigh	to consider carefully or evaluate
	write (or) type	to put in print
Rule	announce	to make known or proclaim
	categorize	to separate according to specified characteristics
	coach	to instruct beforehand
	corroborate	to support with evidence
	define	to fix or mark limits
	depict	to portray or make meaning from
	describe	to represent or give an account
	disclose	to uncover or make known; to reveal
	display	to exhibit or make evident
	divulge	to make public, unveil, or reveal
	explain	to tell, educate, or train
	expose	to portray, reveal, or draw forth
	extricate	to untangle or straighten; to pull from
	locate	to find; to place in a location or category
	organize	to arrange or form into a coherent unit; to integrate
	paint	to make a representation or give an example
	place	to situate or locate

Learned Capability	Verb	Definition
Rule (cont'd.)	present	to show
	proclaim	to give an outward indication of
	prove	to authenticate
	relate	to tell
	reveal	to divulge or make known
	separate	to break up or detach
	show	to demonstrate clearly or make clear
	summarize	to state concisely
	teach	to instruct or train
	tell	to give an account of
	tutor	to coach or guide, usually in a particular subject
	unfold	to open to view; to reveal
	verify	to establish truth, accuracy, or reality; to confirm
Problem solving	acquire	to come to have possession of
	arrive	to appear; to reach a predetermined or undetermined conclusion
	assemble	to fit together
	build	to construct or form
	collect	to bring together into one body or place
	complete	to finish
	compose	to form by putting together
	construct	to arrange parts or elements; to build
	convince	to persuade by argument; establish belief
	create	to produce or bring about by a course of action
	deduce	to derive from
	design	to conceive and plan
	develop	to expound; to make clear by degrees or in detail
	devise	to plan to obtain or bring about
	effect	to bring about, or cause to take place
	eliminate	to exclude based on specified criteria

Learned Capability	Verb	Definition
Problem solving (cont'd.)	enact	to set up, establish, or constitute
	enlist	to secure the support and aid of; employ
	equalize	to make like in quality or quantity
	erect	to put together by fitting materials; build
	establish	to set up or constitute
	excite	to stimulate to action
	exhibit	to present to view
	finish	to complete
	formulate	to form systematically
	give	to furnish what is needed
	inaugurate	to bring about the beginning
	incite	to move to action
	include	to incorporate according to specified criteria
	initiate	to cause the beginning of; set in motion
	introduce	to bring into play; institute
	invent	to originate, find, begin
	launch	to set in motion; initiate
	make	to create or cause to exist, occur, or appear
	originate	to author or cause to exist
	plot	to devise or plan to bring about
	present	to offer to view; show
	produce	to make, yield, render, or bring to bear
	show	to cause or permit to be seen; exhibit
	stimulate	to arouse to action
	supply	to furnish what is needed; give
Cognitive strategy	accede to	to give in to a request or demand
	accept	to regard as having a certain meaning; understand
	admit	to allow or permit; provide for
	advocate	to plead in favor of
	affirm	to validate
	agree	to settle on by common consent; admit; concede
	allow	to permit, admit, consent, say, or state

Learned Capability	Verb	Definition
Cognitive strategy (cont'd.)	approve	to give formal or official sanction
	arrange	to place or distribute in an orderly manner
	authorize	to establish by authority
	champion	to uphold; support
	clarify	to make understandable
	comply	to accept tacitly or overtly
	concede	to accept as true, valid or accurate
	confirm	to give approval to; ratify
	contain	to have within; hold; compromise; include
	corroborate	to support with evidence or authority; confirm
	defend	to protect or maintain a position
	define	to fix or mark limits
	describe	to represent or give an account
	embrace	to include
	employ	to make use of
	enact	to establish by legal and authoritative action
	encompass	to enclose, envelop, or include
	endorse	to express approval publicly
	endure	to remain firm or unyielding
	engage	to attract and hold
	espouse	to give verbal support
	exercise	to make effective; use; exert
	exhaust	to use up or consume entirely
	expend	to make use for a specific purpose
	explain	to make known; to make plain and understandable
	implement	to put into effect, carry out, or accomplish
	incorporate	to unite or work into something that already exists so as to form an indistinguishable whole
	incur	to contract

Learned Capability	Verb	Definition
Cognitive strategy (cont'd.)	legislate	to enact by laws
	list	to enumerate
	manipulate	to manage or use skillfully
	narrate	to tell in detail
	operate	to perform a function; to produce an appropriate effect
	permit	to make possible
	prove	to test the truth or validity of
	ratify	to formally approve and sanction; confirm
	recite	to repeat or read aloud
	recount	to relate in detail; narrate
	rehearse	to present an account of; repeat; narrate; relate or enumerate
	relate	to give an account of; tell
	report	to give an account of
	sanction	to make valid or binding
	simplify	to make more intelligible
	substantiate	to establish by proof or evidence; verify
	support	to substantiate
	uphold	to support against an opponent
	use	to put into action
	validate	to confirm, support, or corroborate
	verify	to confirm or substantiate in law by oath
Verbal information	acknowledge	to make known or take notice
	advance	to move forward
	affirm	to state positively; validate or confirm
	agree	to be consistent or in harmony with
	allege	to assert without proof
	announce	to make known publicly; proclaim
	argue	to contend or disagree in words; dispute
	articulate	to express
	assert	to state or declare positively
	attest	to establish or verify the usage of

Learned Capability	Verb	Definition
Verbal information (cont'd.)	characterize	to describe a quality
	charge	to command or instruct
	clarify	to make understandable
	comment	to explain or interpret
	communicate	to make known
	confess	to tell or make known
	confirm	to approve or ratify
	contend	to maintain or assert
	contribute	to supply information
	decipher	to convert into intelligible form
	declare	to make known formally or explicitly
	decode	to decipher
	define	to explain the meaning of
	delineate	to describe in detail
	describe	to represent or give an account of
	explain	to make known; to make understandable
	expound	to set forth; state
	express	to represent, state, depict, or delineate
	interpret	to explain or tell the meaning of
	justify	to prove to be just, right, or reasonable
	narrate	to tell in detail
	notify	to give notice
	offer	to present for acceptance
	portray	to describe in words
	profess	to declare or admit openly or freely
	propose	to set forth
	rationalize	to bring into accord with reason or cause something to seem reasonable
	recount	to relate in detail or narrate
	speak	to talk
	tell	to state or relate
	utter	to speak
	summarize	to describe briefly and succinctly
	verbalize	to express in words

Learned Capability	Verb	Definition
Verbal information (cont'd.)	vocalize	to speak
	voice	to express in words
Motor skill	attach	to fasten to
	administer	to manage or supervise the use of
	aid	to help
	arrange	to order
	bring about	to cause to take place
	bring on	to cause to appear
	carry out	to achieve
	clean	to remove or eradicate; strip or empty
	complete	to finish
	conduct	to lead
	deal	to distribute
	deliver	to convey
	demonstrate	to show
	direct	to show or point out
	discharge	to unload
	dismiss	to permit or cause to leave
	dispense	to deal out in portions
	display	to make evident
	distribute	to expend by proportion
	do	to bring to pass or carry out
	donate	to give
	dramatize	to present with heightened action
	emerge	to come forth
	empty	to remove the contents of
	endow	to bestow upon or furnish with
	equip	to furnish
	establish	to physically erect
	excrete	to sift out; discharge
	finish	to bring to an end
	force	to cause to happen
	free	to rid of restraints
	give	to yield, grant, or bestow

Learned Capability	Verb	Definition
Motor skill (cont'd.)	impersonate	to assume the character of or act like another
	implement	to carry out; accomplish
	inflict	to impose or perpetrate
	liberate	to set free
	make	to create or construct
	organize	to arrange
	pass	to move ahead of
	perform	to act out or dramatize
	play	to engage in pleasurable activity
	present	to show
	release	to let go
	serve	to wait upon
	sketch	to draw
	stage	to produce for public view
	supply	to provide
	surrender	to give over
	transfer	to convey from one person, place, or situation to another
	work	to expend energy toward labor
Attitude	adopt	to accept formally
	advocate	to plead in favor of
	champion	to support
	complete	to finish
	conclude	to decide
	cull	to select from a group
	decide	to come to a conclusion
	decree	to determine
	defend	to take a position
	determine	to settle or decide
	discover	to make known or visible
	discriminate	to distinguish
	distinguish	to perceive a difference
	divine	to discover or locate

Learned Capability	Verb	Definition
Attitude (cont'd.)	elect	to choose freely
	embrace	to take in or include as part of
	encompass	to include
	endorse	to express approval
	espouse	to support
	fancy	to like
	favor	to lean toward
	include	to take in as part of a whole
	incorporate	to unite or work into something that already exists
	judge	to form an opinion of
	opt	to choose or select
	perform	to act out or dramatize
	pick	to choose or select
	prefer	to like better; recommend
	resolve	to conclude
	select	to choose by preference
	settle	to resolve or decide
	take up	to accept or adopt

SAMPLE ORGANIZATIONAL
ASSESSMENT OF CUSTOMER SERVICE

Scenario

Your customer is a customer service industry company. It is receiving unsatisfactory reviews on customer surveys; complaints about lack of courtesy and personal care of customers are increasing by about 20 percent per year. With an improved economy, it is difficult to hire employees at the current pay grade, which has not kept up with inflation. The position is very stressful, and there is a 70 percent annual turnover rate.

The company operates in thirty-four countries around the world but is based in the United States. There is one major operations center in Europe, one in Asia, and four in the United States (New York, Chicago, Dallas, Los Angeles). Each region has its own distribution center. All ordering and shipping is automated through an integrated computer system. All customer records are computerized.

Employees speak twelve languages and have varied cultural backgrounds. Five thousand employees are engaged in direct customer service. About half of the service representatives interact with customers in person, half by phone. They may be involved in initial sale of products, answering customer questions, responding to customer inquiries, keeping customers informed of status of orders and inquiries, and handling customer complaints.

Revenue is $10 billion per year.

The company's goal is to be number one in customer service because it sees this as the competitive advantage in the market. Your customer needs a solution to help achieve its goals.

Results of Analysis

The results of the analysis are in Table B.1.

Information Structure

The information structure pertaining to the customer service scenario is shown in Table B.2.

Table B.1
Results of Sample
Organizational Assessment of Customer Service

Level	Activity	Question	Information from Analysis
Systemic	Corporate culture	Will the corporate culture support the solution you propose?	Employees believe management is too authoritarian.
		Consider: –Respect for the individual –Leadership style of management –Acceptance and use of employee ideas	Employees believe they do not have enough contact with management. Employees do not believe their ideas are valued.
	Incentives	Are users motivated by the organization to use the solution you propose?	Pay is low. There is a recognition program for good customer service.
		Consider: –Pay structure –Bonuses –Recognition –Performance reviews	There is a profit sharing program for long-term employees. Employees receive performance reviews from supervisors once a year; phone calls are randomly monitored and feedback given.
	Organizational structure	Does the organizational hierarchy support using the solution you propose?	Each supervisor has thirty or more people as direct reports.
		Consider: –Hierarchical structure of the organization –Decision-making authority	Front-line employees have no guidelines regarding their authority or responsibility to solve customer issues.

Table B.1
Results of Sample
Organizational Assessment of Customer Service, Cont'd.

Level	Activity	Question	Information from Analysis
Performance Training	Tools	Do employees have the required equipment to complete their jobs? Consider: –Computers –Software –Forms	Computer system was upgraded two years ago, is reliable and well integrated.
	Work environment	Does the environment where work is done permit people to do their jobs? Consider: –On-the-job training after or in place of formal training –Removal of old systems –Coaching –Management support for solution –Temperature –Ventilation	This is a high-stress job; phone employees handle calls at the rate of twelve per hour with an average call time of five minutes. No further training is provided after initial training other than feedback from performance reviews and monitored calls. Employees work in a modern facility with pleasant surroundings. Employees can take time out if things become too stressful.
	Processes and procedures	Do employees understand how to get their jobs done? Consider: –Are there processes and procedures in place for employees to follow?	Employees use more than one hundred processes and procedures. Processes and procedures are documented in a training manual;

Table B.1
Results of Sample
Organizational Assessment of Customer Service, Cont'd.

Level	Activity	Question	Information from Analysis
		Do employees know whom the internal and external customers and partners are?	updates are provided by placing hard copies of page changes in employee mail boxes.
		Consider: –What are the interdependencies between people and groups to complete work?	Employees know how to contact shippers if customers do not receive products.
		Are ways of getting work done effective?	
		Consider: –Are there too many steps? –Are there unnecessary steps? –Are there unnecessary delays?	
	Quality standards	Is the emphasis on quality and effectiveness rather than quantity and efficiency?	Employees are rated on number of calls completed per minute.
		Consider: –Are employees expected to perform their jobs well? –Do employees know the criteria for performance?	

Table B.1
Results of Sample
Organizational Assessment of Customer Service, Cont'd.

Level	Activity	Question	Information from Analysis
Training	Knowledge	Do employees have the information they need to get the job done?	Employees are given four weeks of classroom training to memorize the procedures. Employees also attend a four-hour course covering customer-service issues.
	Skills	Do employees have the ability to do their jobs?	Employees are given the following opportunities to learn about their jobs: Listening to taped calls Watching videos of personal interaction between employees and customers, then discussing them Watching videos of employees following procedures and then discussing correct and incorrect steps
	Attitudes	Do employees know the importance of doing their job?	Employees are provided an introduction to the company, company history, video of the company founder, videos of upper management talking about the company.

Table B.2
Information Structure for Sample
Customer Service Organizational Assessment

Type of Information	Definition	Information from Analysis
Principle	Guiding forces contained in vision and mission statements	Vision is to be number one in customer service.
Concept	Ideas and definitions	Employees represent the company through customer interface.
Process	Systematic way of doing something	Ordering merchandise by phone. Ordering merchandise at a store.
Procedure	Steps for completing a job or task contained within a process	Steps in completing an order form and submitting it.
Fact	Discrete pieces of information	Access the computer by . . . Areas on the form must be completed correctly.

SCRIPT STANDARDS

General

A script is a recipe that tells the video production crew what they need to know.

This appendix offers a template, a sort of fill-in version of such a recipe, defining the standard parts that need to be determined for the particulars of each script. We offer just enough of a sample script to illustrate commonly encountered ingredients and instructions for the video recipe.

Start with a title:

UNDERLINED AND CENTERED

Now proceed with the body of the script.

1. *Slug line.* Begin each video scene with instructions for the director, the set, and the lighting crew. The slug line indicates interior or exterior, location or set, and lighting—day or night—in ALL CAPS. Example:

FADE IN

INT. RESTAURANT—EXPO WINDOW—DAY

2. Next, indent and describe the scene, including who is in it, what the scene looks like, and what is going on. Include camera directions that are critical to the sequence in ALL CAPS. Use CAPS the first time a character is seen on screen so that the number of characters can be counted in a quick scan of the script, and so that actors can quickly locate the place where their role begins. Example:

CHRIS stands at the Expo window and looks back and forth between the ticket and the plate. He is wearing a server uniform. He pauses and the CAMERA MOVES IN for a TIGHT SHOT of the ticket in his hand.

3. Insert dialogue and sound effects. Always refer to characters in the dialogue with the same names used in the narrative. Dialogue is indented even further, single spaced, with the character in ALL CAPS. Example:

> *SFX:* Sound of a busy restaurant in the background.
>
> > CHRIS
> > Whoops. Did you forget the tomatoes?
> > KATY
> > You've got to be kidding.

Check the dialogue to make sure it is realistic by reading it out loud. Avoid tongue twisters such as "So send us seven servers singing, Sir."

4. If the scene continues onto additional pages, write CONTINUED at the top of the page. Be sure to include a slug line and narrative for each new scene.

Terminology

Here are some common terms used in a video script to provide direction.

- FAVORING or ANGLE ON: Focus on or center a person, place, or thing in a shot.
- NEW ANGLE or ANOTHER ANGLE: Shoot the same scene from another angle.
- WIDER ANGLE: Change the focus of a scene to include more of the surroundings.
- INSERT, CLOSE IN, MOVE IN, or TIGHT SHOT: Used to emphasize an object.
- POV: Shoot from a person's point of view.
- REVERSE ANGLE: Change the perspective, usually the opposite of POV.
- MATCH CUT: Matching something in the shot exactly with something in a follow-on shot.
- MOVING SHOT: Focus on the movement of an object such as a car moving through a restaurant parking lot.

- TWO SHOT or THREE SHOT: Subject of the shot is two or three people.
- SFX: Sound effects.
- TIME DISSOLVE: Show a time progression using a fade-in-and-out technique.
- FADE IN: Begin the video.
- FADE OUT: End the video.

APPENDIX D: EVALUATION

Direct-Interview Instructions	249
Focus-Group Instructions	252
Observation Instructions	254
Self-Completion Questionnaire Instructions	255
Test Specification Form: Completed Sample	256
Test Specification Form: Template	258
Evaluation Report Instructions and Sample	259
Evaluation Report Template	262
Evaluation Glossary	265

DIRECT-INTERVIEW INSTRUCTIONS

Process

During needs assessment, direct interviews are often used to gather information on job-related needs. The procedures for constructing instruments and conducting interviews listed here apply to both assessment and evaluation.

Interviews have several advantages:

1. They are a direct link to people who have unique information about the problem you are investigating.

2. They are structured by the elements of schedule and planning, contain specific rules, and have a specific focus.

3. They allow collection of immediate follow-up information.

Note that although this section focuses on structured interviews, don't overlook valuable information that might come out in informal conversation with individuals. Anything you hear or read may be useful later. Take notes, organize your information, and remember to review it as you proceed with your assessment and analysis.

Procedure

The interviewer must prepare for the interviews, maintain control during them, and analyze the results.

Preparation includes studying available handbooks and dictionaries to learn the jargon of the people you will be interviewing, developing questionnaires for interviews, and presenting the questionnaires to the customer for final approval.

Once the interview questions are approved by management, the next step is to choose who will be interviewed. Customers often want to give you a list of hand-selected interviewees. Discourage them from doing so because these people might not represent a random sample of the population being investigated, and instead might be those who are generally perceived positively by management. Request a list of all persons who are among the population to be interviewed. Randomly select names based on the total number of names on the list, divided by twice the number of interviewees desired for the sample. If you are given a list with one thousand names and wish to have a 10 percent sample (one hundred interviewees), you need to select two hundred names—every fifth name on the list—for a random sample.

Contact everyone whose name appears on this derived list and attempt to enlist their cooperation for the interview.

If the customer insists on hand selecting those persons to be interviewed, explain the drawbacks to this type of selection process but abide by the customer's wishes. However, you should note the selection process in the analysis report.

A confidentiality agreement must be made with the customer, in writing, to show to interviewees. This assures them of the anonymity of their responses and leaves them inclined to give you "just the facts." We have included an example in the Assessment and Front-End Analysis Tools section of Appendix E.

When calling potential interviewees, you need to explain what the purpose of the interview is and enlist their cooperation. During this contact, tell them

- The purpose of the interview
- Their role in the interview
- The confidential nature of the interview
- How the information collected in the interview will be used and who will receive the data
- The potential impact on the organization
- That the interview will be taped (and ask if they have any objections)

Continue calling those on the derived list until you have scheduled the desired number of interviews (in the example above, call until you have commitments from one hundred people). If only half of the people scheduled for interviews show up, randomization is still achieved.

Consider all of these factors when scheduling interviews:

- Schedule a specific time and place for the interviews.
- Leave a break of thirty to forty-five minutes between interviews so that you can go over your notes and fill in information while it is still fresh in your memory (if the interview is not taped).
- Don't schedule interviews before or during lunch, or late in the day.
- Make appointments directly with the interviewee rather than leaving messages.
- Be present when the interviewee arrives.
- Conduct the interviews in a neutral location.

Don't begin questioning immediately. Instead:

1. Put the interviewee at ease by explaining the purpose of the interview again.
2. Show him or her the confidentiality statement from management.
3. Ask if he or she objects to having the session tape recorded.

Explain that tape recording helps get all of the information exactly as the interviewee expresses it and eliminates the need to interpret notes later, which might lead to omitting important points. Very few people object to having the session tape recorded. However, if they do object, you must slow the pace of the interview to get the detailed information through note taking.

After establishing rapport with the interviewee, begin. Here are some suggestions for making the interview successful:

• Arrange the room comfortably. Sit opposite the subject so that eye contact is possible, but avoid putting a desk or table between yourself and the interviewee. A table or desk puts up a subtle barrier that might influence the interview results. Rather, put two chairs on either side of a low, small table that can hold the tape recorder. Be certain that the table has a pad or cover so that if the beverage you offer is set on the table or papers are shuffled, there will be little distortion on the recording.

• Focus your attention on the interviewee; don't let your mind wander. You might want to question the person further on a particular statement.

• Sequence questions from general to specific. Ask for concrete examples about statements made, ask key questions in more than one way, and rephrase questions that the interviewee does not understand.

• Ask for constructive criticism, but keep the criticism focused on the problem, not on specific people. Don't encourage long discourse on private gripes. Use the next question on the questionnaire to ask for a specific example to refocus the interview.

• Ask if the opinions expressed by the interviewee are held generally throughout the organization or whether they are his or hers alone.

• Admit an error if you make one.

• Avoid disagreeing with the interviewee as well as expressing sarcasm, correcting, and contradicting. If you find yourself in a personality conflict or a power struggle, simply terminate the interview.

- Don't bring the interview to a stop abruptly. Conclude the interview by summarizing the points made by the interviewees and thank him or her for the time and valuable information provided.
- Above all, when personally interviewing someone, be a good listener. Remember, you are present to learn. Don't monopolize the talk. Good interviewers have certain requisite skills; you must be able to

Initiate. Use questions or statements to get the session going and keep it moving.

Regulate. Pace the session through periodically summarizing or, if necessary, pointing out time restrictions.

Inform. Clarify a point or offer information that the interviewee might not know.

Support. Discourage the interviewee from attacking the viewpoints of the organization or other members of the group. Regularly remind each interviewee that the purpose of the session is to get his or her point of view, not a critique of the views of others.

Evaluate. Provide a reality check by reflecting back to the interviewee, in summary form, what has been stated.

Remember, one-to-one interviews are expensive in terms of time and money. A well-structured interview minimizes the use of both, while still gaining the maximum amount of information.

FOCUS-GROUP INSTRUCTIONS

Process

If job descriptions and prerequisite skills are not accurate, focus groups should be convened. A focus group consists of current job holders and their supervisors, convened separately or jointly, to determine the KSA required of the job holder.

Procedure

Many of the skills and suggestions that we list in the direct-interview section apply to working with focus groups.

Focus groups are normally organized by the customer, who supplies both the space and the people to attend the sessions. This is usually done at the customer's discretion, but you might want to request that the customer keep the following considerations in mind when selecting focus-group members:

- Members should be those who are considered exemplary workers by their supervisors and peers.

- If the position is being newly created, supervisors who will work with the job holder should participate in writing the job description to delineate which KSA are needed to successfully fill the position.

- Members should be assigned rather than volunteer. This helps ensure that you get a representative sample of the members of the work group.

Regarding this last point, realize that volunteers sometimes have their own agenda precipitating their desire to participate. Even if a personal agenda generates a lot of debate in the focus group, it's counterproductive to the purpose of the session. If the volunteer is highly verbal, has a strong personality, and is very persuasive, he or she might actually dominate the session, which skews the results of the focus group and misrepresents the description of the job holder.

There are several techniques for conducting focus groups, some requiring consensus and some not. What has worked best for us is using a technique that does not require consensus of the group members. This seems to foster discussion and information exchange better than those techniques that do seek consensus. Do, however, prioritize the items in order of relative importance across the entire group. We use a rank-and-order (RAO) technique. With large numbers of items (duties and the like), the first RAO pass might be conducted to arrange the items in some logical structure.

Follow these steps in conducting an RAO procedure:

1. Use a random list of items to be considered by each focus-group member.

2. Request that each member individually prioritize items in the list in order of importance from 1 to n (however many items are in the list).

3. As a group, chart the prioritized number of each item on the list.

4. Sum the group's responses and divide by the number of responses.

5. Rewrite the list in the prioritized format, with numbers closer to 1 at the top, indicating that they are considered more important. (Stop here if this is the second round.)

6. Look for large gaps in the totals that might be natural breaking points for items having high, medium, and low priority.

7. Discuss the highest-priority items with the focus-group members, and elicit expression of why each item has high priority. Ask those members who did

not give a high rank to an item to voice their reasons for the lower priority. Their reasoning might be due to misinterpretation of the statement, or the reasoning might change the opinions of others in the group regarding the relative position of an item. Follow the same procedure for medium-priority and low-priority items. Eliminate any items that the group agrees do not belong.

8. Repeat steps 2 through 5.

The resulting list should be the group's estimate of the requirements for successful performance on the job.

OBSERVATION INSTRUCTIONS
Process
Sometimes it is not convenient or practical to collect job-related information in a situation that is removed from where the work is actually carried out. In these cases, a simple yet effective method of collecting information is observation.

Procedure
You should select a subject-matter expert (SME) to observe and write down everything that the person performing the job does. Observations may be made in person, or the individual can be videotaped for later observation. Your job is to develop a behavioral description that consists of the inputs from the observed behavior, actions, and outputs. When collecting information through observations, these steps are helpful:

1. Identify team members (preferably SMEs) to conduct the observations.
2. Develop observation checklists using the recommended techniques of validity in Chapter Twenty-Seven.
3. Train observers using the recommended inter-rater agreement techniques of reliability in Chapter Twenty-Seven.
4. Identify exemplary (successful) job performers to be observed.
5. Request permission for observation, and give dates and times.
6. Ensure that your observations are as unobtrusive as possible.
7. Mark the checklist, but take a minimum of additional notes. Excessive note taking (if the observer can be seen by the subject observed) can make the subject nervous or self-conscious, which might affect performance.

8. Share observations with the job performers (if appropriate). The fact that information will or will not be shared and the frequency of the sharing should be clarified with the subject prior to the first observation. It would be inappropriate to share information if the subject were going to be observed on subsequent occasions. Sharing information would tip off the subject about what you are observing, which would influence his or her behavior.

SELF-COMPLETION QUESTIONNAIRE INSTRUCTIONS
Process

Questionnaires are an effective way to gain information from a large sample population. Questions must be constructed properly, because poorly constructed questionnaires allow each respondent wide interpretation and therefore yield little valuable information. Constructing useful questionnaires and establishing content validity for questionnaires is covered in Part Four, which is on evaluation.

Questionnaires are limited in that they only elicit the information requested. This limitation can be exacerbated if a questionnaire is returned anonymously. In this case, there is no way to contact the respondent if the answers deviate greatly from the responses of the rest of the sample. It would be valuable to know what unique experiences caused the anonymous respondent to answer as he or she did. One way around this particular difficulty is to send out confidential (instead of anonymous) questionnaires.

Of course, those questionnaires that are intended to be anonymous should remain anonymous. Because this makes it impossible for you to follow up with your respondents, you should carefully consider your options before selecting anonymity.

Procedure

Once you construct the questions you want to ask, have them approved by management or a customer designee with authority to make decisions on the project. There may be some information that you are not allowed to ask because of labor union agreements or governmental regulations. Give your customer a written plan that details how you will conduct the interviews, select participants, assure anonymity, and analyze and report the information.

If questionnaires are sent out confidentially, a number code system should be developed that can trace a specific questionnaire to a list of names to help retrieve this potentially valuable information. Make sure, however, that you inform all respondents that the confidentiality of their responses is strictly observed.

Self-completion questionnaires (surveys) have a couple of peculiar characteristics. First, they may or may not have a high return rate. Send a questionnaire to everyone on the list of names that you have. It is not likely that you will be sending to a large group of anonymous persons (as with general surveys through the mail), but if you are, be certain to keep a record of how many surveys you send out and how many are received.

Second, you need a much larger sample size, at least 80 percent. The reason you need such a high return rate is to ensure randomization. The problem with surveys is that you cannot control who returns them. People who return questionnaires may come from a certain group that is not typical of the general population you are seeking information from or on. They might be more civic minded, might have stronger or lesser feelings on the topic than the general population, or (for any of myriad uncontrollable variables) might be otherwise unrepresentative of the group you are surveying. To ensure reliable results, then, if you are given a list of five hundred names, you need four hundred returned surveys to achieve an 80 percent response rate to optimize the chances that the responses are typical (equivalent to a random sample) of the general population you are surveying.

Consider these points in preparing your questionnaires:

- Ask as few questions as necessary to optimize chances of a high return rate (long surveys are less likely to be returned than short ones).
- Determine the type of response mode to use. Do you want respondents to used open-ended questions, forced choice (yes or no), or scaled scores?
- If you are using scaled scores, do you want to permit a neutral response (use a scale from, say, 1 to 5 or 1 to 7, where 3 and 4 respectively are scores midway on the scale) or not (a scale from, say, 1 to 4 or 1 to 8)?

TEST SPECIFICATION FORM: COMPLETED SAMPLE

This section of Appendix D and the next give you a template to follow in designing a test specification form. First, we illustrate how to use the form by presenting a completed sample. A blank template follows this sample form, in the next section of this Appendix.

The test item is valid:
Yes ☐   No ☐
(check one)

Terminal Objective

Objective 1.3.3
Given a diagram of the electronic instrument, the student will discriminate each functional part by circling each major part with complete accuracy.

Test Item

Circle the part of the diagram that shows the oscillator.

Item Attributes

The stem of the sample item written to measure achievement in this objective should

1. State what the student is to do to demonstrate the knowledge.

2. State what part the student must circle to demonstrate the knowledge.

The responses for the sample item should:
Provide a diagram with the part to be circled readily visible, and clearly able to be circled without interference or confusion with other parts.

Comments:
_____
_____
_____
_____
_____
_____

Signature _____

TEST SPECIFICATION FORM: TEMPLATE ⊙

Please fill in this form using the accompanying completed sample.

Terminal Objective

_____
_____

Test Item

_____
_____

Item Attributes

The stem of the sample item written to measure achievement in this objective should:

_____
_____

The responses for the sample item should:

_____
_____

Comments:

_____
_____
_____
_____

Signature _____

EVALUATION REPORT INSTRUCTIONS AND SAMPLE

The following is a section-by-section description of how to prepare an evaluation report. Following the explanation is a blank template.

Section I: Executive Summary

This section is a brief overview of the entire report, explaining the basis for the evaluation and the significant conclusions and recommendations.

The following is an executive summary of the main findings of the evaluation:

- (Finding number one)
- (Finding number two)
- (And so on)

Section II: Background Information

Introduction. This section includes a general description of the evaluation and the reasons for conducting the evaluation. It is divided into these components:

- Background
- Purpose
- Roles and responsibilities
- Data-collection methods

Background. The [development activity, course, job aid, mentoring exercise, and so forth] was developed by [name and organization] for the [job family or customer] organization. At the customer's request, an [evaluation level] evaluation was performed.

Purpose. The purpose of the evaluation is to [state the purpose of the evaluation level, what you are measuring, and why]. For this project, the evaluation focused on the following questions:

- (Question number one)
- (Question number two)
- (And so on)

Roles and responsibilities. The following table lists the roles and responsibilities of the cross-functional team that participates in evaluating and reporting the results of the project.

Name	Role	Responsibility
	Sponsor	
	Customer	
	Project manager	
	Project team members	
	Subject-matter experts	
	Evaluation specialist	
	Other stakeholders	

Data-collection methods. The evaluation is performed by the project manager and project team members, with the support of the evaluation specialist.
[Describe the role of the evaluation specialist.]

Here is a description of the methods and instruments used to collect the evaluation data.
[Briefly describe the process or tools used to collect, analyze, report, and preserve the evaluation data.]

Section III: Findings

This section summarizes the findings of the evaluation. It is divided into two subsections.

Introduction. _____
_____
_____

Findings. _____

_____

_____

Section IV: Conclusions and Recommendations

This section reports the interpretation of the findings.

Conclusions. _____

_____

_____

Recommendations. _____

_____

_____

Section V: Appendices

This section contains the supporting data from the analysis.

EVALUATION REPORT TEMPLATE ⊙

Section I: Executive Summary

_____
_____
_____
_____
_____
_____
_____

Section II: Background Information

Introduction. _____
_____
_____
_____
_____
_____
_____

Background. _____
_____
_____
_____
_____

Purpose. _____
_____
_____
_____
_____
_____
_____

Roles and responsibilities. _____

_____

_____

Name	Role	Responsibility

Data-collection methods. _____

_____

_____

_____

_____

_____

_____

_____

_____

Section III: Findings

Introduction. _____

_____

_____

_____

_____

_____

_____

Findings. _____

_____

_____

_____

_____

_____

Section IV: Conclusions and Recommendations

Conclusions. _____

_____

_____

_____

_____

_____

Recommendations. _____

_____

_____

_____

_____

_____

Section V: Appendices

_____

_____

_____

_____

_____

_____

EVALUATION GLOSSARY

Concurrent validity Measure of the ability of test items to discriminate between master and novice students. Establishes the superiority of a course in instructional delivery if the course is to be used for certification of competence.

Content validity Measures that use subject-matter experts to review materials to qualitatively validate that there is congruence between the objectives, content, and test items.

Correlation Establishes the relationship among variables regarding whether one variable is dependent on the others for the dependent variable to be true. The result is a number between −1.0 and +1.0. The closer the correlation to +1.0, the higher the positive correlation and the stronger the relationship between the variables.

Criterion-referenced (CR) Measure of performance against a predetermined standard that allows comparison of individuals against that standard.

Difficulty index A rating score by subject-matter experts that identifies how high a degree of expertise is necessary for a student to correctly answer a particular test item.

Distractor analysis Analysis of the possible answers (distractors) on a test to determine if there are certain questions that students are consistently answering incorrectly, and if a certain one of the incorrect distractors is being chosen more frequently than any other.

Face validity Qualitative measures requiring SME validation that course content approximates that of any other course on the subject. It is the minimum validity required to establish that a course teaches what it intends to teach or test. It cannot be the only form of validity used if reliability measures are also required.

Formative evaluation All activities occurring from the time a customer begins contract negotiations until the final product is delivered, ensuring the instructional soundness, quality, and suitability of a training program.

Instrument validity Developing and evaluating test instruments to ensure that the informational data collected is unbiased and replicable during subsequent administrations of the instrument.

Item analysis A test that compares two independent variables to determine if individual test items are valid. Item analysis requires that various statistical tests be applied, depending on the information required.

Mastery curve A distribution curve with a mean near the upper or lower end of the distribution indicating that the majority of the group whose characteristic is shown on the curve has or does not have the attribute. Also known as a leptokurtic curve.

Normal curve A distribution curve that graphically shows the results from a group where each is compared on the same variable; the average (mean) score is near the middle of the distribution with equal intervals (standard deviations) both above and below the mean.

Normal distribution A distribution where the mean is near the middle of the distribution with equal interval (standard deviations) both above and below the mean.

Norm-referenced (NR) Measures of knowledge or performance against a level that is derived from the average of all scores from a large sample of student performance on the test. This measure allows comparison of students who should possess the same characteristic.

Predictive validity Measures of the ability of a test to predict future success in a skill area as a result of success on a test. Establishes superiority of a course in instructional delivery if the course is used for certification of competence.

Qualitative Subjective measure of instructional soundness. May be open to a variety of interpretation.

Quantitative Measure of instructional soundness that employs data and the results of statistical analyses.

Reliability A quantifiable value that describes the degree to which a training program produces consistent results in what it teaches.

Simulations CBT-generated scenarios that contain a high degree of realism. High-level simulations duplicate complex situations where the student actually experiences and reacts to the scenario; midlevel and low-level simulations demonstrate a situation but have students input answers to questions after the scenario.

Skewed distribution A distribution on a curve where scores are clustered around the top or bottom end of the curve with unequal intervals (standard deviations) on either side of the mean.

Standard deviation A measure of the extent to which individual scores differ from the mean.

Standardized Repeated administrations of a test to refine it to the point where it is both valid and reliable (students score consistently on the test), resulting in a normal distribution curve from any group of people who possess or should possess a certain characteristic.

Summative evaluation Testing the effectiveness of the training program along predetermined criteria.

Test-item validity Statistical analysis of test items to ensure they measure the skills learned to a sufficiently high degree to discriminate between high-achieving and low-achieving students.

Validation Procedures employed to ensure the instructional effectiveness of a training program.

Validity A quantifiable value that describes the degree to which a training program teaches what it claims to teach.

APPENDIX E:
TOOLS

Assessment and Front-End Analysis Tools   269

Design Tools   288

Development and Implementation Tools   303

Evaluation Tools   327

ASSESSMENT AND FRONT-END ANALYSIS TOOLS

Confidentiality Agreement	270
Needs Assessment Report Form	271
The Fog Index	272
Technology Assessment Tool	273
Job or Task Breakdown Tool	275
Task Inventory Tool	276
Media Selection Form	277
Extant Data Analysis Tool	283
Extant Data Materials Review	284
Roles and Responsibilities Matrix	286
Analysis Report Tool	287

Confidentiality Agreement ⊙

[on customer letterhead]

I [name of customer], as a representative of [customer's organizational name], agree that the information gained from the participation of company employees in the [insert project name] training project will remain strictly confidential and that individual performance or scores need not be divulged to the company. Individual information will be known solely to [your name or organization], whose representatives will guard that data with strictest security.

Only cumulative results of assessment studies or analyses will be divulged to the company in the form of a final report.

[signature of customer]
[date]

[your signature and organization]
[date]

Needs Assessment Report Form

1. Statement of the problem:

   _____

   _____

   _____

   _____

2. Data collection methods used:

   _____

   _____

   _____

   _____

3. Data analysis:

   A. Job goals:

   _____

   _____

   _____

   _____

   B. Potential solutions:

   _____

   _____

   _____

   _____

4. Recommendations:

   _____

   _____

   _____

   _____

The Fog Index

The Fog Index, developed by Robert Gunning (1968), expresses readability as the number of years of schooling required to read a text with ease. Follow these steps to check readability:

1. Select a representative sample of text.

2. Count the number of words the sample contains.

3. Count the number of sentences it contains.

4. Count the number of difficult words in the sample. Difficult words are those defined as having three or more syllables or ending with -*ly* or -*ing*. However, note the following exceptions:

   Capitalized words should not be counted as difficult.

   Combinations of short, easy words such as *vice-chairman, teacher-coach,* and so on, count as one word.

   Verb forms made into three syllables by adding -*ed* or -*es,* such as *adjusted, inserted, assesses,* should not be counted as difficult.

5. Determine the average sentence length. Divide the number of words by the number of sentences.

6. Determine the percentage of difficult words in the sample:

$$\text{percentage of difficult words} = \frac{\text{number of difficult words}}{\text{number of words}} \times 100$$

7. Use this formula to calculate the Fog Index:

$$\text{Fog Index} = (\text{average sentence length [step 5]} + \text{percentage of difficult words [step 6]}) \times 0.4$$

8. Repeat the process by selecting a couple of other samples. Use random samples from the beginning, middle, and end of the material, or from different authors in the same piece, to see if there is uniformity.

Note: You may average the samples to determine an average readability level. It is permissible to have an escalating reading level from the beginning of a work to the end, as long as the level does not increase by more than about a year and a half.

Technology Assessment Tool ⊙

1. List the types of technology available. For example, if employees have access to e-mail, put a check mark in the "Availability" column next to "E-mail."

2. Document the capability of each technology. For example, if e-mail is used for communication, put a check mark in the "Capability" column.

3. Document the number and percentage of employees who have access to the technology.

Technology Use	Examples of Technology Type	Availability	Capability	Access (percent)
Communication	Phone conferencing			
	E-mail			
	Chat rooms			
	Newsgroups			
	List servers			
Reference materials, online help	Websites			
	Work process and procedures			
	Databases			
	Phone lists			
	Course catalogues			
	Scheduling and appointments			
	Course notes			
	Instructor's notes			
	Abstracts			
	Technical manuals			
	Videos			
	Graphics and photos			

(cont'd.)

Technology Use	Examples of Technology Type	Availability	Capability	Access (percent)
Testing and assessment: online testing, tracking, reporting	Electronic self-assessment databases			
	Electronic tracking databases			
	Electronic reporting databases			
	Security (access, authentication, confidentiality)			
Distribution: sending throughout the organization	CD-ROM			
	Diskette			
	Video			
	Audio			
	Downloading			
Delivery: receiving throughout the organization	Dedicated audio and video servers			
	Multimedia computers			
	Video teleconferencing			
Design and development expertise: infrastructure design, development, maintenance, resources (include anticipated upgrades)	Video production			
	Audio production			
	Graphics production			
	Online help and reference system production			
	CBT authoring			
	Web authoring			
	Testing databases			
	Statistical programs			

Job or Task Breakdown Tool

Here are definitions important to the use of this tool:

Job: A collection of duties and tasks constituting the total job responsibilities.

Duties: Major subdivisions of the job responsibilities performed by an individual. Duties are usually stated as a general area of responsibility, with action words ending in *-ing.*

Task: A specific function or meaningful unit of work that must be performed to accomplish the overall duty. This task achieves a single objective or output.

KSA: Knowledge, skills, and attitudes.

Instructions

1. List each job you identified during job or task analysis in the order each must be performed.

2. List each duty associated with the identified job.

3. List each task associated with each duty in the order each must be performed.

4. Eliminate any jobs and associated duties and tasks you deselect during critical incident analysis.

5. Write the number of the objective associated with the job duty or task after you complete objective analysis.

	Objective Number[a]
Job	Course objective
Duty 1.0	Terminal objective
Task 1.1	Lesson objective
Task 1.2	Lesson objective
Duty 2.0	Terminal objective
Task 2.1	Lesson objective
Task 2.2	Lesson objective

[a]To be completed after objectives are written.

Task Inventory Tool

Here are useful criteria for selecting tasks for training:

Frequency. How often is the task performed?

Number performing. What percentage of the target population is performing or will perform this task?

Difficulty. How difficult is it to learn this task on the job?

Criticality. How important is this task to job performance?

- Noncritical (N): this code identifies tasks not critical to the job.
- Important (I): this code identifies tasks that are important in some situations but not critical.
- Critical (C): this code identifies tasks that must be performed correctly because of their impact on the job.

Time. How long does it normally take to perform this task?

Impact. What is the probability that this task will be performed poorly or incorrectly if the performer is not formally trained?

Delay. How long after training will it be before the trainee encounters this task?

Immediacy or assistance. Must this task be performed on the spot without any assistance?

Media Selection Form 🔘

Instructions

Complete the rating scale as follows:

1. Consider each factor on the rating scale in regard to its importance to the situation you are analyzing, using the key provided.

2. Once you have rated each factor, make a list of those media that are associated with each factor rated 4 or 5. Count the number of occurrences of each medium on the list.

3. List each suggested medium associated with a 1 or 2. Count the number of occurrences of each medium on this second list.

4. Determine which suggested media appear most often with highly rated items.

5. Determine which suggested media appear most often with low-rated items.

6. Eliminate from consideration any media that appear on the second list more often than they appear on the first list.

7. The media that remain are most probably the ones to use in this situation.

Rating Scale

5 = Very important consideration
4 = Important consideration
3 = Neutral consideration
2 = Unimportant consideration
1 = Not a consideration at all

Instructional and Student Factors	Considerations	Suggested Media
1 2 3 4 5		
Content requires interactivity (computer).	Does the content involve computer software, simulation, or practice? Computer-based training simulations can facilitate learning.	Computer-based Web-based

Instructional and Student Factors	Considerations	Suggested Media
1 2 3 4 5 Incidental learning may occur.	Do you need to control for incidental learning?	Instructor-led Distance broadcast Video teleconference
1 2 3 4 5 Collaborative learning is desired.	Do group learning experiences, including opportunities to build relationships or share information, need to occur?	Instructor-led Distance broadcast Video teleconference Web-based
1 2 3 4 5 Content requires interactivity (human).	Will participants gain interpersonal and communication skills from immediate feedback from an observer about their performance? To what extent does the learner need to use or demonstrate interpersonal or communication skills, such as presentation, teamwork, leadership, or facilitation?	Instructor-led Distance broadcast Video teleconference
1 2 3 4 5 Audience requires motivation.	How motivated are the learners? (*Note:* self-instruction or distance education requires higher intrinsic motivation for successful learning.)	Instructor-led Videotapes Web-based Distance broadcast
1 2 3 4 5 Audience requires convenience, training at or near the work site.	Is time away from work not possible because of work schedules, project requirements, variable shifts, or time-sensitive performance? Are participants dispersed and require decentralized training?	Computer-based Video teleconference Performance support Web-based Audio teleconference

Instructional and Student Factors	Considerations	Suggested Media
1 2 3 4 5 Audience has limited access to required technology.	What technology is available? Is there a barrier to technology?	Audio teleconference Instructor-led Computer-based
1 2 3 4 5 Audience has limited access to required expertise.	Is there limited expertise that must be leveraged across the organization?	Computer-based Distance broadcast Videotapes Web-based Video teleconference
1 2 3 4 5 Students are resistant to new media.	How receptive is the audience to using a new medium? To what extent does attitude toward lecture style help or hinder learning? (*Note:* learners often enjoy instructor-led training because it allows them to be with other learners. Although they enjoy it, they may learn less. They may fear technology, may have experienced only mainframe CBT, or may not want to spend more time at a computer screen. Take that fear into account and move toward a technology solution whenever possible.)	Instructor-led
1 2 3 4 5 There is an immediate need for application of expertise to	How critical are the knowledge or skills to performance of job-related tasks?	Performance support

Instructional and Student Factors	Considerations	Suggested Media
the job. Employees must review the information frequently.		
1 2 3 4 5 Wide variation in entry-level background knowledge	How wide is the gap in entry-level knowledge? (*Note:* CBT can branch users to various levels of training.)	Computer-based

Cost Factors	Considerations	Suggested Media
1 2 3 4 5 Content has a short shelf life or is changing rapidly.	Is the content stable? Is it still under construction or development? How does the stability of the content affect frequency of revision? How difficult is it to make revisions using this medium? Revisions to audiotapes, videotapes, and CBT are time consuming and expensive.	Video teleconference Audio teleconference Web-based Distance broadcast Instructor-led
1 2 3 4 5 Global audience with multiple cultures or languages	Will reading, hearing, or understanding English be difficult for audience members? Are there varying levels and types of information need? (*Note:* a variety of nonprint media can deliver text, graphics, sound, and motion while allowing for learner control.)	Computer-based Distance broadcast Videotapes
1 2 3 4 5 Materials must be available in a variety of formats.	Do you need to repurpose materials? (*Note:* video can be reused in a variety of media. Electronic media can be delivered in a variety of formats.)	Videotapes Distance broadcast Video teleconference Computer-based

Cost Factors	Considerations	Suggested Media
1 2 3 4 5 Fewer than two hundred people per year need training or support.	Is the target audience small in number? What is the projected size of the audience over the expected shelf life of the training?	Performance support Instructor-led Video teleconference Audio teleconference
1 2 3 4 5 More than two hundred people per year need training or support.	Is the target audience large in number?	Distance broadcast Computer-based Videotapes Audiotapes
1 2 3 4 5 Must train large numbers of employees quickly.	How quickly must the intervention be developed? How much time is available to build, buy, or revise products? For shortened time frames, consider buying or revising existing products.	Video teleconference Audio teleconference Audiotapes Instructor-led Distance broadcast
1 2 3 4 5 Compressed training time is required.	Is it important to reduce the time participants spend in training? (*Note:* CBT has typical training compression ratios of 50–70 percent.)	Performance support Computer-based Distance broadcast Self-paced workbook
1 2 3 4 5 Must keep development cost per hour of instruction low.	What is the cost per learner for developing or acquiring this medium?	Video teleconference Audio teleconference Distance broadcast
1 2 3 4 5 Must keep travel expenses low.	Is travel a barrier due to budgets, distance, and business considerations? How can travel expenses be reduced?	Performance support Computer-based Web-based

Cost Factors	Considerations	Suggested Media
(cont'd.)		Distance broadcast
		Self-paced workbook
		Computer teleconference
		Audio teleconference
		Videotapes
		Audiotapes
1 2 3 4 5		
Must keep implementation, delivery, maintenance costs low.		Performance support
		Computer-based
		Video teleconference
		Audio teleconference
		Self-paced workbook
1 2 3 4 5		
Testing, evaluation, or tracking of student performance is necessary.	Can the assessment can be self-scored? Is certification necessary? (*Note:* assessment of interpersonal and communication skills requires observation. Some observation requires a trained expert.)	Self-paced workbook
		Computer-based
		Distance broadcast
		Instructor-led
1 2 3 4 5		
Tracking course completion is necessary.	Can media assess course completion?	Computer-based
		Distance broadcast
		Instructor-led

Extant Data Analysis Tool

1. Source of information:

   _____

   _____

   _____

   _____

   _____

   _____

2. Type of information:

   Article _____

   Book _____

   Course material _____

   User manual _____

   Other _____

3. Summary of information found:

   _____

   _____

   _____

   _____

   _____

   _____

   _____

4. Probability of use:

Very low	Low	Moderate	High	Very high
1	2	3	4	5

Extant Data Materials Review ◕

This form presents questions to aid in evaluating training materials. The purpose of the review is to determine if the program content, materials, and learning activities produce the intended business outcome.

List course materials for review:

1. _____

2. _____

3. _____

After your review, check your response to each of the following questions. Add any comments that you feel might be helpful in making a buy-or-build decision. For example, note items of confusion, parts of the course you feel are helpful, questions, or comments about missing or ambiguous content.

Program content

	Yes	No
• Were the primary course objectives accomplished?	☐	☐
• Did you feel the content was clearly presented?	☐	☐
• Was the content relevant to job tasks?	☐	☐
• Was the course content at an appropriate level of difficulty?	☐	☐

Comments:

_____

_____

_____

_____

Learning activities

	Yes	No
• Did the course presentation or exercises meet the primary course objectives?	☐	☐
• Were the media and visuals effective in aiding understanding of the content?	☐	☐

Comments:

_____

_____

_____

_____

Program materials

	Yes	No
• Were the course materials of high quality?	☐	☐
• Did you feel the materials would be easy to use?	☐	☐
• Will the hardware, software, and scheduling required by the course fit your organization's requirements?	☐	☐
• Is the cost appropriate to the project budget?	☐	☐
• Does the program take too much time?	☐	☐

Comments:

_____

_____

_____

_____

Overall reaction

	Yes	No
• Overall, are you satisfied that the course meets your requirements?	☐	☐

Comments:

_____

_____

_____

_____

Reviewer: _____ Date: _____

Roles and Responsibilities Matrix ⊙

Role	Task	Person	Code[a]	Date Due

[a]Codes:

R = Responsible—person has responsibility and authority for completing the task.

C = Consulted—person must be consulted because of their responsibility for a task that impacts this task.

I = Informed—person has no direct input into the task; must be informed after the fact of actions taken and decisions made.

Analysis Report Tool

In this tool, a description of the section content or the source follows each heading, in parentheses.

1. Introduction (brief description of the purpose of this report)

   _____
   _____
   _____
   _____

2. Description of the job analyzed (audience analysis)

   _____
   _____
   _____
   _____

3. Description of the job performer's needs (instructional analysis)

   _____
   _____
   _____
   _____

4. Description of tasks (task analysis)

   _____
   _____
   _____
   _____

5. Attachments:
   - Rejected tasks (critical incident analysis)
   - Objectives list (objectives analysis)
   - Description of delivery media (media analysis)
   - Available materials (extant data analysis)
   - Technical capabilities (technology analysis)
   - Environmental and situational conditions (situational analysis)
   - Cost versus benefit of the solution (cost-benefit analysis)

DESIGN TOOLS

Editorial Review Instructions 289

Editorial Review Form 290

Instructional Review Instructions 291

Instructional Review Form 293

Standards Review Instructions 295

Standards Review Form 296

Technical Review Instructions 298

Technical Review Form 299

Management Review Instructions 301

Management Review Form 302

Editorial Review Instructions ☺

An editorial review ensures that incorrect grammar, spelling errors, and poor writing do not detract from the effectiveness of the multimedia. The thoroughness of an editorial review enhances the quality and consistency of the product.

Review Procedures. The CDS is the guide to conducting review of these elements:

- Correct spelling
- Correct punctuation
- Correct grammar
    Person and number
    Tense
    Noun-verb agreement
- Voice

Recording Errors. Record each error you observe.

Editorial Review Form 💿

Project: _____ Lesson: _____ Date: _____

Reviewer's signature _____

Be sure that you identify any unique specifications in the space provided. On completing your review, check each item to certify that your review included the item.

☐ **1.** Correct spelling: list any words that have unique form.

_____
_____
_____
_____
_____

☐ **2.** Correct punctuation: list any special punctuation specifications.

_____
_____
_____
_____
_____

☐ **3.** Correct grammar: list any specifications regarding

Person _____

Number _____

Tense _____

Noun-verb agreement _____

☐ **4.** Voice: list any unique specifications.

_____
_____
_____
_____
_____

Instructional Review Instructions 💿

An instructional review ensures consistency of instructional strategy and design within and among lessons. The thoroughness of an instructional review enhances student learning through improved overall instructional integrity.

Review Procedures. The CDS is the guide to reviewing these elements:

1. Readability. Written at the appropriate grade level for the audience, as determined from audience analysis.

2. Register. Register is the level of formality or informality of the writing style used in the CBT lessons (that is, formal being highly stylized and impersonal, consultative being instructive and semiformal, and informal being casual). Very formal register is third person singular or plural, using passive voice to a great extent. Casual register uses very familiar language, first person singular or plural.

3. Vocabulary. Use terms and vocabulary appropriate for the audience, as determined from audience analysis.

4. Transitions. The lesson ties previous topics to current topics.

5. Conceptual framework. The lesson contains these events of learning:
   - Introduces the lesson in a way that relates the current lesson to previous and subsequent lessons
   - States the objectives
   - Presents the content by introducing an overview of each topic, breaks the topic into component parts, and ties all components together in a summary
   - Checks often for understanding and extends feedback to learners
   - Provides guided practice where applicable
   - Allows independent practice

6. Congruence. There is a natural flow of information and relation between these elements:
   - Objectives
   - Topics associated with the objectives
   - Topics summarized
   - Topics reviewed
   - Topics tested

7. Question format and feedback. Questions are in the correct format and refer to the correct objective:
   - Quiz questions refer to a lesson objective
   - Test questions refer to a terminal objective
8. Mapping strategies.   All strategies are correctly mapped:
   - Processes
   - Procedures
   - Concepts
   - Principles
   - Facts
   - Systems

Recording Errors. Record each error you observed.

Instructional Review Form 💿

Project: _____ Lesson: _____ Date: _____

Reviewer's signature _____

Be sure that you identify any unique specifications. Check off each item to certify that your review included it.

☐ **1.** Readability (expected level _____)

_____

_____

_____

_____

_____

_____

_____

_____

☐ **2.** Register

_____

_____

_____

_____

_____

_____

_____

☐ **3.** Vocabulary

_____

_____

_____

_____

_____

_____

_____

☐ **4.** Transitions

_____
_____
_____
_____
_____

☐ **5.** Conceptual framework

_____
_____
_____
_____
_____

☐ **6.** Congruence

_____
_____
_____
_____
_____

☐ **7.** Question format and feedback

_____
_____
_____
_____
_____

☐ **8.** All instruction correctly mapped

_____
_____
_____
_____
_____

Standards Review Instructions

A standards review ensures formatting consistency. The thoroughness of a standards review enhances overall quality of the product by fostering a consistent learning environment.

Review Procedures. The CDS is the guide to conducting review of the following elements:

- Standard pages or screen elements (all standard areas of the pages or screen are in the correct position, using correct fonts)
- Standard pages or screen specifications (all standardized pages are used in the correct place and are identical in appearance)
- Standard page colors (all color standards are adhered to)
- Text (standards for text size are adhered to)
- Standard reference terminology (all informational areas of the document are completed)

Recording Errors. Record each error you observe.

Standards Review Form 💿

Project: _____ Lesson: _____ Date: _____

Reviewer's signature _____

Be sure that you identify any unique specifications. Check off each item to certify that your review included:

☐ **1.** Standard page elements (all standard areas of the page are in the correct position and use the correct fonts)

_____
_____
_____
_____
_____
_____
_____
_____
_____
_____
_____
_____

☐ **2.** Standard page specifications (all standardized pages are used in the correct place and are identical in appearance)

_____
_____
_____
_____
_____
_____
_____
_____
_____
_____
_____
_____

☐ **3.** Standard page colors (all color standards are adhered to)

_____

_____

_____

_____

_____

_____

_____

_____

_____

☐ **4.** Text (standards for text size are adhered to)

_____

_____

_____

_____

_____

_____

_____

_____

_____

☐ **5.** Standard reference terminology (all informational areas of the document are completed)

_____

_____

_____

_____

_____

_____

_____

_____

_____

Technical Review Instructions 💿

A technical review ensures that correct information is presented in course materials. The thoroughness of a technical review enhances student learning through improved accuracy and relevance in the courseware.

Review Procedures. The CDS is the guide to reviewing these elements:

- All topics required to thoroughly teach the lesson are covered.
- All topics are covered in the order they should be presented.
- All topics are covered to the proper depth considering the audience.
- All technical terms are accurate and complete as listed in the documentation for the course.
- All technical terms are spelled correctly.

Recording Errors. Record each error you observe.

Technical Review Form 💿

Project: _____ Lesson: _____ Date: _____

Reviewer's signature _____

Be sure that you identify any unique specifications. On completing your review, check each item below to certify that your review included all items.

☐ **1.** All topics required to thoroughly teach the lesson are covered.

_____

_____

_____

_____

_____

_____

_____

_____

_____

_____

_____

_____

_____

☐ **2.** All topics are covered in the order they are listed.

_____

_____

_____

_____

_____

_____

_____

_____

_____

_____

_____

_____

_____

☐ **3.** All topics are covered to the proper depth considering the audience.

_____

_____

_____

_____

_____

_____

_____

_____

☐ **4.** All technical terms are accurate and complete as listed in the documentation for the course.

_____

_____

_____

_____

_____

_____

_____

_____

☐ **5.** All technical terms are spelled and explained correctly.

_____

_____

_____

_____

_____

_____

_____

_____

Management Review Instructions

A management review ensures adherence to goals and to any contractual requirements of the project. Adherence to management requirements affirms sponsorship and ensures that the project meets the needs that management staff perceive.

Review Procedure. Use the contract prepared for the project as a guide to conducting the review of these elements of the materials:

- The materials conform to the requirements outlined in the contract.
- The materials meet management goals and objectives.
- The materials conform to the requirements of the system specification.

Recording Errors. Record each error you observe.

Management Review Form 💿

Project: _____ Lesson: _____ Date: _____
Reviewer's signature _____

Check off each item to certify that your review included it.

☐ **1.** The materials conform to the requirements outlined in the contract.

_____
_____
_____
_____
_____
_____
_____

☐ **2.** The materials meet management goals and objectives.

_____
_____
_____
_____
_____
_____
_____

☐ **3.** The materials conform to the requirements of the system specification.

_____
_____
_____
_____
_____
_____
_____

DEVELOPMENT AND IMPLEMENTATION TOOLS

Shot List   304

Audio Log   306

Audio Revision and Error List   308

Graphics Log   310

Reshoot Request   312

Rerecord Request   313

Graphics Rework Request   314

Functional Review Instructions   315

Functional Review Checklist   317

Online Review Form   319

Review Scheduling Form   320

Storyboard Template Explanation   322

Storyboard Template   323

Web-Based Storyboard Template Explanation   324

Web-Based Storyboard Template   325

Lesson Plan Template for Web-Based or
  Interactive Distance Broadcast   326

Shot List 💿

Here is a key to understanding and using the Shot List:

Shot number	Sequentially numbered shots for the lesson
Storyboard number	The storyboard sequence where the shot is used
Brief description	Two or three words that convey the essence of the shot
Filename	To be filled in with the filename (using proper naming conventions) from the CDS
Used or reshot	This is filled in after the disk is logged in postproduction to determine if the shot was used; if reshot, the number of the new shot should be indicated here.
Disposition	Choices are (1) *buy* (this is the shot chosen for use in the course), (2) *OK* (this shot can be used if there are no better ones available, and (3) *NG* ("no good"; this shot has errors and cannot be used).
Logged	The camera has a running meter that can tell where a shot began (in) and where it ended (out).

Note that sections 1 through 4 are filled out during the shoot by the director's assistant. Sections 5 through 7 are completed during review and logging in postproduction.

SHOT LIST

Lesson Number _____
Unit Number _____
Lesson Title _____

Director _____
Logged by _____
Date Logged _____

1. Shot Number	2. Storyboard Number	3. Brief Description	4. Filename	5. Used or Reshot (Reshoot No.)	6. Disposition	7. Logged	
						In	Out

Audio Log

Here is a key to understanding and using the Audio Log:

Segment number	Sequentially numbered audio segments for the lesson
Storyboard number	The storyboard sequence where the audio is used
Brief description	Two or three words that convey the essence of the audio
Filename	To be filled in with the filename (using proper naming conventions) from the CDS
Used or rerecorded	This is filled in after the disk is logged in postproduction to determine if the audio was used; if rerecorded, the number of the audio file should be indicated here.
Disposition	Choices are (1) *buy* (this is the bite chosen for use in the course), (2) *OK* (this bite can be used if there are no better ones available), and (3) *NG* ("no good"; this bite has errors and cannot be used).
Logged	The audio recorder in the sound studio has a running meter that can tell where a segment began (in) and where it ended (out).

Note that sections 1 through 4 are filled in during recording by the sound expert. Sections 5 through 7 are completed during review and logging in post-production.

AUDIO LOG

Lesson Number _____
Unit Number _____
Lesson Title _____

Sound Director _____
Logged by _____
Date Logged _____

1. Segment Number	2. Storyboard Number	3. Brief Description	4. Filename	5. Used or Rerecorded (Rerecord No.)	6. Disposition	7. Logged In	7. Logged Out

Audio Revision and Error List ⬤

Here is a key to understanding and using the Audio Revision and Error List:

Segment number   Running list of the number of segments where errors
                      occur

Storyboard number   The storyboard identification page where the error was
                      found so that the narrator can quickly identify where the
                      segment is that needs to be rerecorded

Brief description   A description of the error identified

Filename   The audio filename

Old segment   The beginning (in) and end (out) of the old audio
                      segment

New segment   The beginning (in) and end (out) of the new audio
                      segment

Date logged   Date the new audio segment was logged onto the master
                      audio file list

AUDIO REVISION AND ERROR LIST

Record any errors in the audio on this sheet and return it to the audio production team for rerecording.

Requester _____

Lesson Number _____

Unit Number _____

Lesson Title _____

Date _____

Sound Director _____

Logged by _____

Segment Number	Storyboard Number	Description of Error	Filename	Old Segment		New Segment		Date Logged
				In	Out	In	Out	

Important note: Be sure to record the audio file changes on the audio log.

Graphics Log ◉

Here is a key to understanding and using the Graphics Log:

Graphic number   Sequentially numbered graphic segments for the lesson

Storyboard number   The storyboard sequence where the graphic is used

Filename   To be filled in with the filename (using proper naming conventions) from the CDS; each frame in an animation sequence must be logged separately but identified as part of a sequence (animation sequences are specified by the CDS but are normally identified with an alphanumeric extension on the filename).

Brief description   Two or three words that describe the graphic

GRAPHICS LOG

Lesson Number _____
Unit Number _____
Lesson Title _____

Graphic Artist _____
Logged by _____
Date Logged _____

Graphic Number	Storyboard Number	Filename	Brief Description of Graphic

Reshoot Request ⊙

Requester: _____   Date of request: _____
Unit number: _____   Old shot counter in: _____
Lesson number: _____   Old shot counter out: _____
Lesson title: _____

1. Reason for request

   _____
   _____
   _____

2. Explanation of new shot needed

   _____
   _____
   _____

Completion

Date: _____   By whom: _____

New shot in: _____   New shot out: _____

Logged date: _____

Rerecord Request 💿

Requester: _____   Date of request: _____

Unit number: _____   Old segment counter in: _____

Lesson number: _____   Old segment counter out: _____

Lesson title: _____

1. Reason for request

   _____
   _____
   _____

2. New audio (written here as needed)

   _____
   _____
   _____

Completion

Date: _____   By whom: _____

New shot in: _____   New shot out:_____

Logged date: _____

Graphics Rework Request

Requester: _____   Date of request: _____

Unit number: _____   File number: _____

Lesson number: _____   Filename: _____

Lesson title: _____

1. Reason for request

   _____

   _____

   _____

2. Explanation of new graphic

   _____

   _____

   _____

Completion

Date: _____   By whom: _____

Graphic file number: _____   Filename: _____

Logged date: _____

Functional Review Instructions

A functional review of online lessons and courses ensures that the material is free of bugs and is of professional quality. The CDS is the guide to establishing the standards for courseware design and development. The functional review determines if all of the functional aspects of the software execute correctly.

Review Procedures. Obtain a current copy of the lesson storyboards from configuration control (CC). This should be the copy that the author used to execute the lesson. Follow the storyboard closely to be sure that the functions to be checked operate in the manner in which they were designed. Record any errors on the Functional Review Checklist.

Functions. Function buttons must appear on each screen and work the way they are intended. Press each function button on each screen. Functions to check include

- Pause/resume
- Back
- Replay
- Continue
- Hypertext
- Navigation screens
    - Main menu
    - Log on
    - Title (splash) screens
    - Exit screens
- Help
- Quit
- Others (list specifics)

Programming. Movement between screens must be free of glitches, blips, and fatal errors (those that make the program crash).

Test the branching on each screen having options for where the programming is to go depending on inputs. You need to test every branching option by backing up to the original screen each time and choosing each possible option. If backing up is not possible from some screens, mark those areas; you'll have to go through the lesson again. Here are typical examples of branching that must be checked:

- Embedded questions
- Quiz questions of a multiple-choice format; alternate between giving the correct answer first and the incorrect answer first
- Expanded information based on incorrect student input (these may be the most difficult to back out of, because the lesson typically moves back to the main lesson after the information is delivered)

Test the lesson using the longest path first (go through the lesson answering every question incorrectly and taking all remediation available); then review the lesson again taking the shortest path (go though the lesson answering everything correctly).

Keep a tally of the number of questions answered correctly and incorrectly on questions that are to be tracked and scored. Check this against the score given by the computer at the end of the lesson.

Be sure that the branching between lessons also functions smoothly, as intended.

Recording Errors. Record errors on the Functional Review Checklist. Use the color assigned to record errors. Also, be very specific in your description of the error.

Functional Review Checklist ⊙

Lesson number: _____   Date of review: _____

Lesson name: _____

Reviewer signature: _____

Functions

☐ Pause/resume

☐ Back

☐ Replay

☐ Continue

☐ Hypertext

☐ Navigation screens

   ☐ Main menu

   ☐ Log on

   ☐ Title (splash) screens

   ☐ Exit screens

☐ Help

☐ Quit

☐ Others (list specifics here)

   _____

   _____

   _____

   _____

Comments:

_____

_____

_____

_____

_____

_____

_____

Programming

☐ Movement between screens free of jumps, blips, and so on

☐ Branching working correctly

    ☐ Embedded questions

    ☐ Quiz questions

    ☐ Expanded information

☐ Branching between lessons

☐ Quizzes and other recorded items scored correctly

Comments:

_____

_____

_____

_____

_____

_____

_____

_____

Online Review Form 💿

This form is used by subject-matter experts (SMEs), educational soundness reviewers, and pilot audience members for a postproduction quality review of a course. These persons generally will fill out hard copies of these forms as they go through the lessons.

Lesson number: _____

Lesson name: _____   Storyboard number: _____

Reviewer's name: _____   Date completed: _____

Editorial. Comments and notes (validated ☐):

_____

_____

_____

Reviewer's name: _____   Date completed: _____

Standards. Comments and notes (validated ☐):

_____

_____

_____

Reviewer's name: _____   Date completed: _____

Functional. Comments and notes (validated ☐):

_____

_____

_____

Changes validated by: _____   Date completed: _____

Review Scheduling Form

The author fills out one of these forms for each lesson as it becomes available. Each reviewer places his or her name in the first column, then schedules the day and time for reviewing the lesson by initialing the appropriate box on the schedule. The reviewer's initials or signature go in the last column to indicate completion of the review.

REVIEW SCHEDULING FORM

Lesson Number and Title						
Reviewer's Name	Time	M	T	W	R	F	Review Completed
	8:00						
	9:00						
	10:00						
	11:00						
	12:00						
	1:00						
	2:00						
	3:00						
	4:00						
	5:00						

Storyboard Template Explanation ⊙

Here are explanatory notes for the storyboard template that follows:

Lesson title: title of the lesson as it appears on the screen in the header.

Sequence number: a running, sequential page number, such as "1 of 14."

Section: "Introduction," "Objectives," "Lesson," "Summary," "Quiz," "Test," etc.

Visual: describes what the student sees on the screen. This can be described in words or with an illustration. Text and questions should be in the identical or corresponding font and size that students see on the screen. The box at the bottom of the storyboard is to hand-draw any graphic for the screen.

Audio: Any narration, sound effects, or music that the student hears. This can be listed here or referenced to audio scripts. (Write the scripts that accompany the screen on separate pages, using the Script Standards found in Appendix C, and attach these pages immediately behind the storyboard screen.)

Programming: any special instructions to the author (including correct answers to question screens). Most standard programming instructions are in the CDS and do not need to be mentioned in this section.

Branching: explains where the program goes after a student input. This is expressed using the storyboard number. There are three alternatives for branching:

1. Previous: where the program goes if the student goes backward one screen.

2. Next: where the program goes if the student uses Continue to move forward.

3. Variable: a series of if-then statements for variable branching. For example, if the student answers a question correctly, the program moves ahead one screen; if incorrectly, the branching moves to some other screen in the program.

Type: what kind of screen is shown: either graphic (text is normally considered graphic depending on how it is created on the screen) or video.

The remaining parts of the template are completed by the storyboard author.

Video in: identifies the video file number where video begins on the videodisc or CD-ROM.

Video out: identifies the video file number where the video ends.

Files required: files from other sources (graphic, audio, CD-ROM). *Graphic* includes diagrams, drawings, and so on, that reside on the computer software disk but must be called up. *Audio* means logged audio file numbers that must be called up from the audio source.

Storyboard Template 💿

Lesson title: _____   Sequence number: _____

Section: _____

Visual:

_____

_____

_____

_____

_____

Audio:

_____

_____

_____

_____

_____

Programming:

_____

_____

_____

_____

_____

Branching: previous _____ next _____ variable _____

Type: _____

Video in: _____ Video out: _____

Files required: graphic _____ audio _____

```
Graphic




```

Web-Based Storyboard Template Explanation ⊙

Here are explanatory notes for the web-based storyboard template that follows.

Screen number	The sequence of the web page in the course
Screen description	The visual look of the screen; placement of components of the screen such as text, video, buttons
Video	Explanation of the video for the screen
Audio	Explanation of what the audio for the screen describes; use the script format found in Appendix C to create an audio script
Text	The print that appears on the screen
Branching	The screen number, URL, or other location the screen moves to if any of the buttons on the screen are pressed

Web-Based Storyboard Template ⬤

Screen Number	Screen Description	Video	Audio	Text	Branching

Lesson Plan Template for Web-Based or Interactive Distance Broadcast ⊙

Time (in minutes): _____

Objectives (learning outcomes):

_____

_____

Materials required (hardware, software, print materials, handouts):

_____

_____

Preparation (instructor activities before the lesson):

_____

_____

Items to Include	Supporting Information
What to ask (Questions)	_____
What to explain (Instructor script)	_____
What to demonstrate	_____
	_____
Overhead number	_____
	_____
Video segments	_____
	_____
Exhibit name and number	_____
Page number of references and text materials	_____
References to handouts	_____
	_____
Instructor's self-written notes	_____
	_____

EVALUATION TOOLS

Matching Question Checklist   328

Multiple-Choice Question Checklist   329

True-False Question Checklist   330

Completion (Short-Answer) Question Checklist   331

Simulation, Role Play, Performance Test Checklist   332

Essay Question Checklist   333

Test Completion Checklist   334

Tool for Constructing a Bank of Parallel Test Items   335

Matching Question Checklist

☐ Have more possible answers than terms.

☐ Give instructions that are clear and concise in specifying how to match the stimulus to the response.

☐ Co-locate stimuli and responses on one page.

☐ Identify stimuli by arabic numbers (1, 2, and so on).

☐ Have only one correct response for each stimulus.

☐ Identify responses with uppercase letters, commencing with A.

☐ Make the ratio of responses to stimuli three-to-two.

☐ Place the stimulus column left of center, with the response column right of center.

☐ Keep the lists of terms homogeneous.

☐ Title the lists of terms and answers. (No, don't use the titles "Terms" and "Answers." Devise a short title that conveys the concept.)

☐ Form answers using longer phrases than the terms.

☐ Explain the basis for matching stimuli with responses and whether options can be used more than once.

Multiple-Choice Question Checklist 💿

☐ The question stem should contain a verb.

☐ The stem must clearly formulate a problem.

☐ The stem should contain no extraneous information.

☐ Make sure interrogatory stems are complete sentences punctuated with a question mark.

☐ There should clearly be one correct answer.

☐ Specify in the instructions if the student is to select the one correct answer, or the most correct answer.

☐ Don't use the words or phrases *always, never, simply, all of the above,* or *none of the above;* don't use a combination of correct answers ("both A and C").

☐ Have three to five choices per question; using one correct answer and two to four distractors deters guessing. However, if the question does not lend itself to this many distractors, do not add obviously incorrect answers just to equalize all questions.

☐ Increase the similarity between the possible answers to enhance the difficulty of the questions.

☐ Precede choices with an uppercase letter (A, B, C, D, E).

☐ Incorporate video or graphics (for example, selecting three or four parts that are outlined on a video still).

True-False Question Checklist

☐ Make items definitely true or definitely false without requiring additional qualifiers.

☐ Use short stems that eliminate unnecessary material.

☐ Keep statements approximately the same length whether they are true or false.

☐ If opinion is used, attribute it to some source.

☐ Do not make all questions true or all questions false.

☐ Avoid using double negative statements.

☐ Randomize the questions after they are all written so that no pattern can develop, whether intentionally or unintentionally.

☐ The method of responding should be explained at the beginning of the test.

Completion (Short-Answer) Question Checklist 💿

☐ Make wording clear and comprehensive enough to allow a student who is knowledgeable to answer correctly.

☐ Make the missing segment of the incomplete statement important, such as a key element of equipment.

☐ Don't omit so many words as to make the statement unclear.

☐ Specify the degree of accuracy of the answer, and the units for computational problems.

☐ Put the completion portion for incomplete statements at the end.

☐ Use direct questions to test for comprehension of technical terms or knowledge of definitions.

☐ Omit only consecutive words.

Simulation, Role Play, Performance Test Checklist ⊙

☐ Be sure to show positive examples of the situation you are depicting, and have students evaluate it. (Show negative examples only of common errors.)

☐ Use for guided practice.

☐ Analyze the work requirements by observing persons who are highly skilled at performing the task.

☐ Allow practice of the task before evaluation.

☐ Evaluate only the end result, unless there is a specified or preferred way to achieve the end result.

☐ Share the performance criteria with the student.

Essay Question Checklist

☐ Clearly fix the level at which you want to write the question, and use appropriate verbs (*compare, contrast, give reasons for, give original examples for*) in the question.

☐ Explain the overall task in the information that precedes the test.

☐ Be certain that the task involved in completing the question is clearly defined.

☐ Ask for supporting evidence for the student's answer.

☐ To ensure test validity, have all students complete the same questions rather than allowing them to choose from a number of questions.

☐ When you write essay questions for any type of delivery (paper-and-pencil, CBT, and so on), you must develop the scoring criteria ahead of time. What key words are you looking for in students' answers?

☐ Establish a reasonable length for completing a question, in number of pages or in length of time students should spend composing the response. (Restricting time and space allotted to writing essays actually requires students to better compose and express their thoughts.)

☐ Use essay questions for those objectives that cannot be measured adequately through objective questions.

Test Completion Checklist 💿

If all of the items listed can be checked, the test meets the criteria for a well-designed measure.

- ☐ The item measures the behavior required by the objective.
- ☐ The item is clearly supported by text.
- ☐ The stem of the item states a central problem.
- ☐ The item can stand alone out of context.
- ☐ The item is clear, brief, and direct.
- ☐ All distractors are plausible.
- ☐ All distractors are approximately the same length.
- ☐ Options are parallel in category, structure, and length.
- ☐ Options are grammatically consistent with the stem.
- ☐ There is clearly only one correct answer.
- ☐ The choice of words does not give away the correct answer.
- ☐ Key words (*most, best, least, not*) are italicized.
- ☐ The item is free of poor logic.
- ☐ The item is free of sexism.
- ☐ Superfluous words, phrases, or sentences that do not contribute to the meaning of the item are absent.
- ☐ Such words as *always* or *never* are omitted from options, because they are generally false and put the student on alert.
- ☐ Omit ambiguous words that can trick, mislead, or confuse a student into choosing the incorrect answer.
- ☐ No verbatim excerpts from text are included. Items should be paraphrased or presented in the working language of the job so that the students grasp the principle rather than merely recognize a word or phrase.
- ☐ Never use catch-all options (*all of the above, none of the above*).
- ☐ Negative items (*not, except*) are used sparingly.
- ☐ Never use options such as *both a and c* and *neither a nor b*.

Tool for Constructing a Bank of Parallel Test Items ⊙

This form is used in developing equivalent tests that can be administered before and after a lesson or section of a course.

Test developer should complete the following before giving the tests to the judges:

1. Place the number of each terminal objective in the first column.
2. Enter the weight of the objective in column 2.
3. Enter the test item numbers for the test items that match the terminal objective in columns 3, 4, 5, and 6.
4. Provide this form, the terminal objectives, and the test items to the test judge.

Test judges should:

1. Write "Yes" in the last column (Same Level of Difficulty) if all test items for a terminal objective are at the same level of difficulty. Write "No" if any items are not at the same level, and circle the test item number in column(s) 3, 4, 5, or 6.
2. If all test items are at the same level of difficulty, sign the bottom of the form and return it to the test developer.
3. If all test items are not at the same level of difficulty, return the form to the test developer unsigned.
4. The test developer will modify the questions and return them to you for pre-judging.

Project: _____   Date: _____

Evaluator: _____

Terminal Objective Number	Weight	Test Item Number	Test Item Number	Test Item Number	Test Item Number	Same Level of Difficulty

I concur that the test items matched above are parallel in form.

Signature: _____

REFERENCES

Abernathy, D. "Authoring Software: It's the Write Stuff." *Training & Development*, 1999, *53*(4), 54–55.

Alley, G., and Deschler, D. *Teaching the Learning Disabled Adolescent: Strategies and Methods.* Denver: Love, 1979.

Andersen Consulting. *The Future of Airline Training.* Chicago: Arthur Andersen, 1994.

Barron, T. "IDL Options Broaden for Training Providers." *Technical Training*, 1999, *10*(3), 18–21.

Borg, W., and Gall, M. *Educational Research: An Introduction.* (4th ed.). White Plains, N.Y.: Longman, 1996.

Briggs, L. (ed.). *Instructional Design.* Englewood Cliffs, N.J.: Educational Technology Publications, 1977.

Campbell, D. T., and Stanley, J. C. *Experimental and Quasi-Experimental Designs for Research.* Boston: Houghton Mifflin, 1963.

Dick, W., and Carey, L. *The Systematic Design of Instruction.* (3rd ed.). Glenview, Ill.: Scott, Foresman; Little, Brown, 1990.

Equal Employment Opportunity Commission, U.S. Civil Service Commission. U.S. Department of Labor and U.S. Department of Justice. *Uniform Guidelines on Employee Selection Procedures.* Washington, D.C.: Federal Register, 1978.

Gagné, R. *Conditions of Learning and Theory of Instruction.* Austin, Tex.: Holt, Rinehart and Winston, 1985.

Gagné, R., Briggs, L., and Wager, W. *Principles of Instructional Design.* (3rd ed.). Austin, Tex.: Holt, Rinehart and Winston, 1988.

Gilbert, T. *Human Competence: Engineering Worthy Performance.* Washington, D.C.: International Society for Performance Improvement, 1996.

Greer, M. *Project Management Partner: A Step-by-Step Guide to Project Management.* San Francisco: Human Resources Press, 1996.

Gunning, R. *The Technique of Clear Writing.* New York: McGraw-Hill, 1968.

Hale, J. (1998). *The Performance Consultant's Fieldbook: Tools and Techniques for Improving Organizations and People.* San Francisco: Jossey-Bass/Pfeiffer, 1998.

Hammer, M., and Champy, J. *Reengineering the Corporation: A Manifesto for Business Revolution.* New York: HarperBusiness, 1994.

Hammond, S. *The Thin Book of Appreciative Inquiry.* Dallas: Kodiak Consulting, 1996.

Harrow, A. (ed.). *A Taxonomy of the Psychomotor Domain.* New York: David McKay, 1972.

Kirkpatrick, D. L. *Evaluating Training Programs: The Four Levels.* San Francisco: Berrett-Koehler, 1994.

Knowles, M. *The Adult Learner: A Neglected Species.* Houston: Gulf, 1990.

Krathwohl, E. (ed.). *A Taxonomy of Educational Objectives: Handbook II, Affective Domain.* New York: David McKay, 1964.

Lee, W. "Bridging the Gap with IVD." *Training & Development Journal,* 1990, *44*(3), 63–65.

Lee, W. W., Mamone, R. A., and Roadman, K. *The Computer Based Training Handbook: Assessment, Design, Development, Evaluation.* Englewood Cliffs, N.J.: Educational Technology Publishing, 1995.

Lee, W., and Owens, D. "Linking Business Needs to Training Objectives and Delivery Media." *Performance Improvement,* 1999, *38*(8), 30–36.

Lee, W., and Roadman, K. "Linking Needs Assessment to Performance Based Evaluation." *Performance & Instruction,* 1991, *30*(6), 4–6.

Lee, W., Roadman, K., and Mamone, R. *Training Evaluation Model.* 1990. Library of Congress copyright number TXu 455-182.

Mager, R. *Preparing Instructional Objectives.* Palo Alto, Calif.: Fearson, 1962.

Martuza, V. *Applying Norm-Referenced and Criterion-Referenced Measurement in Education.* Boston: Allyn & Bacon, 1977.

Noonan, J. "How To Escape Corporate America's Basement." *Training,* 1993, *30*(12), 39–42.

Shrock, S., and Coscarelli, W. *Criterion-Referenced Test Development: Technical and Legal Guidelines for Corporate Training.* Reading, Mass.: Addison-Wesley, 1996.

Skinner, B. *The Technology of Teaching.* New York: Appleton, 1968.

ABOUT THE AUTHORS

William W. (Bill) Lee is director of performance technology at American Airlines for the AMR Training Group in Fort Worth, Texas. He holds a bachelor of science degree in education from Clarion University of Pennsylvania (1968) and both a master of education degree in education (1972) and a Ph.D. in curriculum and instruction from Penn State University (1986). He has held positions in higher education at Penn State University, Clarion University of Pennsylvania, and Virginia State University. He is presently on the faculty of the University of Oklahoma and University of Texas at Arlington. He received the 1997 Distinguished Achievement award from the Dallas Chapter of the American Society of Training and Development (ASTD). He has been on the board of directors for the Dallas chapter of ASTD, with which he has been affiliated since 1991. He is a contributing editor for *Performance Improvement Quarterly Journal* of the International Society for Performance Improvement (ISPI).

Lee is the lead author of *The Computer Based Training Handbook: Assessment, Design, Development, and Evaluation* with coauthor Robert A. Mamone. He has published many articles in professional journals and has made presentations at numerous national and international conferences. He holds a number of copyrights on training materials and instruments. His areas of specialization include testing and measurement, performance analysis, media analysis, business process improvement, and organizational and professional development.

Diana L. Owens is a consultant and principle owner of Training Consulting Softek, an independently owned company specializing in multimedia training development, in Garland, Texas. She has worked for EDS, American Airlines, TGI Friday's, and other corporations. She holds a bachelor's degree in art education from the University of Nevada at Reno (1982) and a master of science degree in human resource training and development from Chapman College (1986). She is an active member of the Dallas chapter of the American Society of Training and Development. She is the author of several articles published in professional journals and has made presentations at national and international conferences. Her areas of specialization are leadership development, performance analysis, project management, and multimedia interface design.

INDEX

A

Abernathy, D., 143

Access: to multimedia PCs, 23, 24; to web, 165

Action verbs, 43, 228–238

Active X, 166

Actors, 151

Additional development, 84

Administrative resources, media selection and, 59

Adult learning: components of, 30; theory of, 29–30. *See also* Learning approaches; Learning domains; Learning principles; Learning strategies

Advance organizer, 124

Affective domain of learning, 38, 39; levels in, 39; in performance objectives, 44, 45

Allen Interactions, 143, 157

Alley, G., 40

American Society for Training and Development (ASTD), 70

Analysis. *See* Data collection and analysis; Front-end analysis; Needs assessment

Analysis of variance (ANOVA), 210

Analysis Report Tool, 15, 78, 287

Analysts: performance, in instructional design project team, 96; requirements for, in rapid analysis method, 71, 72, 74

Animation: design and use of, 111; in web-based training, 176

Animators, 152

Anticipated or future need, 6, 75

Application developer, 98

Application-system prototype, early, 140

Appreciative-inquiry technique, 9

Approval, of CDS document, 85

Art director, 147, 152

Artificially imposed restrictions, 208, 211

Assessment. *See* Evaluation; Front-end analysis; Needs assessment; Organizational assessment; Testing and assessment

Assessment technology. *See* Testing and assessment

Assignments, student, 117

AST Computer's Ovation Program interface design, 105–106, 108

Asymetrix, 143–144

Asynchronous training, 168, 171–174

Attain Enterprise Learning System, 143, 172, 175–177

Attitudes: change of, 51; defined, 29; identification of, in organizational assessment, 73; verbs for, 237–238. *See also* Knowledge, skills, and attitudes

Audience analysis, 17–19, 36; activity one (analyze demographics and special requirements), 18; activity two (determine attitudes toward content), 18; activity three (analyze language skills), 18–19; activity four (document results),

19; advice for, 19; procedure for, 18–19; process of, 18; purpose and uses of, 14, 17, 116; in rapid analysis method, 76; step/action checklist for, 220

Audience characteristics, 17–19, 36; content structure and, 115–116; interface design and, 103. *See also* Audience analysis

Audio cards, 175

Audio Log, 151, 306–307

Audio preproduction, 147

Audio producer/specialist, 94, 147

Audio production, 151, 180

Audio Record, Stop, and Play buttons, 105

Audio Repeat button, 104

Audio Rerecord Form, 151, 313

Audio rerecording, 151, 162–163, 313

Audio Revision and Error List, 151, 308–309

Audio scripts, 90, 147, 245–247

Audio specialist, 147

Audio standards, 110, 147, 245–247

Audio teleconferencing, 51, 52

Audiotape: advantages and limitations of, 57; defined, 49; indications for, 50, 51

Auditory approach to learning, 101

Auditory discrimination level, 40

Author: configuration control responsibilities of, 133, 134, 135; roles and responsibilities of, 94; roles and responsibilities of, in postproduction stage, 153, 154; roles and responsibilities of, in preproduction stage, 145; roles and responsibilities of, in production stage, 149

Authoring software/authorware. *See* Software

Authorware 5.0, 143, 157, 172, 175–177

Automated response, 118

B

Back button, 104

Backtracking, 212

Backups, 162

Bandwidth, 166–167, 174

Barron, T., 182

Basic movements, 40

Benchmarking, of project time, 91–92

Biserial measures, 199–200, 210

Bookmarking, 104

Borg, W., 190

Brainstorming: for design ideas, 129; as instructional strategy, 122

Branching, 167, 171–172, 176; student-controlled, 109–110

Briggs, L., 5–6, 37–38, 44

Bulletin board service (BBS), 66

Buy-in, 85–86, 142

C

Camera operators, 151

Campbell, D. T., 190, 215

Capability verbs, 43, 44

Capturing, 118

CD-ROM production, 161

CDS document. *See* Course Design Specification

Champy, J., 77

Change and complexity, systemic assessment and, 72, 79

Characterization level, 39

Chat rooms: analysis of technology for, 21; in web-based training, 56–57, 168

Check disk or files, 150

Chi-square measure, 210

Clip art photo, customized, 147, 148

Clothing, distance-broadcast instructor, 182

Cognitive domain of learning, 37–38; levels in, 38; media selection for, 50–51, 52; performance objectives in, 43, 44, 45; terminal objectives in, 45–46

Cognitive strategy level, 38; verbs for, 232–234

Color usage, 111

Communication technology: analysis of, 21; types of, 21

Comparative need, 6, 75

Completion (Short-Answer) Question Checklist, 331

Compression/decompression rates, 174

Computer-based learning environments. *See* Computer-based training

Computer-based training (CBT): activity one (create storyboards), 159–160; activity two (create and assemble media elements), 160–161; activity three (perform online reviews), 161–162; advantages and limitations of, 54; advice for, 162–163; authoring software for, 143–144; described, 49, 156; development methodology for, 145–155; development of, 156–163; development platforms for, 157–158; future of, 163; procedure for developing, 159–162; process of developing, 158; sample interface designs for, 105–108, 109; software templates for, 156–157; step/action checklist for, 224–225

Computer-managed instruction (CMI), templates for, 142

Concept mapping, 127–128

Concrete concept level, 38, 45; verbs for, 228–229

Concurrent development, 84

Concurrent validity, 197, 265

Confidentiality, 22–23, 28

Confidentiality agreement, 7, 250, 270

Configuration control (CC) plan, 131–135; activity one (establish a configuration control plan), 131–132; defined, 86, 131; importance of, 132; procedure for, 131–132; process of, 131; sample, 132–135; step/action checklist for, 224

Configuration control gatekeeper (CCG), 132, 133–135

Congruence, 190, 291

Consensus, 253

Consistency: in development, 142; in interface design, 103, 111–112; recording and, 110; team approach for, 86. *See also* Standards

Construct validity, 198

Content: categorization of, 126; determining audience attitudes toward, 18; as event of instruction, 124; content structure and, 113; verbal, 114–115. *See also* Content structure

Content structure, 113–130; activity one (break content into units), 126; activity two (map information), 126–127; advice for, 128–129; defined, 86; elements of, 126–127; instructional delivery strategies for, 120–123; principles of learning and, 113–120; procedure for, 126–128; process of, 123–125; step/action checklist for, 224

Content validity, 191, 195, 197, 199–200, 265

Control groups, 215

Control over learning, 30

Coordinated abilities, 40

Corporate culture, organizational assessment and, 73

Corrective feedback, 119, 124

Correlation, 199–200, 203–204, 210, 265

Coscarelli, W., 190

Cost analysis, 68–70; activity one (conduct a CBA), 69; activity two (determine the ROI), 69; activity three (document the results), 69; advice for, 69–70; for interactive distance broadcast, 182–183; procedure for, 69; process of, 68; purpose and benefits of, 14, 68; step/action checklist for, 223; for web-based training, 174–175

Cost saving: in audio or video production, 150, 162–163; rapid prototyping for, 142–143; in technology analysis, 25; of Web-based training, 173. *See also* Time saving

Cost-benefit analysis (CBA), 14, 68–70; formula for, 69; resources for conducting, 70

Costs: of audio studios, 162; benchmarking, 91–92; factors of, associated with media, 59; of interactive distance broadcast, 182–183; of maintenance, 61; of off-the-shelf versus new materials, 66, 67; per training unit, 60; of web-based training, 174–175

Costume designers, 151

Course Design Specification (CDS): activities for creating, 84; approval of, 85; elements of, 85, 86; implementation of, 139–143; implementation of, in computer-based training, 159, 160–161; phased approach and, 84–85; team involvement in, 85–87, 99; template for, 87. *See also* Design

Course flowchart, 127–130

Course management system, 156, 157

Course maps, 127–130, 145, 173

Creative director, 94–95

Credits screen, 141

Criterion-referenced (CR) measurement, 190, 199, 203, 208, 209, 210, 265

Critical-incident analysis, 34–36; activity one (determine the tasks), 35; activity two (categorize the tasks), 35; activity three (rule out certain tasks), 36; activity four (document the results), 36; advice for, 36; defined, 34; process of, 34–35; purpose of, 14; in rapid analysis method, 76; step/action checklist for, 221

Cues, for transitions, 117

Cultural differences: analysis of, 18–19; interface design and, 103

Current state/desired state analysis. *See* Needs assessment

Customer service organizational assessment, 239–244

Cyltek Systems, 157–158

D

Data capture, 215, 216

Data collection and analysis, 214–217; activity one (set up database), 215; activity two (develop evaluation plan), 215–216; activity three (collect and run the data), 216; activity four (interpret the data), 216; advice for, 216; procedure for, 215–216; process of, 214; step/action plan for, 226

Database: for evaluation, 215; for needs assessment and front-end analysis data, 10

Data-collection methods, instruments, and tools, 269–287; for critical-incident analysis, 34; for evaluation, 201–217; for extant-data analysis, 66, 67; instructions for using, 249–261; for

needs assessment, 7, 10–12; for situational analysis, 28; validity establishment and, 199–200

Decision-making structure, organizational assessment and, 73

Decisions based on evaluation, 216, 217

Deductive learning strategy, 120; instructional delivery strategies and, 121–123

Defined concept level, 38; verbs for, 229–230

Deliverables, list of, for schedule, 89

Delivery: analysis of environment for, 27; analysis of media for, 48–64; analysis of technology for, 23; factors of, associated with media, 60; instructional strategies for, 120–123

Demographics, audience, 18

Demonstration: as instructional strategy, 121; as learning principle, 115

Deschler, D., 40

Design, 81–135; configuration control in, 131–135; importance of, 83; learning approaches and, 101–102; of content structure, 113–130; media specification for, 100–112; outcome of, 84; overview of, 83–87; project schedule for, 85, 88–92; project team for, 85–87, 93–99; senses and, 101–102; step/action checklist for, 223–224; tools for, 288–302; for web-based training, 167–170. *See also* Course Design Specification; Media specification

Designer's Edge, 143–144

Design-time prototyping, 140

Desired state/current state analysis. *See* Needs assessment

Detailed lesson flowchart, 128, 130

Development and implementation, 137–184; advice for, 143–144; of computer-based learning environments, 156–163; elements of, 140–141; of interactive distance broadcast environments, 178–184; of Internet/intranet/web-based learning environments, 164–177; methodology for, common components of, 145–155; overview of, 139–144; of performance support systems, 170–177; postproduction stage of, 153–154; preproduction stage of, 145–149, 161; principles of, 140; production cycle for, 145–155; production stage of, 149–153; rapid, methodologies for, 140–143; software packages for, 143–144, 156–157, 165–166, 168–170; step/action checklist for, 224–225; tools for, 303–326

Development platforms: integrated, for computer-based training, 157–158; for web-based training, 172–173

Development-team resources, media selection and, 59

Difficulty index, 204, 265

Direct-Interview Instructions, 201, 249–252

Directions for students, 117

Director, assistant director, 151

Discrimination level, 38, 43, 46; verbs for, 228

Discussion, lecture and, 121

Discussion groups. *See* Newsgroups

Display treatment, 111

Distance broadcast/distance learning: advantages and limitations of, 55; defined, 49, 178; development of, 178–184; indications for, 50. *See also* Interactive distance broadcast

Distance learning project scheduling, 85

Distractors and distractor analysis, 191, 199, 205, 265

Distribution: analysis of technology for, 23; factors of, related to media selection, 61

Doc-to-Help, 22

Documentation: of audience analysis, 19; of cost analysis, 69; of critical-incident analysis, 36; of evaluation, 216; of extant-data analysis, 66, 67; of front-end analysis, 15; of general project information, for schedule, 89; of media analysis, 58; of needs assessment, 9, 13; of rapid analysis, 78; of situational analysis, 28; of task analysis, 32; of technology analysis, 24; of validity measures, 196; of video and audio treatment standards, 110

Domains of learning, 37–41; objectives-writing and, 41–47

Dreamweaver, 172, 175–176

Duties, identification of job-related, 31

E

Editor, 95

Editorial review, 91, 153; instructions for, 289

Editorial Review Form, 290

Educational TV system, 23

Effectiveness evaluation. *See* Evaluation

Electronic mailboxes, 56

Electronic performance support systems (EPSS), 50, 79; advantages and limitations of, 57–58; defined, 49

E-mail: analysis of technology for, 21; needs assessment questionnaires via, 11; in web-based training, 168

Embedded questions, 209

Employee attrition level, 70

Employee Satisfaction Survey, 70

Encryption, 22–23

English as a Second Language, 18, 19

Entertainment/edutainment, 62–64, 122–123

Environment, 27, 73, 241; media specification and, 100–101, 103

Environmental analysis. *See* Situational analysis

EEOC (Equal Employment Opportunity Commission) Guidelines, 193

Error correction, in computer-based training development, 162

Essay Question Checklist, 333

Evaluation, 185–217; data analysis for, 214–217; data collection for, 214–217; decisions based on, 216, 217; external and internal influences and, 215–216; instrument development for, 201–213; levels of, 188–189, 190; levels of, connected to purpose of, 190–194; measurement planning for, 201–213; overview of, 187–189; purpose of, establishing, 190–194; step/action checklist for, 225–226; summative versus formative, 188, 197, 265, 267; tools for, 327–335; validity establishment for, 195–200. *See also* Testing and assessment

Evaluation glossary, 265–267

Evaluation matrix, 191

Evaluation plan, 215–216

Evaluation Report, 216, 259–264

Evaluation specialist, 95

Events of instruction, 123, 124–125, 126

Evolutionary development, 140

Examples, providing for learners, 115

Exemplary performers: observation of, in rapid analysis, 75; for task analysis, 31–32

Exit button, 104

Experimental and control groups, 215

Expertise: for delivery implementation, 163; leveraging available, 143; technology, analysis of, 23–24

Expressed or demanded need, 6, 75

Extant Data Analysis Form, 66

Extant Data Materials Review, 284–285

Extant-data analysis, 65–67; activity one (identify sources of information), 66; activity two (collect information and course materials), 66; activity three (compare information), 66; activity four (make buy-or-build decision), 67; activity five (document your decision), 67; advice for, 67; procedure for, 65–67; process of, 65; purpose and benefits of, 14, 65; step/action checklist for, 222

F

Face validity, 191, 195, 197, 265

Facilities. *See* Situational analysis

Federal Aviation Administration (FAA), 192

Feedback: defining standards for, 110; as event of instruction, 124; following, with appropriate technique, 119; for instructional design improvement, 188; in content structure, 118–119; for monitoring, 118. *See also* Evaluation

Felt need, 5–6, 75

File transfer protocol (FTP), 23

Firewalls, 174

Flash, 172

Flash Card button, 104

Flipcharts, 180, 181

Focus groups: for critical-incident analysis, 34, 36; instructions for, 252–254

Fog Index, 19, 272

Follow-on development, 141–142

Font specifications, 111

Formative evaluation, 188, 197, 265

Frame identifier, 104

Frames: parallel development of, 141; timing of, 116

Frequency counts, 205–206

Front-end analysis, 3–4, 14–79; advice for, 15–16; of audience, 17–19; of cost, 68–70; critical incident, 34–36; of extant data, 65–67; of media, 48–64; objectives formulation and, 37–47; overview of, 14–16; of physical and environmental situation, 26–28; rapid analysis method of, 71–79; rationale for, explaining to customers, 15–16; step/action checklist for, 220–226; of tasks and KSAs, 29–33; of technology, 20–25; tools for, 269–287; types of, listed by purpose, 14

Functional review, 153; instructions for, 315–316

Functional Review Checklist, 153, 317–318

G

Gagné, R., 37–38, 43, 44

Gall, M., 190

Games, 122–123

Gap analysis. *See* Front-end analysis; Needs assessment

Gap identification, in rapid analysis method, 71, 75, 78

Global audience: analysis of, 18–19; design and development for, 19

Glossary button, 104

Goals and course objective, 42

Graphic artists, 95, 149, 152

Graphic designer, 95, 147

GIF (graphic interchange format) files, 176

Graphics: design and standards for, 111; media selection and, 51; preproduction of, 147, 148; in web-based courses, 176

Graphics Log, 152, 310–311

Graphics rework, 152, 314

Graphics Rework Request form, 152, 314

Greer, M., 91

Grips, 152

Guided learning, 115–116

Guided practice, 124

Gunning, R., 19, 272

H

Hammer, M., 77

Hammond, S., 9

Handouts, 181, 182

Hardware/software issues, in web-based training, 174–177

Harris poll, 212

Harrow, A., 39

Help button, 104

Help files, 171; analysis of, 22

Help screen, 141

High-level course flowchart, 128, 129

Hot links, 172, 176

Humor, 18, 64

Hyperlinks, 176–177

Hypertext Markup Language (HTML), 22, 167, 172, 175–176

I

ID review, 90

Impact level of evaluation, 189, 215

Implementation. *See* Development and implementation

Implementation representative, 95

Incentives, organizational assessment and, 73

Incorrect answers, feedback on, 119, 124

Independent practice, 125

Individual goals, evaluation based on, 191, 193

Inductive learning strategy, 120; instructional delivery strategies and, 121–123

InformaQ, 157–158

In-person interviews, 11. *See also* Interviews

Instructional delivery strategies, 120–123

Instructional design phase. *See* Design

Instructional design process: assessment and analysis phase of, 5–79; design phase of, 81–135; development and implementation phase of, 137–184; evaluation phase of, 185–217; phases of, with time ratios, 15–16; phases of, with validity types, 197–198; step/action checklist for, 219–226

Instructional designers: roles and responsibilities of, in preproduction, 145, 161; roles and responsibilities of, in production, 151, 152, 161–162; roles and responsibilities of, in project team, 96; training technologists versus, 20

Instructional review, 153; instructions for, 291–292

Instructional Review Form, 293–294

Instructional structure. *See* Content structure

Instructor-led training: advantages and limitations of, 53; described, 49; distance broadcast, 178–184; indications for, 50

Instrument development, 201–213, 226. *See also* Data-collection methods; Evaluation; Measurement plan; Testing and assessment

Instrument validity, 265

Integrated development platforms, 157–158

Interaction: clarity in direction for, 117; defining standards for, 108–110; in distance learning, 178–180; in instructional delivery strategies, 121–123; instructor monitoring and, 118; multimedia and, 108–109; in web-based training, 164, 167–170, 171–173

Interactive designer, roles and responsibilities of, 95

Interactive designs, 159

Interactive distance broadcast (IDB): activity one (develop IDB script and materials), 180–181; activity two (shoot and edit video), 181; activity three (rehearse the session), 181–182; activity four (conduct the session), 182; advice for, 182–183; development and implementation of, 178–184; development methodology for, 145–155; issues of, 178–180, 182–184; lesson plan template for, 326; procedure for developing, 180–182; process of developing, 180; step/action checklist for, 225

Interactive Learning International Corporation, 143

Interface design, 103–108, 111, 112; elements of, 103; options for, 104–105; samples of, 105–108, 109; sources of, 105; for web-based training, 168–170, 173. *See also* Media specification

Internal rate of return (IRR), 174

Internet: advantages and limitations of, 165–167; development of learning environments on, 164–177; intranets and, 165–167. *See also* Web-based training

Inter-rater agreement, 195–196, 198, 200

Interviews: for critical-incident analysis, 34; for evaluation, 201–202; instructions for, 201, 249–252; for needs assessment, 11

Intranets: advantages and limitations of, 165–167, 174; development of learning environments on, 164–177; Internet versus, 165–167. *See also* Web-based training

Introduction, 114, 127

Involvement, 30

Item analysis, 204–205, 266

J

Java, 22

Job aids, 49. *See also* Performance support systems

Job descriptions: analysis of, 9; flowcharting, 10; position titles in, 31. *See also* Task analysis

Job or Task Breakdown Tool, 32, 275

JPEG (joint photographic expert group) files, 176

Judges, panel of, 199, 206

K

Kendall's tau, 210

Keypad for distance learning system (ILINK), 178, 179

Kinesthetic discrimination level, 40

Kirkpatrick, D. L., 188, 190, 199

Knowledge, skills, and attitudes (KSAs): defined, 29; identification of, in organizational assessment, 73, 243; objectives and, 42; task analysis of, 30–32

Knowledge acquisition, 120

Knowledge level of evaluation, 189, 193, 199, 211–212

Knowledge objects, 176

Knowles, M., 29–30

Krathwohl, E., 39

Kuder Richardson (KR–20), 210

L

Language skills: analysis of, 18–19; content structure and, 116

Leader, project, 97

Leadership skills, quantification of, 70

Learned capabilities, in performance objectives, 43, 44, 45, 46

Learning and instructional strategies, 120–123

Learning approaches/preferences, 101–102

Learning domains, 37–41; objectives-writing and, 41–47

Learning objectives. *See* Objectives; Objectives analysis

Learning principles, 113–120

LearnLinc, Inc., 143, 168–170, 173

Lecture, 121

Lee, W. W., 5, 30, 196

Length: lesson, 126; of measurement instruments, 206–207

Lesson and Topic buttons, 105
Lesson length, 126
Lesson objectives, 42, 46, 126. *See also* Objectives;
    Objectives analysis
Lesson outline, 126–127
Lesson plan, for web-based training, 172, 326
Lesson Plan Template, 326
Lesson shells, 156–157
Lesson title, 126
Lesson weight, 126–127, 207
Lighting designers, 152
Linear presentation, 121
List servers, analysis of technology for, 21
Listening: in interviews, 252; in rapid analysis
    method, 74, 78
Logistics, media selection and, 60

M

Macromedia, 172, 175, 176
Mager, R., 37
Main menu, 141, 160
Maintenance: analysis of technology, 23–24; costs
    of, 61; factors of, associated with media, 61
Mamome, R. A., 196
Management review, 91; instructions for, 301
Management Review Form, 302
Mann Whitney, 210
Mapping, concept, 127–128
Marketing program interface design, 105, 106
Martuza, V., 190
Mastery curve, 266
Matching Question Checklist, 328
Materials: adult learning theory and, 30; archiv-
    ing, 132; costs of, associated with media, 59,
    61; for interactive distance broadcast, 180–181,
    182; motivation in, 119; real-world connection
    of, 119–120; review and configuration control
    of, 131–135; using off-the-shelf versus creat-
    ing new, 66–67
Materials developer, 94
McLuhan, M., 62

Measurement plan, 201–213; activity one (select
    the types of measurement), 202–203; activity
    two (develop the measurement instruments),
    206; activity three (calculate the length of each
    instrument), 206–207; activity four (calculate
    how items are weighted), 207; activity five (de-
    cide when the instruments should be adminis-
    tered), 208, 209; advice for developing, 208, 210–
    213; procedure for developing, 202–208; process
    of developing, 202; step/action plan for, 226
Measures of validity. *See* Validity
Media: advantages and limitations of, compared,
    53–58; cost factors associated with, 52, 59; de-
    livery factors associated with, 52, 60; elements
    of, creating and assembling, 160–161; listed
    and described, 49; maintenance factors associ-
    ated with, 61
Media analysis, 48–64; activity one (match out-
    comes and media), 48–52; activity two (match
    media advantages and limitations), 52–58, 59,
    60, 61; activity three (compare results of selec-
    tion), 52, 58; activity four (document the re-
    sults), 58; advice for, 58, 62–64; procedure for,
    48–58; process of, 48; purpose of, 14; rational
    approach to, 58, 62–64; step/action checklist
    for, 222
Media list, in lesson outline, 127
Media Selection Form, 52, 58, 277–282
Media specification, 100–112; activity one (define
    look and feel of the theme), 102–103; activity
    two (design the interface), 103–108, 109; ac-
    tivity three (define interaction and feedback
    standards), 108–110; activity four (document
    video and audio treatment standards), 110;
    activity five (indicate text design and stan-
    dards), 111; activity six (prepare graphics),
    111; activity seven (decide on animation and
    effects), 111; advice for, 111–112; defined, 86;
    goal for, 100–101; learning/sensory approaches
    and, 101–102; procedure for, 102–111; process
    of, 102; step/action checklist for, 224

Mentoring, 50, 143

Menu button, 104

Metacognitive domain of learning, 38, 40–41; media selection for, 52; in performance objectives, 44

Microsoft Internet Explorer, 166

Microsoft Project, 91

Microsoft Scheduler Plus, 91

Microsoft Word, 171

Milestones, list of, for schedule, 89

Mock ups, 103

Mock-up or talk-through simulation, for needs assessment, 12

Models and modeling, for development, 140–143. *See also* Templates

Monitoring, 118

More Info button, 105

Motivation: importance of, 120; material for, 119; self-, 211; training for, 51

Motor domain of learning, 38, 39, 40; levels in, 40; media selection for, 50; verbs for, 236–237

Multimedia: elements of, for specification, 100; interaction in, 108–109; media and, 48; principles of learning applied to, 113–120; web-based technology and, 165, 173–177. *See also* Media; Media specification

Multiple-Choice Question Checklist, 329

Multisensory approach, 101, 102

Music, 147

N

Narration, 147

Navigation components: design of, 103–108, 109; directions for using, 117; templates for, 157

Needs: levels of, in organizational assessment, 73, 79; types of, listed and described, 5–6

Needs assessment, 3–4, 5–13; activity one (determine present condition), 7–8; activity two (define the job), 8; activity three (rank the goals), 8; activity four (identify discrepancies), 9; activity five (determine positive areas), 9;

activity six (set priorities for action), 9; advice for, 9–13; data-collection methods for, 7, 10–12; defined, 5; organizational, in rapid analysis method, 72–74; procedure for, 7–9; process of, 6–7; step/action checklist for, 219–220

Needs Assessment Report Form, 9, 271

Netscape Navigator, 166

Network capacity issues, 166–167

Newsgroups (discussion groups), analysis of technology for, 21

Next button, 104

Nontraditional learning situation, 30

Normal curve, 266

Normal distribution, 266

Normative need, 5, 75

Norm-referenced (NR) measurement, 190, 195–196, 203, 208, 209, 210, 266

O

Object, in performance objectives, 43

Objectives: adult learning theory and, 30; communication of, to learners, 114, 124; domains of learning and, 37–41; elements of, 43; measures based on, 202–203, 211; media selection and, 48–52; ordering, 41, 42; types of, 41, 42; writing, 41–47

Objectives analysis, 37–47; activity one (decide on domains), 42; activity two (decide on level), 42; activity three (write goal statement), 42; activity four (write performance objectives), 42–43; activity five (engage in discussion), 45; activity six (separate terminal objectives), 45–46; activity seven (separate lesson objectives), 46; advise for, 46–47; procedure for, 42–46; process of, 41; purpose and uses of, 14, 37, 211; step/action checklist for, 221–222; theory related to, 37–41

Observation: for critical-incident analysis, 34; instructions for, 254–255; for needs assessment, 11–12; in rapid analysis method, 75–76, 78

Observers, 12, 255

Occupational Safety and Health Administration (OSHA), 192

Off-the-shelf materials: cost analysis of, 66–67; for rapid development, 142, 143–144; as sources for content structuring, 129; statistical testing or validity of, 194, 208. *See also* Software; Templates

Olfactory approach to learning, 102

ONETOUCH Systems, Inc., 178, 179

Online lessons, reviews of, 153–154

Online reference materials, analysis of, 22

Online Review Form, 153, 160, 162, 319

Online reviews, 161–162. *See also* Reviews

Open exploration, 115–116

Ophthalmology training interface design, 106–108, 109

Organization level, in affective domain, 39, 45

Organizational assessment, 72–74, 79; sample, of customer service company, 239–244

Organizational conditions, for rapid analysis method, 71

Organizational development, 74

Organizational goals, evaluation based on, 191, 192–193

Overheads, 180

P

Pacing: brisk, 116; student-controlled, 109–110

Panel of judges, 199, 206

Paper questionnaires, 11

Parallel development, 140–142

Parallel test items, tool for constructing, 205–206, 335

Pass-fail level, 208

Pearson Product Moment (Pearson r), 210

Perceptual level, 39–40, 44

Performance analyst, 96

Performance appraisals, 193

Performance improvement: critical-incident analysis and, 34, 36; evaluation of, 193, 211–212, 215–216

Performance level of evaluation, 189, 199, 211–212, 215

Performance needs assessment, 72, 73, 241–242

Performance objectives, 42–45; defined, 42; elements of, 43; separating lesson objectives from, 46; separating terminal objectives from, 45–46; writing, 42–45

Performance support files, analysis of, 22

Performance support systems (PSS), 50; advantages and limitations of, 57–58; defined, 49; development and implementation of, 170–177; as instructional delivery strategy, 123. *See also* Web-based training

Performance tests, 199, 211–212, 215–216, 332

Performance-centered application, 171

Periodicals, 66

Personal computers (PCs), multimedia: user access to, 23, 24; for web-based training, 174–175

Phased approach, indications for, 84–85

Phone conferencing, 21

Phone interviews, 11. *See also* Interviews

Photographers, 152

Photography: clip art, 147, 148; defining standards for, 110; in web-based courses, 176

Physical environment. *See* Situational analysis

Pilot test, 163

Planning, design as, 83. *See also* Configuration control plan; Course Design Specification; Design; Evaluation plan; Measurement plan

Plug-ins, 165–166, 172, 176

Point-biserial correlation, 199–200, 210

Position title statement, 31

Positive feedback, 124

Postproduction stage, 146, 153–154

Posttest, 211–212

Practice: guided, 124; independent, 125

Praise, 119. *See also* Positive feedback

Predictive validity, 198, 204, 266

Preparing Instructional Objectives (Mager), 37

Preproduction, 145–149, 161

Preproduction meeting, 145, 146, 149, 161

Presentation strategy, 127

Pretest, 203–204, 211–212

Principles of Instructional Design (Gagné, Briggs, and Wager), 37–38

Print button, 105

Problem-solving level, 38, 45; verbs for, 231–232

Processes and procedures, assessment of, 73, 241–242

Production baseline storyboards, 161

Production costs, media selection and, 59

Production cycle, 145–155. *See also* Development and implementation

Production stage, 146, 149–153. *See also* Development and implementation

Professional development, 193

Programmer. *See* Author

Programming templates or models, 90

Project management, 91–92

Project manager: requirements for, 91; roles and responsibilities of, 97

Project plan, 77. *See also* Course Design Specification

Project schedule/scheduling, 77, 85, 88–92; activity one (document general project information), 89; activity two (list project deliverables), 90; activity three (schedule project activities), 90–91; advice for, 91–92; defined, 86; procedure for, 89–91; process of, 89; purpose and uses of, 88–89; step/action checklist for, 223; sticking to, 143

Project tasks, matching team members to, 93, 99

Project team, 93–99; activity one (list team roles), 93–99; activity two (assign roles), 99; activity three (match tasks to members), 99; advice for, 99; defined, 86; involvement of, in project scheduling, 91; involvement of entire, in design phase, 85–87; procedure for defining roles and responsibilities in, 93–99; process of defining roles and responsibilities in, 93; roles

and responsibilities in, 90, 91, 93–99; roles and responsibilities in, during production cycle, 145–155; step/action checklist for, 223. *See also* Roles and responsibilities; Team approach

Promotion, 193

Prompts, 117, 176

Prototype screen interface, 90

Prototypes and prototyping, 83–84, 140–143. *See also* Templates

Psychomotor domain of learning, 38, 39–40; media selection for, 50; in performance objectives, 44; sublevels in, 40

Publisher, 94

Purpose of evaluation, 190–194; activity one (determine purpose of the solution), 192–193; procedure for establishing, 192–194; process of establishing, 190–191; step/action checklist for, 225–226

Q

Qualitative measures, 205–206, 266; quantitative measures versus, 203

Quality, assessment of quantity versus, 73, 188, 242

Quality assurance (QA) reviews, 15, 146, 153–154; of storyboards, 160, 161–162; of web pages, 173. *See also* Configuration control; Reviews

Quality reviewer or evaluator, 97, 140, 149

Quality-control representative, 161–162

Quantification, 70

Quantitative measures, 203–205, 266; qualitative measures versus, 203

Questioning: in multimedia interaction, 110; in rapid analysis method, 75, 77–78; sequencing of, 118; structure for, 118–119

Questionnaires: for critical-incident analysis, 34; for evaluation, 201–202; instructions for, 255–256; for needs assessment, 11

Questions, test. *See* Test items
Quiz items, 209

R

Rank difference, 210

Rank-and-order (RAO) technique, 253–254

Rapid analysis method (RAM), 13, 16, 71–79, 142; activity one (prepare for the analysis), 77; activity two (ask primary questions), 77–78; activity three (listen and record), 78; activity four (observe actual performance), 78; activity five (report results), 78; outline of, 74, 75–76; procedure for, 77–78; process of, 74; purpose and benefits of, 71; step/action checklist for, 223; success factors for, 71–74

Rapid prototyping, 84–85, 140–144. *See also* Development and implementation; Software; Templates

Rational approach, 58, 62–64

Reaction level of evaluation, 189, 199. *See also* Evaluation

Readability analysis, 19, 272

Real-world connection, 119–120

Receiving and responding level, 39

Recitation, 121

Recording: in multimedia systems, 110; in rapid analysis method, 78. *See also* Documentation

Reference technology, analysis of, 22

Referral, 13

Reflex movements, 40

Registration, student, 157

Regulatory requirements, 192–193

Rehearsal of distance broadcast sessions, 181–182, 183

Reinforcement, 120

Relevance, 30

Reliability, 266

Remediation, 125

Reporting and reports, in rapid analysis method, 76, 78

Reproduction, costs of ongoing, 61

Reshoot Request form, 150–151, 312

Resources: design and, 93; list of, in lesson outline, 127; media selection and, 52, 59. *See also* Project team

Responsibilities. *See* Roles and responsibilities

Retention, organizational assessment and, 73

Retest, defined, as event of instruction, 125

Return on investment (ROI), 68, 69; evaluation and, 189, 192; formula for, 69; for interactive distance broadcast, 183; resources for conducting, 70

Return rate on surveys, 201–202

Review forms, 153–154, 160

Review in learning, 113–114

Review Scheduling Form, 153, 320–321

Reviewers, roles and responsibilities of, 133–135, 153–154

Reviews and review cycles: configuration control plan for, 131–135; implementation of, 140; online, 161–162; of online lessons, 153–154; postproduction/quality, 146, 153–154; scheduling of, 90–91, 153; step/action checklist for, 224; of storyboards, 160, 161–162; tools, forms, or templates for, 91, 288–302; types of, 90–91; for validity establishment, 195; of web pages, 173

Revision: configuration control and, 131–135; costs of, 61, 87; design phase and, 87; factors of, related to media selection, 61; front-end analysis and, 15–16; of Web-based courses, 173

Roadman, K., 5, 196

Robohelp, 22

Role modeling, 51

Role playing, 123, 332

Roles and responsibilities: assigning, to team members, 99; for configuration control, 132–135; matching tasks and members to, 99; during preproduction stage, 145–149; during production stage, 149–153; in project management, 90, 91; in project team, listed and described, 93–99; in rapid analysis method, 77

Roles and Responsibilities Matrix, 77, 90, 99, 286

Routing sheet, 134

Rule level, 38, 44; verbs for, 230–231

S

Sampling, 212–213, 249–250

SAP, 171

Satellite delivery, 178, 182, 184. *See also* Interactive distance broadcast

Schedule, project. *See* Project schedule

Scheduling: of interactive distance broadcast, 180, 183–184; of interviews, 250; of testing and assessment, 208, 209

Scope creep, 89, 143. *See also* Standards

Screen shells, 156–157

Screens: color usage on, 111; design of, 103–108, 109; parallel development of, 141; Z pattern for, 103–104. *See also* Design; Interface design; Media specification

Script standards, 149, 245–247. *See also* Audio scripts; Video scripts

Securities Exchange Commission (SEC), 192

Security, issues of: in distribution, 23; in testing and assessment, 22–23, 170

Self-completion questionnaire instructions, 255–256

Self-improvement, 193

Senses, learning and, 101–102

Servers, 173, 174

Set designers and decorators, 151

Shockwave, 22, 176

Shot list, 150, 304–305

Shrock, S., 190

Significance, tests of, 205, 210

Simplicity, 111–112; of web-based training, 166

Simulation, 266–267; checklist for, 332; for needs assessment, 12; for training delivery, 50, 52, 120, 123

Simulation, Role Play, Performance Test Checklist, 332

Situation, stimulus, 43

Situational analysis, 26–28; activity one (analyze environment), 27; activity two (analyze training delivery), 27; activity three (document results), 28; advice for, 28; procedure for, 27–28; process of, 26; purpose and benefits of, 14, 26, 211; in rapid analysis method, 76; step/action checklist for, 221

Skewed distribution, 267

Skill assessment models, 157

Skills: defined, 29; evaluation for, 193; identification of, in organizational assessment, 73; media selection for, 50; performance objectives for, 43–45; prerequisite, 36. *See also* Knowledge, skills, and attitudes

Slides, 181

Smile sheets, 199, 201–202

Soft skills: objectives-writing for, 45; quantification of, 70

Software packages and tools: authoring and authorware, 104, 111, 143–144, 172, 175–177; for development of computer-based training, 156–157; for development of performance support systems, 171; for development of web-based training, 165–166, 168–170, 172–173, 175–177; for online performance support systems, 22; for project scheduling, 91; statistical, 205, 211, 215, 216; for test development, 22, 157. *See also* Off-the-shelf materials; Templates

Sound designers, 152

Sound effects, 147

Special effects, 111

Special requirements, audience, 18

Special-interest groups (SIGs), 66

Specifications. *See* Course Design Specification; Media specifications

Splash screens, 160

Sponsor, 97

SPSS, 216

Standard deviation, 267

Standardized tests, 267

Standards: defining animation and special effects, 111; defining audio and visual, 110; defining graphics, 111; defining interaction and feedback, 108–110; defining text, 111; importance of, 100, 111–112, 118; script, 149, 245–247

Standards review, 91, 153; instructions for, 295

Standards Review Form, 296–297

Stanley, J. C., 190, 215

Statistical software packages, 205, 211, 215, 216

Statistical tests and theory, 70, 195–196; for data collection and analysis, 214–217; for measures development, 208–213; types of, listed, 210; for validity testing, 195–196, 199–200

Steam turbine training interface design, 105, 107

Storage: costs of, 61; issues of, related to media selection, 61

Storyboard Template, 323; explanation for, 322, 324; for web-based training, 324–325

Storyboards, 90; authoring software for development of, 143–144; for computer-based training, 159–163; development of, 145–149, 159–163, 173, 181; for interactive distance broadcast, 181; production baseline, 161; review of, 160, 161–162; for web-based training, 173, 324–325

Stratus interface design, 105, 106

Streaming, 166–167, 174

Structure. See Content structure

Student-controlled pacing and branching, 109–110

Subjective versus objective criteria, 190

Subject-matter experts (SMEs): for establishing validity, 199, 200; for observation, 254; reviews by, 133–134, 319; roles and responsibilities of, 98; roles and responsibilities of, in preproduction, 149; roles and responsibilities of, in production, 151, 152; for task analysis, 31–32

Success, building in student, 115

Summary: defined, as event of instruction, 125; in lesson outline, 127

Summative evaluation. See Evaluation

Surveys, 199, 201–202, 212–213

Synchronous training, 171–173

Systemic assessment, 72–74, 79, 240

Systems designer, 98

Systems engineer/programmer, 98, 152–153, 154

T

Tactile discrimination level, 40

Tactile or kinesthetic approach to learning, 102

Talking heads, 178, 181

Task analysis, 29–33; activity one (state the position title), 31; activity two (identify all job-related duties), 31; activity three (identify all tasks), 31–32; activity four (order the tasks), 32, 33; activity five (document the results), 32; adult learning and, 29–30; diagram of, 31; procedure for, 31–32; process of, 30–31; purpose of, 14; in rapid analysis method, 76; situational analysis and, 27; step/action checklist for, 221

Task Inventory Tool, 32, 276

Tasks (job-related): critical-incident analysis of, 34–36; media selection and, 50–51; ordering of, 32, 33; performance objectives for, 42–47; statements of, 31–32. See also Critical-incident analysis; Project tasks; Task analysis

Taxonomy of Educational Objectives, A (Krathwohl), 39

Team approach, 99; to Course Design Specification development, 85–87; to objectives writing, 46; to project scheduling, 91. See also Project team

Technical review, 90, 133–134, 195; instructions for, 298

Technical Review Form, 299–300

Technical skills objectives, 43–44

Technical Training, 182

Technical-support group, 163

Technology analysis, 20–25; activity one (analyze available communication technology), 21; activity two (analyze available reference technology), 22; activity three (appraise assessment technology), 22–23; activity four (analyze distribution technology), 23; activity five (analyze delivery technology), 23; activity six (analyze technology expertise), 23–24; activity seven (document results), 24; advise for, 24–25; procedure for, 21–24; process of, 20–21; purpose and benefits of, 14, 20; step/action checklist for, 220–221

Technology Assessment Tool, 24, 273–274

Technology resources checklist, 24

Telephone-line delivery, 178, 183. *See also* Interactive distance broadcast

Templates: for design, 87; for development, 140–143; for development of computer-based training, 156–157; for development of web-based training, 172, 175–177; programming, 90. *See also* Off-the-shelf materials; Software

Terminal objectives, 42, 45–46, 202, 206, 207

Test, defined as instructional event, 125

Test answer analysis, 205–206

Test Completion Checklist, 334

Test development: measurement plan for, 201–213; software or templates for, 22, 157; tools for, 327–335; validity measures and, 195–200

Test items: analysis of, 204–205; types of, 209; validity of, 191, 195–200, 204–205, 267; weighting of, 207

Test Specification Form, 199, 256–258

Testing and assessment, 185–217; analysis of technology or, 22–23; artificially imposed restrictions on, 208, 211; data collection and analysis in, 214–217; in lesson outline, 127; scheduling and frequency of, 208, 209; security issues of, 22–23, 170; in web-based training, 170. *See also* Evaluation

Text, 50, 51; design and standards for, 111, 180; for interactive distance broadcast, 180, 181

Themes: defining, 102–103; fantasy versus job-related, 103; interface design and, 103

Theory. *See* Adult learning; Learning approaches; Learning domains; Learning principles; Learning strategies; Statistical theory

Time saving: configuration control for, 132; Course Design Specification template for, 87; front-end analysis for, 15–16; rapid analysis method for, 13, 17, 71–79; rapid development methodologies for, 83–84, 140–143; scheduling and tracking for, 91–92; software packages for, 143–144, 156–157

Time tracking, 91–92

Time zones, 180, 183–184

Title screens or frames, 141, 160

Tool for Constructing a Bank of Parallel Test Items, 205–206, 335

Toolbook, 143

Tools: organizational assessment of, 73; for performance objectives, 43

"Topic level one" screens, 141

"Topic level three," 141

"Topic level two," 141

Topic-level model, 141–142

Tracking, 91–92, 118; templates for, 157

Training needs assessment, 73, 74, 243

Training on demand, 164

Training technologists versus instructional designers, 20

Transfer of learning, 120; consistency for, 86; job-related themes for, 103; as rationale for training, 211; training delivery environment and, 27

Transitions: defined, as event of instruction, 124; smooth, 117; verbal content and, 114–115

True-False Question Checklist, 330

T-test, 210

Two-way audio and video, 182

U

URLs (universal resource locators), 176–177
User authentication, 22

V

Validity: advice for establishing, 199–200; establishment of, 195–200; evaluation purpose and, 191, 194; of off-the-shelf products, 194, 208; procedure for establishing, 196–198; process of establishing, 196; statistical theory and testing of, 195–196, 199–200; step/action checklist for, 226; terms related to, 265–267; types of, 196, 197–198
Valuing level, 39, 44
Verbal content, 114–115
Verbal information level, 38; verbs for, 234–236
Verbs, 43, 44, 228–238
Version control, configuration control plan for, 132–135
Video broadcast schedule, 90
Video cards, 174–175
Video director, 147, 149, 151
Video editor or technician, 98
Video producer/specialist, 98–99, 147, 149, 151
Video production, 147, 149–152, 176, 180, 181
Video reshoots, 150–151, 162–163, 312
Video scripts, 90, 149, 245–247
Video standards, 110, 245–247
Video teleconferencing, 23, 51, 52, 175, 183; advantages and limitations of, 55–56
Video terminology, 246–247
Videographers or video team, 149–151
Video-on-demand systems, 174
Videotape: advantages and limitations of, 57; defined, 49; indications for, 50, 51
Videotaping, for needs assessment observation, 11–12
Virtual teams, 175
Visual approach to learning, 101

Visual discrimination level, 40, 44
Visual examples, 115
Visuals, for interactive distance broadcast, 180–181
Vocabulary definition, 116

W

Wager, W., 37–38, 44
Walk the talk, 78
Web browsers, 165; encryption on, 22–23; plug-ins for, 165–166, 172, 176
Web search: for collecting extant information, 66, 67; tips for, 67
Web-based training (WBT): activity one (determine type of course and platform), 171–173; activity two (bring components together), 173; activity three (review the course), 173; activity four (implement the site), 173; advantages and limitations of, 56–57, 164, 165–167, 173–174; advice for, 173–177; described, 49, 164; designing for, 167–170; development and implementation of, 164–177; development methodology for, 145–155; future of, 177; indications for, 50, 51; interaction in, 164, 167–170, 171–173; issues of, 165–167, 173–177; lesson plan for, 172, 326; procedure for developing, 171–173; process of developing, 171; software for development of, 143, 165–166, 168–170, 175–177; step/action checklist for, 225; storyboard template for, 324–325; testing in, 170; text-based courses in, 168, 173–174
Weighting: of lessons, 126–127; of test items, 207
Wizards, 176
Workforce, improved, 192
Workshop, 52
WorldTutor, 143, 157

Z

Z pattern, 103–104

HOW TO USE THE ACCOMPANYING CD-ROM

SYSTEM REQUIREMENTS

Windows PC

- 486 or Pentium processor-based personal computer
- Microsoft Windows 95 or Windows NT 3.51 or later
- Minimum RAM: 8 MB for Windows 95 and NT
- Available space on hard disk: 8 MB Windows 95 and NT
- 2X speed CD-ROM drive or faster
- Netscape 3.0 or higher browser or MS Internet Explorer 3.0 or higher

NOTE: This CD-ROM requires Netscape 3.0 or MS Internet Explorer 3.0 or higher. You can download these products using the links on the CD-ROM Help Page.

GETTING STARTED

Insert the CD-ROM into your drive. The CD-ROM will usually launch automatically. If it does not, click on the CD-ROM drive on your computer to launch. You will see an opening page. You can click on this page or wait for it to fade to the Copyright Page. After you click to agree to the terms of the Copyright Page, the Home Page will appear.

MOVING AROUND

Use the buttons at the left of each screen or the underlined text at the bottom of each screen to move among the menu pages. To view a document listed on one of the menu pages, simply click on the name of the document. To quit a document at any time, click the box at the upper right-hand corner of the screen.

Use the scrollbar at the right of the screen to scroll up and down each page.

To quit the CD-ROM, you can click the Quit option at the bottom of each menu page, hit Control-Q, or click the box at the upper right-hand corner of the screen.

TO DOWNLOAD MICROSOFT WORD DOCUMENTS

Open the document you wish to download. Under the File pulldown menu, choose Save As. Save the document onto your hard drive with a different name. It is important to use a different name, otherwise the document may remain a read-only file.

You can also click on your CD drive in Windows Explorer and select a document to copy it to your hard drive and rename it.

IN CASE OF TROUBLE

If you experience difficulty using the *Multimedia-Based Instructional Design* CD-ROM, please follow these steps:

1. Make sure your hardware and systems configurations conform to the systems requirements noted under "Systems Requirements" above.

2. Review the installation procedure for your type of hardware and operating system. It is possible to reinstall the software if necessary.

3. You may call Jossey-Bass or Jossey-Bass/Pfeiffer Customer Service at (415) 433–1740 between the hours of 8 A.M. and 5 P.M. Pacific Time, and ask for Jossey-Bass CD-ROM Technical Support.

   Please have the following information available:
   - Type of computer and operating system
   - Version of Windows being used
   - Any error messages displayed
   - Complete description of the problem.

   (It is best if you are sitting at your computer when making the call.)